E-Learning Success:
From Courses to Careers

e-learning queen's

E-Learning Success:
From Courses to Careers

Susan Smith Nash, Ph.D.

*t*P
Texture Press
2012

ACKNOWLEDGEMENTS

The articles in this book first appeared in www.elearners.com and elearnqueen.blogspot.com. Some were also included in AAPG Division of Professional Affairs' quarterly journal, *The Navigator*, and *Feminist Cyberspaces* (forthcoming from Cambridge UP).

E-Learning Success: From Courses to Careers
Copyright © 2012 Susan Smith Nash

Texture Press
1108 Westbrooke Terrace
Norman, OK 73072
www.texturepress.org

Executive Editor: Susan Smith Nash, Ph.D.
Education Topics Editor: Elaine Bontempi, Ph.D.
Associate Editor: Valerie Fox, Ph.D.
Copy Editor: Seth Lynch
Publicity / Public Relations Manager: Arlene Ang

For ordering information,
please visit the Texture Press website at
www.texturepress.org

ISBN: 978-0-9850081-0-9
LCCN: 2012930118

Cover illustration and interior drawings
by Susan Smith Nash

Book design by Arlene Ang

CONTENTS

Chapter 1
Benefits of E-Learning

Chapter 2
Strategies to Help You Succeed in Your Courses

Chapter 3
E-Learning Technology

Chapter 4
Cultures, Contexts, and Readings

Chapter 5
Careers

Chapter 1

Benefits of E-Learning

A Tornado Ate My House...
And It's Finals Week!
A True Story

On the first day of final's week, a tornado ate my son's house. The timing could not be worse. It was finals week for both my son and his wife. They had just remodeled the house, with new paint, tile, carpet, fixtures, bathrooms, and roof repairs. And yet there were many silver linings. E-learning was one of them.

Both Michael and his wife, Shandell, have been taking online courses, and they are in their third year. Michael is studying mechanical engineering and Shandell is studying psychology. Her first love is marine biology, with an emphasis on animal behavior. Michael wants to put together his interest in computers, programming, and mechanical engineering in order to develop new technologies. He joined the Marines immediately after high school, served four years in the infantry, and was in combat missions in Afghanistan. After he finished his commitment of four years, he moved back to Oklahoma ("Tornado Alley") and started working on an associate's degree using his MGI Bill benefits. He received his Associates in Mathematics and in Pre-Engineering, and is now working on his bachelor's degree.

Shandell works at Wet Pets, a store specializing in saltwater aquariums and habitats. E-learning has allowed her to be able to work and keep a job that she loves and which gives her experience in areas that connect to her overall career goals.

They never imagined that their approach to their education had a build-in natural disaster "fail-safe." Further, they never expected that their experience would be one that had been shared by many learners in the path of natural disasters (hurricanes, floods, grass fires, tornadoes, and more).

You always think of the natural disasters as happening to the other guy—the person you see on a news clip or on the Weather Channel—whose talking about the close call he had. He usually says something like this: "We saw the dark clouds, lightening, hail, and then we heard the weatherman say, 'Take your tornado precautions now!' We were spared, though. The tornado took out all the houses in our neighborhood, but skipped over ours. We were lucky!"

My son's story was just the opposite. The huge multi-vortex tornado dipped out of the sky and the various funnels wove through his neighborhood doing all kinds of damage. The tornado saved the worst for Michael and Shandell's house—a vortex came through and stripped off the second floor, destroyed the house, the outbuildings, the trees, and the fence. In less than a minute, the house was reduced to a tear-down.

The tornado that hit Norman, Oklahoma on May 10, 2010, was an F3 on the Fujitsu scale. The most intense is F5, although many say that the mile-wide May 3, 1999, Oklahoma City tornado was an F6. It was crazy. It even stripped the grass right off the ground. I saw the aftermath, and it reduced entire neighborhoods to toothpicks. Photographs never do it justice—the sheer expanse of destruction just takes your breath away. I remember seeing the aftermath of the Oklahoma City bombing before the Murrah building was demolished and it had the same impact. Seeing the destruction fill your field of vision is staggering. Then, there are the other sensory factors—the smells, the sounds, and the feel of it all. Very creepy.

The tornado that ate my son and daughter-in-law's house originated 3.2 miles south of Norman, and was one-half mile in width. The length of the path was at least 16 miles. It was caught on video by a weather helicopter team, and it was truly spectacular.

It was a multi-vortex tornado, which meant that it was composed of many little "fingers" of varying intensity and direction. A multi-vortex tornado can be much more damaging than a single vortex because of the randomness of the direction and velocity of the winds, plus the pressure change.

Shandell and Michael were studying for finals at the time. They had the Weather Channel, and were wondering if they should take cover due to the huge storm system hitting Oklahoma and reports of a tornado forming near Norman.

Fortunately, they were not at home at the time. In fact, they had been trying to sell the house, and, thinking it would sell better empty, they had moved most of their items to a small house owned by Shandell's father that Michael had rehabbed by himself over the last eight months.

There is no doubt that if they had been at home, there would have been serious injuries, perhaps even a fatality. It was amazing to see what was embedded in the walls, and how the shed, beams, and neighbor's fence were wrapped around different things.

So, there were two silver linings:

1. No one was home when it hit and the house was largely empty.
2. They were taking online courses and had moved to a paperless environment so that all their work was stored online.

It may not be apparent at first where you'll benefit from taking courses online. Here are some of the unexpected benefits:

1. Your course is online and you can access it from any computer and any location, if you have sufficient bandwidth, speed, and no firewalls.
2. The work you turn in is archived online. If you lose your computer or flash drives, all you have to do is go in and retrieve your archived versions.
3. The readings and texts are online. E-books can be re-downloaded and/or accessed online.
4. You can share your information with your classmates, and all your discussions and collaborations are archived. There is no need to reconstruct that.
5. You can study at any time and at any place with asynchronous courses, so you can take care of the damage and disruption of natural disasters while not missing a beat with your courses (although, needless to say, a natural disaster a big distractor and time-eater).

Natural disasters have ripple effects, and they tend to affect all the members of the extended family, not just the individuals involved. Having to lose an entire semester due to lost homework/schoolwork compounds the tragedy. However, in the case of online courses, to be able to maintain a bit of "even keel" and "business as usual" and keep moving forward with one's academic progress is a huge morale booster.

I'm saddened by the loss my son and his wife sustained, and yet, with all that happened, I just have to be grateful. It could have been so much worse. The heavens smiled, as did good luck and technology/e-learning!

Autism and E-Learning

When Brender was just 18 months old, Liza, his mom, knew something was very different about him. While other toddlers would interact with each other at the daycare center, Brender would not. He would not look at the other children, nor would he smile. When anyone tried to move him from his place, or take away his favorite green plastic blocks, he would scream so loudly that it appeared he might go into convulsions.

After many visits to the pediatrician and many rounds of tests, it was determined that Brender had a form of autism. According to the Centers for Disease Control (CDC), what Brender suffered from was one of a group of disorders known as autism spectrum disorders (ASDs). ASDs are developmental disabilities that result in impaired social interaction and communication. ASDs are also typified by the presence of unusual behaviors and interests. Many of Brender's behaviors were connected with Asperger's Syndrome.[1]

After speaking with the pediatrician and obtaining information, Liza soon realized that Brender was likely to have difficulty in a typical, traditional educational setting; the schoolhouse scene would be difficult for him.

According to WebMD, children with Asperger's Syndrome may exhibit the following behaviors and cognitive challenges:

- Not pick up on social cues and may lack inborn social skills, such as being able to read others' body language, start or maintain a conversation, and take turns talking.

---

[1] www.webmd.com/brain/autism/tc/aspergers-syndrome-symptoms

- Dislike any changes in routines.
- Appear to lack empathy.
- Be unable to recognize subtle differences in speech tone, pitch, and accent that alter the meaning of others' speech. Thus, your child may not understand a joke or may take a sarcastic comment literally. Likewise, his or her speech may be flat and difficult to understand because it lacks tone, pitch, and accent.
- Have a formal style of speaking that is advanced for his or her age. For example, the child may use the word "beckon" instead of "call" or the word "return" instead of saying "come back."

After Liza was able to obtain her initial information, she worried about the future. What happens when autistic children reach their teen years? Where can they study? What happens when they grow to be adults? Are they still considered autistic?

Autism is in the rise. According to the CDC, 1 out of 150 individuals from all socio-demographic groups is affected by ASDs (www.cdc.gov/ncbddd/autism/index.html). There are competing theories about why the number is increasing. Some claim the number is not increasing at all—that it is something that has always present in our society, but we never had a clear-cut label to define it. Others say it's on the rise, and they blame childhood vaccinations. Others blame food additives, while others point to environmental toxins and overstimulation due to our fast-paced world.

Whatever the issue, the rising number of children, teens, and adults with autism is stretching the resources of schools and entire communities. As the children turn to teens and adults, there is a tragedy in the making as some autistic adults are unable to participate fully in society, and may fall prey to drugs, alcohol, crime, and ultimately prison. Clearly, an education program that offers hope would be a blessing.

Liza found that traditional school settings are very difficult for children with autism. Not only is it difficult for them to focus on classwork because of the numerous distractions in the world around them, they are often targets of bullying and ridicule. In the past, it was very common for an autistic child to go to a special school for the developmentally disabled. They would rarely graduate. Even autistic teenagers who had very high test scores in cognitive functioning, and who showed an aptitude for certain tasks, fell by the wayside and failed to graduate.

Children with autism can often succeed in academic programs, and can graduate from high school when their environment can be managed to avoid the triggering, precipitating actions, and when they are provided with curriculum that has been designed expressly with the challenges of autism in mind.

The key to success is often assistive technology, and finding a program that is computer-based, which allows the autistic teen to feel calm and in control of his or her environment.

Adults who were diagnosed as autistic when they were children can also often succeed in online programs, particularly when accommodations are made to avoid certain types of assessment, and when they are provided with the right kind of assistive technology for their needs.

Assistive Technologies for Autistic E-Learners

According to Susan Stokes[1], in a study published in 2007, some of the most effective educational programs for children with autism involve using organizing one's learning space, maintaining order, and keeping firmly grounded in the concrete world.

E-learning is ideal. Online courses that incorporate schedules, clearly laid-out calendars, and an interface that is generally free of distractions, such as flashing images, scrolling banners, or other moving items, can be very helpful for students with autism.

Further, connections to the concrete world via images and photographs are also very helpful because they help the autistic e-learner feel grounded and connected. Assistive technologies can help autistic e-learners communicate.[2]

_____

[1] www.specialed.us/autism/assist/asst10.htm

[2] www.brighthub.com/education/special/articles/2723.aspx

Learning Environments for Autistic E-Learners

The ideal learning environment involves:

- At home, room with computer, few distractions
- The library
- Study room

Curriculum Considerations for Autistic E-Learners

Building block approach

- **Math:** can focus on the equations and solution sets. In contrast with most adult learners, it is not necessary to make connections to real-world applications. Repetition of problems, and very straightforward problem-solving approach. Avoid simulations or graphics with flashing colors, moving lights.
- **Statistics, skills, complex tasks:** In this case, be sure to provide clear, step-by-step instructions, and include many opportunities for repetition and practices. Repetitions of the tasks will build confidence.
- **Accounting:** Clear presentation of the formulas and the spread-sheets. Clear directions, and provide guidance for each formula. As in the case of statistics, be sure to provide clear, step-by-step instructions, and include many opportunities for repetition and practices. Repetitions of the tasks will build confidence.
- **Writing:** Connect to experiences, and write with concrete details. When possible, use flow charts, checklists, and other clear, easy-to-follow procedural guides.

The Future

When Liza found out about the assistive technologies that have been developed, and the instructional strategies behind effective e-learning, she turned to Brender and gave him a big hug. Not expecting her gesture, he, of course, recoiled. All the more reason to work with Brender, thought Liza.

Homeschooling was an obvious starting point. If no one could help her in the local school system, she could always set up something at home. Liza, however, was in luck. Her school system had recently expanded the special needs facilities, and they had computer labs with assistive technologies. Students could take online courses, and receive special guidance and tutoring. Brender would be well served there, and Liza could take him to school and not fear for his safety or his future.

Autistic learners have hope. With assistive technologies, well-designed e-learning programs, and a support system with tutors and guides, autistic e-learners can obtain an excellent education and achieve their potential.

College Credit By Exam:
Shave Time and $ From the Degree Quest?

My husband is in the military and he told me about a program where he can take exams and if he received a passing grade, he'll receive a certificate that many colleges and universities will accept and award him college credit.

He took about 12 exams, and he passed 9 of them. They are in the general education area, and he's earned 27 hours! He's thrilled—it's saved him a lot of time and money. It's almost a full year's worth of work.

I started to feel pretty skeptical though. Is it too good to be true? Which colleges and universities will accept them?

Are there any ways for me to get credit by exam? I'm not in the military.

Any insights you might provide would be very helpful.

Sincerely,
Test-Ready in Texas

****

Dear Test-Ready:

I have good news for you! There are a number of ways to obtain credit by exam. While not all colleges and universities will accept all exams, there are hundreds that do. In fact, there are some colleges that will let you earn an entire degree via exam.

Many colleges will accept up to 30 hours of general education credit earned via approved credit-by-exam and applied toward an associate's degree.

Perhaps the most well-known exams are the CLEP exams.

- **DSST**
  - ▸ www.getcollegecredit.com/index.html

  DSST (also known as DANTES) exams are available in 38 unique subjects and they cost approximately $80 per exam. The college or university that administers them usually charges an administrative fee, and there is usually a transcript fee as well. DSST exams are primarily in the lower-division baccalaureate area, and are often ideal for individuals who have been in a homeschool environment and would like to accelerate the path to college credit as they enter college. For many active-duty military personnel, there is no fee to take the exam.

- **ECE (Excelsior College Exams)**
  - ▸ www.excelsior.edu/ecapps/exams/creditByExam.jsf?gw=1

  Excelsior College offers 24 non-nursing exams. It also offers 17 nursing exams for working adults who would like to earn a nursing degree. The exams are generally for individuals who are already working as nurses, who wish to obtain an Associates Degree in Nursing. ECE exams cost around $100 per credit hour, which is a significantly cheaper than tuition—even in-state tuition.

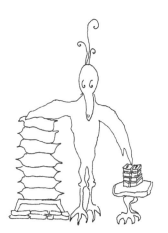

- **CLEP**
  - ▸ www.collegeboard.com/clep

  CLEP tests, which have been developed by the College Board are administered by more than 1,200 colleges and universities worldwide. The colleges that administer the exams often accept credit by exam, and, depending on your degree, you can make significant progress toward your degree by taking exams. While not all exams will apply to all degrees, and it's important to meet with an academic advisor, CLEP tests can offer a huge advantage. In addition, the practice exams and study materials are excellent reviews for students preparing for regular online or face-to-face courses. CLEP exams are offered in 34 different subject areas.

I hope this has been helpful, dear Test-Ready. If you'd like to shave time and money off the full cost of your college degree, I recommend credit by exam. Be sure, though, to spend time with the practice materials and to review the materials by purchasing the practice materials and a copy of the text, where possible.

Are there times when I would NOT recommend credit by exam?

To be honest, I think it's a good idea to take the courses when you're passionate about the subject and you're looking forward to sharing your ideas with peers and an instructor. If the course requires a portfolio, there is all the more reason to take the course rather than testing out.

I'd say the best thing is to have a heart-to-heart talk with your advisor, and also to take stock of your overall goals and interests. The best approach might be a blend of online courses, virtual internships, and credit by exam. Keep an open mind—education is an adventure that prepares you for an exciting future!

Teen Moms and Online Education

The individuals in this article are based on actual e-learners who participated in interviews, but names and details have been changed.

"Being an unwed teen mom is absolutely the most expedient way to economic perdition," droned the economics professor on the radio. Tiffany and Britta were driving back home after going to the local community college for a job and career fair, and also a free flu vaccine clinic.

"What does he mean? I mean, I get the general drift, but what does he exactly mean?" asked Tiffany.

Tiffany reflected back on her own experience. It was like an episode from Glee—head cheerleader from a strict, religious family experiments with alcohol, finds herself half passed out, and then, to her dismay, pregnant. After being rejected by her family, she has nowhere to go. She ends up at a home for pregnant teens, then on food stamps and public assistance, ashamed and afraid to return to high school, or to look ahead to college.

Tiffany's friend, Britta, sighed. "I have heard the statistics. Apparently, a lot of teens who have kids early have a very tough life. They have more than one child. They never have a job. They never get out of public housing."

Britta mentioned statistics from the U.S. Census. "The numbers are tough. Looking at moms on food stamps—40% never married. They are younger when they have their first child, and have more children. Four out of 10 do not have a high school diploma, and they stay jobless, with low family incomes," continued Britta.

"Can't one get out of the trap with education?" Tiffany pulled out a flyer she had picked up at local community college. "Check it out. They have special programs for moms with young children."

It would take some planning. She would need to obtain grants and student loans, and have a stable location for an online connection. Also, it would be helpful to have a job. She thought about a website she had read which contained a guide for moms starting college (Back to School Survival Guide).

As Britta looked at areas with high job growth, she recognized new opportunities in the area of health care, as well as energy and new industries.

"It would be great to have a dad around," said Tiffany. "But I'm not going to let that stop me. Do you realize that almost 7 million women with a child under age 3 were working in 2008?"

She went on to discuss the statistics from the U.S. Bureau of Labor Statistics. In 2008, there were 6.8 million working moms with a child under the age of 3, not married, no spouse present. The statistics did not indicate how many were attending classes toward a degree or certificate program, but she imagined that number would be very high as well.

"I'm motivated to take courses," said Tiffany. "Even if I have to take remedial courses and go through a long GED process. I'm thinking about the future."

She and Britta drove the rest of the distance home in silence. They were both thinking the future looked good.

REFERENCES

‣ www.census.gov/population/socdemo/statbriefs/sb95-22/sb95-22.html
‣ www.bls.gov/news.release/famee.t06.htm
‣ edis.ifas.ufl.edu/FY1057

Top Ten New Directions in E-Learning

Improvements in connectivity, technology, and infrastructure are changing the way that online programs are approaching e-learning. The philosophy of e-learning is evolving as well, and the activities that you'll be asked to do are changing. They are responding to research results on effective e-learning.

Research Findings:

- E-learners interact in many ways; the more convenient and relevant the interaction, the better. Interaction needs to:
    - » be learning-outcome focused.
    - » be oriented toward building trust in a learning community.
    - » employ flexibility to allow students to respond in a way that is most convenient and comfortable.

- The more "humanized" the e-instruction, the better.
    - » Instructor presence needs to be personalized.
    - » Learners need to be able to share relevant information about themselves.
    - » Video, audio, and multimedia should serve to humanize the interaction.
    - » Skype, Twitter, social networking should be used in moderation to avoid distractions or even cyber-stalking.

- Courses that allow students to individualize their learning experience result in higher satisfaction, retention, and engagement
    - » "Building block" approach to a term paper on a topic of the student's choice.

» E-portfolio that can be shared in a forum or e-gallery motivates students.

» Allow students to rank the efficacy of online activities.

» Creating an assignment that engages the interest of the student makes that student a stakeholder who cares about the subject. As such, the learner is less likely to engage in academic dishonesty: copy and paste, plagiarize, or buy a paper.

Here are the top ten ways in which e-learning is evolving:

1. **Learning Outcomes Accommodate Learner Flexibility**

   Student-centered activities focus on the way that learners use technology, and the things they tend to have and use. One can use diverse techniques and devices to do the same thing.

2. **Instructional Strategies are Interaction-Driven**

   Interaction-driven learning activities include synchronous and asynchronous activities, and they are collaborative as well.

3. **Multiple Access Technologies**

   Use your cell phone and mobile device (handheld, GPS, cell phone)

4. **Peer Review and Galleries Rather than Isolated Grading by Instructor**

   Portfolios rather than term papers. Discussion board requires substantive and meaningful interaction.

5. **Social Networking Evolves**

   Dedicated Facebook/MySpace networking; new networks (LinkedIn, Bebo, etc.); collaborations via course wikis, etc. encourage people to share information.

6. **Webinar-type Formats (rather than static PowerPoints)**

   Audio content synched with presentations.

7. **Research Requires Critical Analysis (Debunking, Determining Bias, Disinformation)**

   Bigger and better online libraries; a larger array of blogs

8. **Multi-Disciplinary Focus for Careers, Jobs**

   Courses integrate case studies and skills for/from emerging careers

9. **Green Is Everywhere**

   Environmental and energy related concerns inform course content, infrastructure decisions, delivery modalities

10. **Plagiarism and Academic Integrity Concerns Lead to New Prompts**

    Instead of using the kinds of writing prompts and research paper assignments that can be easily copied and pasted from the internet, or acquired from termpaper.com-type source, colleges and universities are changing the nature of assignments to incorporate more personal experience, case studies, and personal analysis.

Chapter 2

Strategies to Help You Succeed in Your Courses

About E-Learning in 2010:
What You Need to Know

Whether you're new to e-learning, or a seasoned e-learner, it's a good idea to keep in mind that the new decade is starting with a bang, and we're seeing interactivity and collaboration like never before in online courses.

Part of the reason for that is the fact that online courses are continuing to boom, and most course developers follow best practices that hold that interactivity is key to a great online experience.

More than that, though, we're seeing e-learning move rather rapidly to "u-learning" (ubiquitous learning) that allows you to use a multitude of devices to interact with classmates, instructors, and data repositories so that you can approach your course and coursework in the best possible way for your situation.

So, you may be incorporating Twitter in your interaction with your peers. Or you may find that constant connectivity distracts you. As a result, you may be printing out your lessons and working on them while you're not online.

Whatever your ideal learning style and study style, it's good to review the following "Pick Six" tips for success in the new world of e-learning.

- **Tip 1: Collaborate Quickly**
    - ✓ Log in early.
    - ✓ Go into all the course documents.
    - ✓ Introduce yourself.

- **Tip 2: Create a Learning Community**
  - ✓ Make connections with instructors and peers.
  - ✓ Post to the discussion board.
  - ✓ Collaborate with fellow students.
  - ✓ Set up groups with people with shared interests.

- **Tip 3: Try Ubiquitous Learning**
  - ✓ Social networking, Facebook, etc.
  - ✓ Access any place / any time / any device.
  - ✓ Use Twitter when it works for you to share links, update deadlines.

- **Tip 4: Practice Assessment/Outcomes**
  - ✓ Check out the online quizzes.
  - ✓ Practice activities.
  - ✓ Collaborations.
  - ✓ Web quests.

- **Tip 5: Avoid Overcommitment and Multitasking Overload**
  - ✓ Workflow management
  - ✓ Blocking time
  - ✓ Chunking tasks
  - ✓ Logical progression of tasks
  - ✓ Avoid distractions

- **Tip 6: Plan Your Work**
  - ✓ Early bird approach—set deadlines for yourself well ahead of the official deadline.
  - ✓ Update your calendar frequently.
  - ✓ Plan your work strategically.

One of the most important things to keep in mind as you take your online courses is to maintain a good attitude and to be receptive to new ideas, and try new techniques and technologies. You'll enjoy it!

Ace Your Essay Exams

I am taking a couple of courses this semester that requires essay exams. I feel pretty confident when I do multiple choice, and also short answer exams that require me to write a paragraph-long answer.

When it comes to essay exams where I'm expected to write several pages on a topic, I freeze. I feel overwhelmed by the details, and I never know how/where to organize the essay. It doesn't help that I am under time pressure, too. It's terrible and I need to figure out a strategy before it's too late.

What should I do?

Sincerely,
Essay-Challenged in Essex Junction

****

Dear Essay-Challenged,

Don't worry—you're not alone. Writing a coherent, well-organized essay that responds to the test question and demonstrates your knowledge is tough, but you can do it. Follow these tips and ace that essay exam!

1. Restate the essay question in your own words.
2. Develop a thesis statement that reflects the rephrased essay question.
3. Create an outline.

- Definition section: List the terms you'll need to define and/or explain.
- List the topics that support your thesis. These will be your body paragraphs.
- Under each supporting topic, make a bullet point list of evidence and also thinkers/theorists.
    1. Discuss the supporting topic.
    2. Make connections, share insights, provide analysis, point out problems or inconsistencies.
  - Conclusion should not simply restate your thesis. Discuss your findings, insights, and analysis, and make recommendations.
4. Write your essay, and follow your outline carefully. Do not let yourself get distracted or go off on a tangent. You are limited in terms of time, so make each part of your essay really count. Write quickly from your outline. You can clean it up later if you have time.

The key to success with an essay exam is good preparation. Not only should you practice outlining and writing a draft essay, you should also practice working under the pressure of an exam. Simulate the testing environment. Set a time limit and practice. Do this at least two times before your exam. You'll be amazed at how much calmer and more confident you'll be.

Ace Your Pre-Nursing Science Courses
with the TOPICS Approach

I'm having a hard time studying for my science and math courses. I'm worried because I have to do well in them. If I don't, it is possible that I won't be accepted into the nursing program I'm applying for.

I'm very committed to my goal—maybe I'm too committed. I'm so nervous about doing well that I seem to go in all directions and I feel scattered.

What should I do?

Sincerely,
Hoping to be a Nurse

****

Dear Hoping,

Don't worry. What you're experiencing is very common. It boils down to a type of performance anxiety that centers around the tasks that are most mission-critical to your goal.

At this point in time, it appears that your science and math courses are the most critical—and, not surprisingly, that's where you're feeling blocked and unable to focus.

The good news is that there are a number of approaches you can take that will help you succeed in science and math courses.

One of my favorites is called the TOPICS approach. TOPICS is an easy-to-remember acronym which stands for the following:

- **Time management:** Map out the tasks that you need to do (homework, concepts, readings, activities), and then find out how much time each will take.

- **Online Focus:** Make sure your focus stays online. If you're working on a topic that makes you uncomfortable, use the power of your online course to learn from your instructor, your class-mates, and the activities. Use the discussion board and other fo-rums to discuss issues, and also "study buddies" to prioritize your activities, and learn the best approach.

- **Performance Management:** Are you spending time on all the activities, and all the content, or are you giving preferential treat-ment to the things you enjoy? Be sure to cover all the topics, not just the ones you enjoy.

- **Internet and Mobile:** Use mobile devices and Wi-Fi and to ac-cess review materials. Be sure to access ones that cover all levels of Bloom's taxonomy, starting with identification (digital flash-cards, etc.) and moving to higher level tasks such as analysis and evaluation, which could include case studies.

- **Content Management:** Make a checklist that covers the content you need to know.

- **Skills Management:** Make a checklist that covers the skills that you need to cover.

One of the keys to success is to keep your approach simple and straight-forward.

Active Learning
and Your Online Course

When you hear the term "active learning," the image of a frantically busy you, posting and tweeting as you zoom through all the activities in the course, probably comes to mind.

"Active" is not simply "busy" though. To really learn the things you need to know in order to be successful and achieve the stated outcomes of the course, you're going to have to be active in very specific and targeted ways. A frenzy of activity, or an unfocused approach to your course will almost always result in less than desirable results.

For "active learning," you will focus on the following items:

- Reflect on what you're reading.
- Practice what you're learning, especially as they have to do with skills.
- Practice the tests.
- Interact with your peers in a productive, outcome-focused way: share drafts of papers, respond to learning objective-focused discussion posts.
- Look ahead and plan your study time.
- Budget your time.
- Break down your tasks in manageable bites.
- Reward yourself when you finish tasks.
- Start problem-solving tasks early, and keep them in mind as you read.

Active learning means active thinking. The best approach is to relate out-side events or activities to subjects you're dealing with. Incorporating situated learning is good, too—you can connect to real-life examples and prior knowledge.

If you have any questions, it's worthwhile to look up Chickering and Gamson's work. Their "Seven Principles for Good Practice in Under-graduate Education" (*AAHE Bulletin*, March 1987) is a classic. Although the article refers to traditional classroom-based learning, the principles here definitely apply.

As you read, think about what you're reading and make connections. When you're faced with problem solving, don't save it for last. Jump on the opportunity to engage in higher-order thinking tasks, such as analysis, synthesis, and evaluation.

Active learning, when it's focused and relates to your personal life and goals, can be a lot of fun.

Active Reading
in Your Online Course

I have a lot of reading to do in one of my online courses, and I'm starting to get lost.

How can I develop a strategy for remembering what I've read and using the information to do well in my quizzes and exams?

Sincerely,
Lost in Long Island

****

Dear Lost,

The best approach to your course materials is to do something called "active reading." Active reading is a strategy you can use to start creating order out of chaos by making clear ties between your readings and the course objectives.

Step One:
Make a list of your readings. Map them to learning objectives.

Step Two:
As you read each article, book, or chapter, jot down how and where the main ideas in the articles tie to the unit and course learning objectives. Determine the purpose or goal of the article you're reading: persuasive, informative, how-to, process.

Step Three:
In each article, look for main ideas and then draw a connection between the main ideas and supporting details/evidence.

Step Four:
Look at your required work for the unit and the course. See how the activities tie in with your readings. Annotate, highlight, jot down ideas, then make/sketch connections.

Step Five:
Review your notes, the readings, and the course content. Create a bullet point list of the main concepts in the unit, and then list which readings contain information to support/illustrate them.

Step Six:
Make a list of key thinkers/writers. Whose ideas form intellectual pillars? List their names, dates, and their ideas and key works.

Step Seven:
Make a list of case studies, examples, etc. in your readings that illustrate and/or provide evidence for some of the main concepts in the course.

You may be wondering at this point, what exactly do you do to make sure that you're reading in an active manner. One way is to constantly ask questions, and to keep a checklist.

Here are a few questions to ask yourself:

- Why am I reading this? What is it that I need to know? How should I read in order to pull the information I need?
- How should I start reading the document? How should I go about skimming it? How can I scan the document to pull out the main ideas and then the supporting evidence? What are the details that I should pay attention to? Which ones can I safely disregard?
- How can I pick out the main points and avoid being distracted?
- What can I do to use the table of contents or index in order to organize knowledge and to create a structure for my knowledge?
- How can I develop an outline or a special format for taking notes and organizing the information in my mind so that I can easily retrieve the key points?

- What is the point of tables of content, glossaries, and indices with respect to active reading? How can the table of contents help me organize my thoughts? Which points should I focus on? Which should I keep to the side?

Try these techniques, and I'm confident that you'll feel more focused, organized, and in control with respect to your course.

Annotated Bibliography:
Key to Research Paper Success

Online research has me bothered, bewitched, bewildered—and not in a good way!

I'm taking an online course in Broadway Musical Culture that gives me the opportunity to listen to the old standards and to trace the music history of the show tunes I love. So, I've started looking up articles, and things started to go well.

At first, my research went well. Then, I quickly became completely confused. Which sources are good? How can I evaluate the credibility of an article?

On top of that, I'm supposed to write an annotated bibliography. What is it? What's the point? This project is very frustrating. Help!

Sincerely,
Baffled in Bedford

****

Dear Baffled,

Let's take a look at your question and untangle the situation. Here is a step-by-step approach to conducting an online literature search while evaluating the credibility and developing an annotated bibliography.

Follow these steps and you will forge a solid foundation for your paper.

Step 1. Identify the topic of your search.

This step seems obvious. At the same time, you might be surprised to know how often this step is not taken seriously. It's important to identify the topic/focus of your paper and to start formulating your primary thesis. Granted, this may change or evolve as you write your paper, but the more tightly focused you can be, the better.

Step 2. Identify the appropriate databases to search.

One of the best things you can do early in the game is to make a list of available databases and to jot down the kinds of articles you're likely to find in each one. This will help focus your search. For example, if you're interested in writing a paper on childhood obesity in the United States, then you'll need to look in a database that contains statistics as well as journals and articles on health and wellness, social trends, and more. In this case, be sure to look at U.S. repositories of information and reports published by the Department of Health and Human Services, the U.S. Census, and more. **www.fedstats.gov** and **www.childstats.gov** are two great portals. For articles, your library may have Pro-Quest, EBSCO, Gale, and more.

Step 3. Analyze your articles for reliability.

Here are things to look for in the books, articles, and reports you read as you do your research.

- **Accuracy and Timeliness:** When was the article written? What kinds of support are they using as evidence for their position? Look closely at any data or statistics used to support the argument. Are they from reliable sources, and are they recent? Are they presenting the raw numbers, or are they interpreting them?

- **Completeness:** Are the statistics and the information giving you just one side of the story? How complete is the view?

- **Bias or Agenda:** What is the author's reason for writing? Is there an attempt to convince you of a particular point of view or perspective? Is there an obvious agenda? Do you see selective referencing? Do you see only one side of an issue represented?

- **References to Recognized Experts:** Who is your author citing as an expert? Is it a recognized expert? Is it a member of a fringe group? Is it a relative or personal acquaintance? Once you start determining the source of the author's expertise, you'll know the best way to approach the information.

Step 4. Write a paragraph description of each article.

Avoid a simple summary. Instead, make connections between the article and your primary thesis. What does the article say about what you're discussing? What kinds of information does it contain? Statistics? Case studies? Theoretical underpinnings? New perspectives and ways to look at things? Where? When? If you relate the article to your paper, you'll find it to be extremely useful as you start building your paper. Think of the one-paragraph description as a digital note card.

Step 5. Examine the references of the articles.

One way to determine where the main ideas and perspectives are coming from is to take a look at the references. Does your paper rely on Wikipedia for its information? If so, run! Discard that article and look further. What you're going for is an idea of who the "big thinkers" are, as well as their "big ideas."

Step 6. Start developing second-order references.

Second-order references are a secret weapon. Start looking up the references of the references. You'll be amazed at what you find. You'll be able to trace the entire history of an idea, and you'll see where some of the controversies and breakthroughs occurred. You'll also see where information and findings started to be swept under the rug. It is often useful to make a list of "second order references" and to list your article, and then just jot down the works you found in their bibliography/works cited list that really popped out for you. Then you'll be able to keep the information organized nicely in your mind—little mental file cabinets—of intellectual treasures and discoveries that you encounter in your research.

Step 7. Start identifying the "key thinkers" and "key ideas" that occur with regularity in your articles.

All of your research will start taking you to a deeper understanding of the big picture as well as the smaller details. You'll be fascinated and delighted by the depth and breadth of your understanding of a topic once you start to be able to map out the key thinkers and the key ideas.

As you work on your paper, you'll find that the research phase of your paper is perhaps the most valuable part of the process.

Are You Learning-
or Performance-Oriented?

How It Matters in an Online Course
and How to Avoid Learned Helplessness

I'm taking an online math course that requires me to do a lot of interactive quizzes and games. I am also required to show how to do very simple diagrams. At first it seemed fun, but now I don't know.

I'm able to do tasks easily, but I am frustrated. It feels like busywork, and that I'm not learning anything. I'm bored. I want to read articles and learn something about the underlying principles and theories.

I'm demotivated. I can't do anything to change it.

Help! What should I do?

Signed,
Underwhelmed in Iowa

****

Dear Underwhelmed:

Don't worry—you're not alone! Chances are the reason you're frustrated is because you're learning-oriented rather than performance-oriented. You exhibit strong mastery orientations regardless of your confidence. What motivates you is the idea of learning. It's more the concept than the skill.

Also, you may be on the track to a condition called "learned helpless-ness," which should be avoided at all costs.

The difference between learning-orientation and performance-orientation was first explored in the 1970s and 1980s by educational psychologist Carol Dweck who was trying to find out why some students started to develop what came to be known as "learned helplessness."

When certain students were asked to perform certain tasks—especially ones that could lead to feelings of failure and public humiliation—those same students became unwilling and unable to perform at all—no matter what task they were presented with. In essence, they froze and seemed paralyzed by indecision.

The same experiments were performed on dogs in a laboratory setting. When the laboratory subject was forced to endure aversive stimuli, they became unable or unwilling to avoid subsequent applications. The key is that they became helpless when they believed the situation was out of their control.

What I'm most worried about, Underwhelmed, is that you're having such an aversive reaction to the tedious activities that you're becoming unwill-ing to try them, even if you know that you are probably going to be able to perform well.

Yes, I'm worried that if you're in a similar class in the future, and you're forced to endure what is to you aversive stimuli (having to do a lot of busy work), you may simply quit and not continue.

In this case, I'd like to encourage you to be very proactive. It seems to me that you're more of a learning-oriented person, rather than performance-oriented.

According to Dweck, the way to motivate you is to find ways for you to pursue knowledge within your course, even if you're able to do the activi-ties without much worry.

Go to the resources page and read the background and any optional readings.

Then, contact your instructor for recommended readings.

Finally, in the discussion board area, be in touch with your fellow students. See if there is anything that they'd like to share from their readings

or personal experience.

Please try my suggestions as quickly as you can. I don't want to be alarmist, but I think your situation has the potential to go very badly very quickly. You must do an "e-learning intervention" right away.

REFERENCES

Dweck, Carol S. (1990), "Self-Theories and Goals: Their Role in Motivation, Personality, and Development," in *Perspectives on Motivation: Nebraska Symposium on Motivation*, Richard Dienstbier (Ed.), Lincoln, NE: University of Nebraska Press, 38, 199-235.

Attitudes, Value, Beliefs
and Succeeding at E-Learning

The Affective Domain and E-Learning Success:
Attitudes, Values, Beliefs, Opinions, Interests, Motivation

If you're used to face-to-face courses and traditional formats, you proba-bly feel fairly comfortable and confident. But why do you feel so good about what you're doing? You probably have a good attitude about the course, the delivery format, and the instructional strategy.

Chances are, you have a good attitude because you've succeeded in many similar situations and you're not worried a bit about what you have to do. You trust the teaching method, and you're convinced that you can learn, and that you can demonstrate what you've learned.

When it comes to online courses—e-learning that involves Web-based learning, mobile learning, or perhaps a combination of handhelds, laptops, and interactive devices—you're not so comfortable. In fact, you might feel awkward, uncomfortable, even defensive and nervous.

Why the difference?

It all boils down to the "affective domain." That's the term that instruc-tional psychologists use to describe the realm of feelings and emotions as they apply to learning.

The affective domain includes attitude, values, beliefs, opinions, interests, motivation, and even basic emotions such as fear, joy, anger, and sadness.

The elements in the affective domain are almost always key determinants in whether or not you, the e-learner, succeed in your course, and whether or not you perceive you had a positive experience.

How can you use this information to improve your chances of success, even enjoyment in your course? You can start by building a framework for the affective domain, and equipping yourself with what you need.

What are the elements to include in the framework? How can you construct them so that you're able to manage them? Here are the elements, and here are suggestions for putting them together.

1. **Attitude.**
   Attitude can be viewed in general terms as one's tendency or predisposition to respond positively or negatively toward things, people, places, events, concepts, and ideas (Koballa, 2008). The first step is to become aware of your attitudes toward distance learning, online instructors, the software, the technology, and your fellow students. Once you identify where you may have a negative reaction, then, find out what is shaping your attitude. Once you identify the points of stress, are you able to change your attitude by adjusting your attitudes or beliefs? Often, your self-investigation will reveal that many of your attitudes are shaped by fear of the unknown and/or fear of failure. Find activities that help you assuage your fears. Talk to someone. Practice the technology. Buy better equipment. Read your materials. Tell yourself that you like adventure, and you thrive in an intellectually challenging environment.

2. **Values.**
   Keep in mind that values tend to be less malleable than attitudes. Your values tend to be strong and enduring. So, with that in mind, use your values as muscle. Put your values to work. If you value education, knowledge, learning, and respect, remind yourself of that. Keep in mind that your regard for education can help you overcome your fears.

3. **Belief and attitude work together.**
   They mediate, modify, and alter behavior. This is a powerful insight. Think of the implications. If you don't believe in the efficacy of e-learning, then your behavior will demonstrate that. You

will not attack your lessons in an enthusiastic way. You'll hang back and resist purchasing the equipment you need. You'll behave unenthusiastically in the collaborative activities you need to do (discussion board, sharing messages/IM/tweets, posting portfolio materials).

4. **Need to change your attitude?**
Look to your instructor for help and guidance. Studies have shown that a positive attitude from your instructor can work wonders (Glynn & Koballa, 2006). If he/she demonstrates a positive belief in you, and has a supportive, encouraging approach to you, you're likely to start forming more positive beliefs about yourself and your ability to succeed. Further, you're more likely to enjoy what you're doing.

5. **Becoming a self-starter (self-efficacy).**
A well-designed instructional strategy or lesson plan will capture your interest, engage your feelings, and entice you to start trying out the activities, even before instructed to do so.

6. **Believing in yourself and your power to positively change your situation (self-determination, self-belief).**
One way to bolster your confidence is to actively tell yourself how your academic activities are worthwhile and meaningful. Further, you should tell yourself how much they will positively impact or influence your personal life. Map out the ways in which your academic activities will lead to your achieving your goals. Then, be sure to practices sufficiently in order to alleviate any assessment anxiety you might have.

7. **Motivation.**
There are number of tried and true ways to bolster your motivation in an e-learning context.

   • First, is to reinforce to yourself the positive benefits of what you're doing.
   • Second, look at what you'll get. What are the rewards? Are they extrinsic (Raise? Promotion? New job?) Are they intrinsic? (Do you love the topic? Are you interested in the subject?)
   • Finally, how can you set goals? What is the best way to break

down the task into small tasks?

8. **Self-determination gives you a better sense of control.**
    In e-learning, having the flexibility to the tasks at a convenient
    time and location, and to have choices about the topics you write
    about, what you study, what you discuss, can make a huge differ-
    ence. When possible, remind yourself of where and when you
    have choices. That will build your sense of self-determination.

As you read these points and suggestions, you may be feeling a bit of
anxiety. If so, relax. Keep in mind that a certain level of anxiety is, in reality, motivating. So, whenever you feel nervous about new challenges or
changes in your online education experience, tell yourself it is a good
thing. You're keeping your edge. You'll succeed.

Authentic Learning:
The Real World Makes All the Difference

You may have come across the term, "authentic learning" and wondered that if there is "authentic" learning, could there possibly be "inauthentic" learning?

Then, the horrible specter of the possibility that everything you've learned could be somehow "inauthentic"—in the realm of the false, unreal, and useless—may start to hound you. On some level, you probably consider some of the required general education courses to be an annoying distraction on the path to your overall goal.

But, don't let the idea of authenticity or inauthenticity worry you. Before you start down the path of questioning the whole of your educational experience, let's look at how to make sure that your learning experiences are everything they can be, and that they are "authentic.

Basically, authentic learning involves centering what you do around real-world tasks. For example, if you're taking a course on learning how to install a hot water heater, it's best if you're able to work with actual information and mechanical specifications. Otherwise, what you're learning could be useful in terms of basic principles, but you're not going to be as engaged as you could be.

Also, authentic learning suggests being able to exchange information with your peers and to discuss concepts that are meaningful.

Authentic learning is a kind of natural learning that flows from the concepts and the applications. Motivation tends to be intrinsic because the learners are highly interested in the knowledge and the outcome, and they see immediate value in their lives.

One criticism of authentic learning could be that it can seem a bit utilitarian, and to privilege applications rather than concepts.

In order to power up your learning by incorporating authentic learning, be sure to do the following:

- Center your learning around authentic tasks.
- Rely on your instructor to provide grounding and the proper sequence/scaffolding.
- Engage in social networks (informal and formal) to discuss the problems and tasks.
- Make sure you have ample resources to follow up (library, tools, equipment).
- Let yourself explore and actively inquire.

Authentic learning is a wonderful approach to topics that are highly applied and require you to solve problems.

Avoiding the "Yes, But..." Trap: Overcoming Negative Self-Talk

I was doing really well, on my way to my online degree, but something happened a few weeks ago, and I'm not quite sure what to do.

I was working on a group project, and I started to notice that we weren't able to make any kind of progress at all. Every time someone would suggest something, someone else would come up with some reason why it wouldn't work. For example, I wanted to go out and take photos, put them on Flickr, and then link to them for illustrations for our group project. It seemed like a good idea to me, and easy to do—but that was shot down. It wasn't just my suggestion—everyone else got shot down, too.

What could be happening? We get together quite well online, and no one is rude—it's just that we're at a total impasse.

Sincerely,
Stuck in St. Simeon

****

Dear Stuck:

Even though it is a polite atmosphere, and everyone seems to be getting along quite well, there is something insidious going on. You're starting to see negative self-talk in all your group members.

Negative self-talk is very serious and you have to act quickly before this behavior spreads to your online academic career and your life in general.

The "Yes, but…" game essentially states "I can't do it" or even worse, "You can't do it!" to all who care to listen. There is a feeling of resistance and a kind of stubborn refusal to be solution-centered, which is very disturbing.

Chances are, you and your group members are not even aware of what you're doing. You may not know that you're not only blocking each other, you're blocking yourselves by not even trying the different suggestions.

The "Yes, but…" game is just one of many ways to engage in negative self-talk. There are many ways to sabotage yourself. The key is to learn how to pull yourself out of the tailspin. One of the best approaches is to incorporate strategies from self-regulation. Here are a few great ways to get started:

1. **Keep social opportunities open.** Make sure everyone feels they are contributing something and that it's being recognized and acknowledged. Give people a chance to go out on a limb and be creative.

2. **Set goals that can be measured.** When your group starts mapping out its project, be sure to ask people to do something that can be measured. Usually that translates into something that can be produced. For example, a mini-report could be part of it. Another could be feedback on each other's contributions.

3. **Be sure to include deadlines.** Nothing's worse than having a lot of things to do, but no sense of when to do them. The lack of deadlines is a great way to get people stuck in a procrastination trap.

4. **Make sure challenges are at the right level of difficulty.** If you ask your team members to do something that's too easy, they'll become bored and will stop being engaged. On the other hand, if it's too difficult, it can be demotivating. After all, no one likes to feel as though they'll most likely fail at what they've been asked to do.

5. **Make sure the tasks are relevant.** Help people see the potential transfer implications in what they're doing, and how they can apply what they're doing.

So, Stuck, please don't give up—there are a lot of things that you can do.

Building Your Problem-Solving Skills for Your Online Courses

In your online courses, problem solving comes into play in a number of areas. First, the fact that you're taking a course online requires you to respond to challenges and to solve problems as you negotiate the learning management system and determine the ways that you're expected to satisfy course requirements. Second, your assignments and papers may require a number of problem sets and analyses, from case studies to actual processing of data. Finally, you may be asked to work in groups or with a partner in order to develop a research paper or portfolio that addresses a problem set or case study.

In an online environment, the fact that you're working alone and communication while communication is in certain ways easier, with email, text-messaging, and other ways to send and receive messages both synchronously and asynchronously, there is no escaping the fact that there will always be a bit of anxiety and ambiguity.

For that reason, it's very important to look closely at the problem solving you're expected to do and to develop a method for tackling the problem.

A convenient and very useful approach to problem solving is to break down the problem itself into core aspects.

The Problem's Four Aspects

Here are the ways to break down the problem and to state the components in a way that will help you progress toward a solution.

- **Goal:** state toward which the goal is directed; must be able to measure whether or not the goal has been met
- **Givens:** objects, conditions, and constraints
- **Means of transforming:** ways to change the initial states
- **Obstacles:** does not have experience or knowledge of a solution

Problem Solving as Search

One of the best ways to approach your problem is to take a look at a number of different approaches and to try the one that works for you.

- **Heuristic Approach**
  Look at all possible states and choose the one that is "best." "Hill climbing"—start with the givens at each step, choose the operators to always move "up" to the goal:
  - examine all operators (test with foot)
  - find out the state (what's the angle of the hill?)
  - choose what takes you there most quickly

- **Problem Reversal**
  Not all problems can be solved by choosing what brings you progressively closer to the goal.

- **Means-Ends Analysis**
  This involves a gap analysis—look at where you are and compare it with where you want to be. Find the largest difference/gap & discuss how to meet the gap. You need to know which operators (vectors) to use to meet the gap.

- **Working Backward**
  This is a good approach if the number of directions from the goal is small and the number of givens is large. In this case, it is simpler to work backwards to the beginning.

- **Problem Solving as Representation**
  In this case, the way the problem is represented is crucial— representation of the problem is the problem space, which contains states and operators/vectors. Sometimes representation is easier because it can be displayed graphically and is less challenge to memory.

- **Hierarchies**
  Sometimes you can solve problems by creating hierarchies based on importance. Time management is a good example.

As you take stock of your problems, be sure to break down your problem in order to look at it from multiple perspectives. You'll have a great deal of success as you become increasingly nimble with your analytical processes.

HUMAN PROBLEM SOLVING REFERENCES:

Classic text: Newell and Simon (1972). *Human Problem Solving.* Englewood Cliffs, NJ: Prentice-Hall.

H. A. Simon (1978) *Information Processing Theory of Human Problem Solving.* W. K. Estes (Ed.), *Handbook of Learning and Cognitive Processes*, (Vol. 5). Hillsdales, NJ: Erlbaum.

Wickelgren, W. A. (1974) *How to Solve Problems: Elements of a Theory of Problems and Problem Solving.* San Francisco: W. H. Freeman.

Lovett, M. C. (2002). *Problem Solving.*

H. Pashler & D. L. Medin (Eds.) *Steven's Handbook of Experimental Psychology*, 3rd Ed., Volume 2. (pp. 317-362). New York: Wiley.

Career-Tuning Your Term Papers

I am not motivated to write my term papers. They seem like a waste of time, and I just can't seem to get myself in gear in order to do them. Consequently, when it comes time for my papers, I am not excited about it.

Is there any way that I do something so that the term papers mean more to me? I would love to think that my term papers could be useful to me in the future.

Sincerely,
Troubled by Term Papers

****

Dear Troubled,

I can totally understand your frustration—it's frustrating when you're trying to equip yourself for the future and tool yourself to meet changing times.

But, how would you feel if you could write papers on any topic, and you could list them in your resume?

My personal opinion is that all writing is good. After all, writing involves thinking, and every time that you conduct research on a topic, analyze a problem, draft outlines, and structure an argument, you're engaging in an exercise that helps you deepen your knowledge base and to sharpen your analytical skills.

As you start to look ahead, ask your professors if you have any latitude when it comes to writing your papers. If so, you're in luck. You can tailor your papers so that you can use them later as showpieces as you go to an interview. Just think of the impact of presenting a paper along with your resume. You'll demonstrate in a single gesture that you're creative, you have good communication skills, you can express your thoughts well, and that you're willing to go to extra effort in the pursuit of high quality.

For example, let's say you're interviewing for a position as a marketing support staff position at Whole Foods. You could bring the paper you wrote on sustainability and green business practices. While the person who is interviewing you may not read every word of your paper, chances are, they'll be impressed.

If they're doing a Google search on you to see what you've been up to, you can easily post your papers on your Facebook account, and link to websites where you've uploaded your papers. You can also record a few podcasts and also interview someone (or yourself) on the topic and post a few spontaneous videos on YouTube.

Or, let's say that you're interested in positions that have to do with developing the community. You could do the same with papers/research you've done on such issues as domestic violence intervention, child welfare, taking care of the aging, and more.

The more projects that you have that involve web-based research, Web 2.0, etc. interaction, mobile communications, the better.

So, just to recap, what are the best things for you to put on display?

- Research papers
- Portfolios that include multimedia assets/objects

Now, at this point, you may be asking yourself if you might be overdoing it if you try to do more than a simple research paper for your final paper. Before you plunge in, be sure to clear it with your instructor. Sadly, if you don't, your instructor may think that you're repurposing material from a different course, or that you've found resources from somewhere else. So, to allay suspicion before it even occurs, clear everything first.

In fact, be very open with your motives. Explain to your instructor what you want to do and why. She or he will be impressed—and, you may be surprised what sorts of doors it may open.

Here is a list of multimedia activities you may wish to do:

- videos
- audio podcasts
- web apps
- mashups
- blends of diagrams/maps/charts/graphics

If you're into a topic—start posting feeds and Twitter alerts. After all, you never know when you might attract the eye of someone who would like to inquire about your availability for a position or even consulting/contract work.

So, in conclusion, dear Troubled, I'd like to say that there is no reason to feel troubled. Your ingenuity and your drive will serve you well, even in the worst of times.

Conquering Procrastination

I admit it. I'm a procrastinator. I often get mad at myself for putting myself through what I consider to be unnecessary stress. If only I could work differently!! I get "stuck" right up until the night before the paper or project is due, and then, suddenly, things click. I put on headphones, look at the clock, then block out the world. I know I have to perform, and suddenly it all comes together.

So, time and time again, I pull together a paper at the last minute.

I usually get good grades, but I can't even begin to describe to you the level of stress I endure. It's so bad that I'm even thinking about just saying goodbye to my dream of a college degree. I love what I'm studying, but I just can't handle this nightmare existence.

What should I do?

Time-stressed in Texas

****

Dear Time-Stressed,

You've pointed out what is probably the most damaging aspect of pro-crastination. It's not the fact that you're missing deadlines. It's what it does to your self-esteem and your self-confidence. If you're not careful, you'll start to believe the negative things you say to yourself when you're frustrated.

Procrastination leads to a classic downward spiral: You miss a deadline, you tell yourself negative things, you panic, you can't face another deadline, you paralyze yourself with dread and avoidance.

Before you get entrenched in avoidance, what are some of the things you never avoid? Do you like to do things with friends? Do you like to share news and photos? Do you update your Facebook page regularly?

Start making a list of the things that you do without any prodding at all. List the activities you enjoy, and the ones that make you feel a sense of anticipation and flow.

Then, look at the elements you typically procrastinate with. Is there any way to give yourself a boost and somehow combine them? For example, do you wait to study until the night before the exam? Do you avoid writing papers?

One way to overcome work and study avoidance is to do it in a group. Even if you're isolated and can't easily meet face to face, use Skype or video chat to discuss your paper with a study buddy. You can also share drafts and also share links to reviews.

You talked about how you're thinking about giving up on your dream. Believe me, you're not the only one. You need someone to help keep you motivated. Develop a network of friends, or find a "coach" of sorts—it does not have to be as formal as a mentor or advisor. Just do something to break out of your isolation. Procrastination is not something you have to battle alone.

I really appreciate your honesty. As you may know, college students are renowned for getting caught up in cycles of work avoidance and procrastination.

There have been a number of studies on college students and procrastination. They tend to start in the same way—they ask the question, "What is procrastination?" Basically speaking, it is failing to do something even when you know that the failure to act or perform will result in negative consequences.

Who procrastinates? As I mentioned before, college students are notorious for procrastinating, but the behavior can be found any group—particularly when there are tasks to be performed that are imposed upon an individual and which do not align with that person's interests, goals, or career.

Why do people procrastinate? Some psychologists have looked at procrastination as a kind of self-harming. They say that, like other self-harming activities, procrastination becomes almost a compulsion, and the procrastinator can't seem to stop repeating the negative behavior.

I'm not sure I believe the self-harming explanation for all of procrastination. In my opinion, there's a lot more avoidance going on as well as a lack of motivation. After all, people have needs for affiliation, and if their needs aren't being met, they're potentially in bad shape.

But if self-harming is really what lurks behind the mask of procrastination, it follows that some of the technique used to counter self-harming—self-forgiveness, support groups, talk therapy—might work.

Other studies discuss the role of rewards in breaking procrastination patterns. Others say that procrastination is all about flawed goal-setting. If you set your goal too high, you may be demotivated and frustrated when your attempts fail. Further, you may keep putting off the big task, while you easily knock off the little tasks.

Effective goal-setting—tiny tasks, each with a reward—can be very useful in terms of modifying behavior and beliefs about yourself.

At any rate, Time-Stressed, I hope that this has been a useful response. Ultimately, procrastination is something you'll learn to overcome. It's all about finding the right tactics just for you.

Then, bit by bit, you'll regain confidence again—and you'll feel much more comfortable about embracing your dream of a college degree.

You can do it!

Coping with Major Life Losses: When Grief and Loss Hit You in the Middle of the Term

I'm dealing with grief and it is affecting me more than I ever imagined. I thought I would be ready for it, but I am not. I can't concentrate and I keep having intrusive thoughts.

Perhaps the worst of it all is the fact that—out of the blue—I'll be hit by a wave a sadness. It is not the kind of sadness that makes you burst out weeping. Instead, it's something that gives me a sinking feeling. I feel a bit of weight in my stomach and am overwhelmed by a listlessness that takes over.

My reactions, thoughts, and responses are so slow I might as well be paralyzed. You can imagine how damaging this is for my academic activities. I'm getting hopelessly behind in my courses.

Grief is hard.

My mother died. It was not a surprise. She battled cancer for more than twenty years. She was in and out of remission, and in the meantime had episodes of pneumonia and extreme difficulty breathing. Consequently, she was very frail. Things were bad when she fell and broke her hip and shoulder. She was in the hospital for a month, then went home and in hospice care and died five months later.

Hospice is supposed to make things better, but in my view, it didn't help much. The sedatives and pain management made her more frail and further suppressed her appetite. At the end, my mom was absolutely skeletal. Despite 24-7 home health care from an independent home health agency, combined with hospice for pain management, my mom died a ghastly, painful, and traumatizing death that my sister and dad witnessed.

Yes, she was under hospice pain management care, and you'd think I'd realize the end was near. Frankly, I expected my mom to outlast me. After all, she had cheated death many times over that 22-year battle with thyroid cancer and all its ugly metastases.

She died within two weeks of a conversation in which my dad and I explored ways to find economic alternatives to the $15,000 he was paying each month to the private home health care company. I thought of ways to use independent contractors and to bring the cost down from $15,000 to $4,000 per month. My mom seemed to think it was a good idea.

I had all kinds of emotions and irrational thoughts after she died. My first thoughts were angry ones—why did she refused to eat or drink? Why not hang on longer? Then, I felt guilty—did I do something to make her give up?

Right now, I am stuck. I try to stay out of an emotional freefall—people tell me to stay busy. But it's not working. What can I do?

Guilty in Graduate School

****

Dear Guilty:

It is good that you are self-aware and that you are willing to confront the feelings that are surging within you at unexpected times.

Everyone is different. Don't expect to read one book and think it will apply to you in every regard. That said, there are a few aspects of grief that seem to be fairly common to the human experience. You may feel the following negative emotions:

- Denial
- Anger
- Guilt
- Intrusive thoughts of the past
- Paralysis
- Avoidance

As you start to transition out of the raw pain, you may find that healing involves the following:

- Transformative thoughts
- Forgiveness
- Self-forgiveness
- Renewed focus, with a legacy-inspired mission or goal

It's not unusual for you to be underperforming at this time. In fact, you should underperform! After all, you're dealing with something devastating. As you look inside, here are a few ways to cope:

1. Give yourself time to heal. Maybe take fewer courses.
2. Find strategies to deal with intrusive thoughts.
3. Work with your strengths and rely on your preferred learning styles.
4. Find a support team and collaborate with your peers.
5. Incorporate your experiences and feelings and use them in your papers and projects when you can.
6. Take courses that interest and inspire you.

I know my approach may seem a bit formulaic, but trust me—it works!

Please give yourself plenty of room to be, to feel, and to let yourself fly free. Generously acknowledge your love, your memories, and your sadness with respect to your losses. Fill yourself with love and acceptance. Then, apply the wonderful flow to yourself and others. Give yourself credit. Kudos is due. Don't let yourself give in to any negativity. Take the high road. Be grateful and share.

As you consider my suggestions, don't delay in contacting your advisor. This is a difficult time and it's a very important moment—contact your advisor while you're feeling emotional distress. You'll be amazed at how much trust and true bonding you can experience.

Courage in an Online Course:
Developing the Creativity You Need to Succeed

If you're taking an online course for the first time, you're probably nervous about it, and are not quite sure how to proceed. Don't worry. You're not alone. Everyone who has taken a course has felt uncertain and out of their comfort zone. Sometimes it is due to the unfamiliar technology, and sometimes it is due to uncertainty about the human interactions in the course—with the instructor and with other students.

Remember that you're creating a new world for yourself, and your new world has new possibilities and potential. As you move forward, you will gain momentum and strength from the creative force, all of which means you will be well equipped to handle changes and opportunities in the future. But it's not easy. In many ways, taking an online course is a reflection of what is going on in our world, as we continue to be in flux with technology, the workplace, the global economy, and our sense of who we are in the world.

These are scary times. However, one can argue that all times are scary. You're under a lot of pressure to be successful.

Being successful is not easy—you're required to have a number of skills, and it's often hard to find a mentor or a friend who can walk you through the basics. You need a guide who can give you confidence and can steer you away from pitfalls such as poor time management, poor sequencing of courses, and inadequate preparation (textbook, technology, connectivity, prerequisite courses).

But where is such a guide? You'll find guides in all shapes and forms as you move forward in the world, and in your online course. Sometimes your guide will be your advisor. Sometimes your guide will be a fellow student.

More times than not, you will be your own guide.

To be your own guide requires courage; specifically, the courage to create. In his landmark book, *The Courage to Create* (1975), author Rollo May discusses four types of courage, which he considers essential for creativity and for living in the world. It's amazing that a book published so long ago, roughly contemporaneous with then-popular, but ultimately ephemeral works such as *Future Shock, I'm OK, You're OK, The Peter Principle*, and others. Rollo May's work is timeless because he connects with and responds to dominant approaches to psychology and a kind of existentialism that resonates with a world in constant flux.

May looks at what it takes to maintain a condition of positive creativity in the first chapter of *The Courage to Create*. They break down into four types of courage: physical, moral, social, and creative. In many ways, the four types of courage apply to online courses (as well as to the Web-based world in general).

- **Physical Courage:** This does not relate to violence or combat, but it has to do with the physical body. It also involves skills that require dexterity and coordination. In earning an online degree, you are required to have physical courage as you use your computer, and perhaps other technologies—cellphones, digital cameras, MP3 players, GPS devices, and more.

- **Moral Courage:** For this, you are required to take a stand against violence, and take a stand for what is good for the community. It often requires one to get involved. In an online course, you may need to take a position as you write essays or a research paper. You will be asked to look at a topic from many points of view, and it is important for you to be able to determine your own values, ethical stance, and personal behaviors when confronted by real-world situations.

  If you're in a nursing program, you may be asked to look at your values with respect to terminally ill patients who request euthanasia. If you're in a business course, you may be asked to discuss sustainable business, and how to make sure your choices are environmentally sustainable.

- **Social Courage:** Risk yourself, and be willing to develop supportive social relationships within the course. You will find that one of the best ways to learn in an online course is in conjunction with others. This requires, however, that you confront some of your deepest fears—those of vulnerability and abandonment. Do not abandon yourself. As you turn in your work, share your thoughts and work publicly, and process the thoughts and comments of others, it is very important to develop self-confidence and self-reflection.

  Courage means slowing down and telling yourself you will not rush to judgment—either of others or of yourself. Give yourself second, third, fourth chances—as many as you need. Be patient with yourself. Develop positive self-talk, and recognize how your words affect your mood. Focus on developing an "I can do it!" attitude, and, similarly, find ways to foster a "You can do it!" mood in collaborate online activities, including discussion boards, Twitter, wikis, blogs, podcasts, and more.

- **Creative Courage:** According to May, creative courage involves discovering and appreciating new forms, patterns, and symbols. For May, the reason this is a type of courage is because it asks us to question and shake the pillars of our own mental structures.

  Do you assume something to be the case? Ask again. What causal relations do you assume to be true (without even questioning)? Where are there familiar patterns or configurations of knowledge that you accept (while rejecting the unfamiliar). Rollo May would ask you to take a second look. Question your assumptions. Propose new or different patterns. Suggest a different causal relationship. As you do so, you will become aware that the limits of your world have shifted out—your world, and your possibilities—have just expanded.

Courage in online learning gives you a chance to forge a new reality. As you do so, you change the parameters of your own conditions of living. You will also be adept at change, and at identifying opportunities as they present themselves to you. Rollo May's insights into courage and the elements needed for creative minds and acts resonate now more than ever.

BIBLIOGRAPHY

May, Rollo. 1975. *The Courage to Create*. New York: W. W. Norton. Pedigo, Susie. 2009. (Book summary on: **www.intuitive-connections.net/2004/book-couragecreate.htm**)

Discussion Boards: Delightful or Dangerous?

If the path to your online degree requires a great deal of interaction on a discussion board, you probably enjoy it. It's a great place to get to know your fellow e-learners, and it helps you keep from feeling that you're absolutely alone in the e-learning space. At the same time, if you have questions, it's often easier to ask a classmate instead of asking the instructor. No one wants to feel foolish, and it's good to have a buddy system. You're in a situation where you get to discuss the course and gain a deeper appreciation of different approaches and perspectives to the work. Beware, though—there can be pitfalls in the discussion board, and potentially dangerous areas.

Discussion Boards Pros

- Connect personal experience with course content.
- It is always interesting to hear what others think about the same reading, and the same assignment. When you read an article or do online research, you may wonder if your thoughts are on track with what you're supposed to be getting out of the writing.
- Chance to ask questions, feel comfortable with ambiguity.
- Develop learning community.
- Peer reinforcement and collaboration.
- Connection between readings / course content & learners' lived experience.
- Evoking and building on prior knowledge.
- Post and share learner support items.
- Share or create portfolios and galleries of images, projects, presentations, etc.

Discussion Board Cons

Can you trust everything you read in the discussion board? Which posts are reliable, and which are not? Learning critical thinking skills and how to judge the reliability of information is a skill you'll find very useful in a world of blogs, wikis, Twitter, and other interactive ways to share information and opinions. Sometimes something is believed simply because everyone wants it to be true. We can see that all the time in e-mail chain letters on urban myths. Below are a few issues to keep in mind as you respond to prompts and as you read classmates' posts.

Cognitive Domain Dangers: Can You Trust What You Read?

The cognitive domain covers the knowledge and information you're learning in your course, and it also refers to where and how mental processing takes place. One of the most fundamental lessons of learning is that learning is continuous—you are always learning, even when you may not think you are. So, with that in mind, remember that it is as easy to learn wrong information and practices.

You've seen it in your daily life—the news flash that goes viral, rumors of celebrity deaths or causes of deaths, rumors about the financial health of a bank or a company. People behave as though these rumors are true.

You might not think that the same thing would happen in an online course, but it can because the discussion board is essentially a social network and the same behaviors occur there.

Perhaps the most problematic aspect of the discussion board is that one tends to let go one's critical thinking skills and begin to trust things that are posted.

One of the most radical cognitive issues ushered in by Web 2.0 applications is that that participants tend to stress community member-contributed knowledge. This gives way to a mentality of "knowledge is a construct, mediated by the community," which can be dangerous.

- Like YouTube videos going viral, the information shared may be incomplete, inaccurate, misleading.
- Like blogs and social networking sites, what you share is not necessarily anything more than an opinion, but it possesses authority and could confuse people.
- Like social networking sites, the attention-getting and emotion-grabbing are more appealing; the faux chases out the real (if one is not careful).
- Can distract from the outcomes / outcomes assessments.
- Learning objects can be the anchors—tie to the assessments that will be required.

Core Strengths of the Discussion Board: Affective Domain

Before you give up entirely on the discussion board, keep in mind that the discussion board emulates real life and the social networks (in the real world and in the virtual world) that you interact with. Learning takes place by sharing information and emulating the positive behaviors of others.

- Sense of community (need for affiliation)
- Develop positive self-concept
- Motivating—goal-setting, affirmation, recognition
- Develops sense of self-efficacy
- Self-determination

The strongest benefits occur in the affective domain—the part of learning that engages your feelings and emotions. This is where you find ways to motivate yourself and to satisfy innate needs that you as a human being possess.

Effective Goal-Setting in Your Online Course: Revisiting Locke and Latham and the SMART Approach for Maximum Impact

One of the most effective ways to successfully complete your online courses is to make progress by setting and achieving a series of systematic, clear, and manageable goals.

Do you regularly set goals? How? What are they?

A goal is "something that the person wants to achieve" (Locke & Latham, 1990, p.2). There are a number of types of goals, which range from short-term to long-term goals. It is important to have both.

Long-term vs. short-term goals

A long-term goal is one that can take quite a bit of time to achieve and is complex in nature. It often consists of a series of embedded steps or activities. An example of a long-term goal is a college degree: "My overall goal is to earn a master's degree in criminal justice."

A short-term goal could be to complete a paper or series of assignments. They could be a part of a course needed for graduation.

Mastery goals are better than performance goals

Mastery goals (also called learning goals) focus on gaining competence or mastering a new set of knowledge or skills. For example, "I've decided to study the sonnets from Shakespeare's 'Dark Lady' period."

A performance can lead to frustration because they subject the individual to potential criticism. For example, "I'm going to avoid double-faulting today."

Here are attributes of mastery goals:

- Focus on effort and learning
- High intrinsic interest in activity
- Attributions to effort
- Attributions to effort-based strategies
- Use of effective learning and other self-regulatory strategies
- Active engagement
- Positive affect on high effort tasks
- Feelings of belongingness
- "Failure-tolerance"

How can goal-setting be your secret weapon in your online work?

What are the essential qualities of goals you can really use?

- Positive
- Precise
- Written down
- Realistic
- About performance (not ultimate outcomes)

    » **Step 1:** Identify what you have to accomplish
    » **Step 2:** List the tasks.
    » **Step 3:** Break down the tasks into sub-tasks.
    » **Step 4:** Prioritize
    » **Step 5:** Develop a plan—SMART goals.

        S Specific
        M Measurable
        A Attainable
        R Relevant
        T Time-bound

REFERENCES

Alderman, M. K. (1999). *Goals and goal setting. Motivation for achievement: possibilities for teaching and learning.* New Jersey: Lawrence Erlbaum Associates.

Ames, C. (1992). "Classrooms: Goals, structures, and student motivation." *Journal of Educational Psychology.* V. 84, N.3, p. 261-271.

Ames, C., & Archer, J. (1988). "Goals in the classroom: students' learning strategies and motivation processes." *Journal of Educational Psychology.* 80(3), 260-267.

Locke, E. A., & Latham, G. P. (1990). *A theory of goal setting and task performance.* Englewood Cliffs, NJ: Prentice-Hall.

Feeling Confident
about Your Peer Activities Online

Collaborating with your fellow e-learners can be a high-stakes proposition in an online course. After all, discussion board postings and other peer activities can count as much as 30 percent of your grade. For that reason, you might feel a great deal of anxiety and wonder just what you should do to get a good grade and to have a positive experience.

Your peer activities generally include discussion board entries, group projects, and collaborations (wikis, portfolios). All can cause tremendous anxiety if you're worried that you'll be judged by your peers, or if you wonder if they'll turn in work. You may have visions of the group projects in the past where you ended up doing all the work, and all your group members simply rode on your coattails.

However, in an online learning, peer activities are often what students like most. They enjoy them because they give students a chance to get to know each other and to connect. Further, they can help learners achieve learning objectives and feel more comfortable about assessment (quizzes, papers, etc.).

Typical Peer Activities:

- Analyze the text and readings and post your thoughts.
- Compare and share research results.
- Share thesis / topics of term papers.
- Share drafts of term papers.
- Relate course content to your own experience.
- Identify potential controversial areas and share insights, opinions, and other experiences.

What learning objectives are accomplished through peer activities?

Sometimes it's easy to start by thinking about why your course requires peer activities. You'll have the chance to do the following:

- Develop critical thinking skills by analyzing your own answer as well as responding to others.
- Explore problem-solving in a collaborative way as you bounce ideas off each other.
- Discover new approaches and perspectives as you consider other points of view.
- Synthesize information from several sources.
- Identify points of controversy and disagreement, and develop a way to debate/discuss and come to conclusions.
- Find out how other people organize knowledge and develop your own schemata for filing and retrieving information from your long-term memory.
- Make connections between the content and the real world of people's lives and experiences.

Of course, the quality of the experience of the discussion board depends on the quality of the prompts. You can't do much with "yes/no" answers, so if you happen to be in a course that has a preponderance of "same answer" or "yes/no" questions, contact the instructor and ask her to modify the questions immediately.

Also, if the questions require simple reporting of information or current events, it will be tempting for students to copy and paste excerpts from the Internet rather than putting in their own thoughts and analysis. The discussion prompts should always rehumanize the e-learning space, which is to say that it should make the student put a piece of his or her own heart and soul into the posts.

If discussion board prompts are well written, they can help you achieve the learning objectives for the course, and to successfully perform outcomes and outcomes assessments.

Discussion board posts can help you prepare for your quizzes and papers:

- Course content organized in a way that you can remember.
- Compare and share research results.

- Share online research techniques and articles (along with a precis or synopsis).
- Peer reactions to a text or a problem trigger your own thoughts that you can use to write a paper.
- Stories related to course content and concepts are easier to retrieve (we're hard-wired to remember narratives, especially if they are personal stories).

Tips for Effective Discussion Board and Peer Activity Success:

- Post early, post often: Don't wait until the last minute, and don't be the last poster. If you do, you're not really in the game. You're running the risk of being a "lurker" or a "late to the party" person. Neither is conducive to learning.
- Stay with the group: Conversely, the early birds who post on all the threads the minute they're open, just to disappear and never be seen again, are equally out of the game. In certain ways, they get even less out of the assignment since they're not reading anything that anyone is posting.
- Make sure your posts are engaged and relevant: Detailed, personalized posts are great. When you respond to student posts, make sure your posts are responsive to what they're saying and that you contribute to the conversation.

Final Thoughts:

Peer activities can be the best part of an online course, but to get the most of them, you must make a commitment to truly engage with the content and your fellow students. If you are not really paying attention to what the question is asking you consider, or if you're not really reading your fellow students' posts, it will show. You'll seem disengaged, and worse, you probably will feel a lack of connection to the course and the content. In order to get the most of your experience, relax and think of how much you'll enjoy finding new ways to communicate with learners and really engage with the content and the topic. Peer activities make learning continuous and fun.

Getting the Most
from Student and Sample Essays

I've been reading the sample essays and the textbook for my course, but I'm worried. It is all a blur. What am I supposed to be looking for?

Help!

Jillian G. in Tampa

****

Dear Jillian,

You're on the right track. One of the best ways to meet expectations is to find out what your instructor is looking for. If there are sample essays, be sure to look at them close. They can help guide you as you write your own essays for the course.

Here are steps to follow:

Step 1:
Identify the kind of essay you're looking at. Is it a compare/contrast essay? Taking a position? Process? Extended definition?

Step 2:
Look at the structure. How does the essay start? What do they do to engage the reader? Why does it seem interesting to you?

Step 3:

What is the primary thesis of the essay? How do you know? How does the author make it clear? How does the author structure the thesis in a way that signals how/where the body paragraphs can be structured?

Step 4:

What do the body paragraphs look like? How does each topic sentence tie back to the primary thesis?

Step 5:

How long are the body paragraphs? How, exactly, do they support the goal of the essay? What kind of information can be found in them? Look for main ideas and supporting details/evidence.

Step 6:

What kind of tone does the author have? Is it formal or informal? What is successful about it? How is it interesting?

As you start to write your own essay, be sure to identify what kind of essay it is that you'll be writing. Relate it to the sample essays you've been reading. Then, start to brainstorm and generate content. Here are a few steps:

- Identify your writing goal.
- Jot down a few primary thesis options.
- Annotate, highlight, jot down ideas that tie to your primary thesis.
- Make/sketch connections to your own experience, articles you've read, case studies, or statistics.

After you've written a draft of your paper, it is always a good idea to have a "second set of eyes" go over it. Exchange it with fellow student for peer review. As you read each others' papers, keep the following questions in mind:

1. How well does the paper I'm reading compare with the various samples? Does it follow too closely and thus lose originality?
2. How does the paper capture my attention and keep me wanting to continue reading?
3. What kinds of support are presented? Am I convinced? Is the

argument a solid one? How? Where? When?

4. Is the author too careful? Does he/she fail to express original views or ideas? How and where might the author introduce new and different types of support, arguments, and insight?

5. Where are ideas underdeveloped?

6. Where do the ideas start to go off topic and on a tangent?

I think that if you follow these rather simple procedures, you'll be very happy with the outcome.

Good luck, and remember to enjoy writing!

Getting the Most from Webinars

It is possible that the online course you're taking involves signing up for a webinar. Or, alternatively, you may be asked to do research for a paper, and in doing so, you've found a webinar that addresses your topic. Webinars are fantastic because they can present up-to-the-minute information from renowned experts in a way that lets you interact with them synchronously, or, to go back and review on-demand at your own convenience.

Some learning organizations use webinars for "guest lecturers" who elaborate a topic that has been discussed in course. Or, they guide learners in making connections between concepts and real-world concerns. For example, the topic of the webinar might be on the importance of budgeting when creating a financial plan for yourself and your family.

While the number of speakers can vary, as can the type of presentation, the key elements to keep in mind are the following questions:

- Before the webinar, how can I prepare for it? Is there any pre-reading to do? Should I brief myself on the assessments?
- How does this webinar tie into the overall course outcomes and learning objectives?
- What am I expected to do after the webinar is over?
- How am I supposed to work with the material that was presented?
- How can I get the most out of the fact that I can interact with the speaker and the audience members? What are the kinds of questions I can ask?
- Will there be any kind of follow-up discussion?

Webinars come in many shapes and sizes.

When many people think of webinars, they think of an online product demo or a software training session. They are useful, but limited in scope. The training webinar is just the beginning, however. Recent uses of webinars include virtual workshops and forums, as well as information sessions and question and answer sessions.

Webinars in educational settings:

When many people think of webinars, they think of an online product demo or a software training session. They are useful, but limited in scope. The training webinar is just the beginning, however. Recent uses of webinars include virtual workshops and forums as well as information sessions and question and answer sessions.

- **Guest Lecturers:** Your professor can invite a guest lecturer to discuss an aspect of the course for which he or she has special expertise or experience. Webinar attendees are able to gain new insights and perspectives.

- **Live Events:** Tap into a subject matter expert: the webinar may incorporate a live feed from an event, which can be incorporated into the interface where the webinar attendees are asking questions. This is often done in virtual worlds, and the live event streams in on a screen while audience members communicate via their avatars.

- **Archived Webinars:** The value of the webinar lives on as it become a learning object, and used as instructional material for asynchronous courses.

Typical Speakers and Types of Presentations:

- Single speaker or multiple
- Questions / active responses
- Focus on content (not on background)
- Technical – avoid sales pitches "infomercials"
- Connect to current events
- Respond to current concerns

Characteristics of Webinars

- Interactive
- Participatory
- PowerPoint presentation with voice presentation
- Questions from audience
- May have streaming media / live feed from webcam
- May use special platforms (Elluminate, Adobe Connect, Omnovia, Web Ex, Go to Meeting)

- May use messenger/communications (Skype, MSN Messenger, Google chat)
- May supplement with landline audio
- Can share information (upload/download files)
- Typical length of a webinar: 1 - 1 ½ hours
- Typical number of presenters: 1 - 3 presenters, with a host
- Typical size of the room: varies, but strategies for responding to questions will have to vary if there are more than a hundred active participants typing questions for the presenters.

Webinar platforms range from simple (and almost free) to highly functional and expensive. Webinars tend to use web conferencing software and the live presentation is often archived and hosted for on-demand access.

Webinar Software:

Adobe Connect
Large volume users often use Adobe Connect because it is easy to use, the platform is very stable, and it can accommodate a large number of attendees without any detectable perturbation. Some of the features in the interface are fairly basic.

WebEx // GoToMeeting
WebEx and GoToMeeting are ideal for file sharing and having multiple participants evaluate and discuss a document. It is good for collaborative

workflows and for quality review.

Elluminate

The features in Elluminate are ideal for virtual classroom instruction requiring high levels of audience participation and interaction, including voice and shared tools.

Omnovia

Users tend to love this interface because there is nothing to download, and participation is straightforward. Presenters have a wide array of tools to choose from, including file sharing, streaming media, polling, and whiteboard. It does not offer all as many attendee participation options as other interfaces.

Web Conferencing via Skype, MSN Messenger

Skype and MSN Messenger are often first choices because they are widely used and accepted, and it is very easy to allow attendees to see the presenter as he/she speaks. Skype is often used in a classroom setting where the presenter turns on his/her webcam, talks into a headset for voiceover IP (internet telephony) and then guides the attendees who are clustered in a single room. The presenter walks them through a set of slides that are projected onto a screen for the audience. There can be problems when there are more than 3 or 4 participants/attendees.

Pre-preparation for Webinars

- Research
- Discussion/blog
- Social networking announcements / info sharing

Post-webinar reinforcement

- Discussion questions
- Review questions, send to professor

Future Trends

- Asynchronous and Synchronous blend – live presentation followed by day of independent study.

- Archived and bundled as course content.
- Archived with opportunity to interact via discussion board or blog.

As mobile technologies improve, we'll probably see more webinar-type events via BlackBerries, iPhones, or other pda's, and the ability to interact will probably pull in different applications. For example, you may be viewing the webinar through an Omnovia interface, but be simultaneously communicating via Twitter, MSN, AOL, or Yahoo. There are advantages to having the chat go on in a different interface because it is easier to save the chat archive. In any case, webinars are a valuable supplement to online courses, and they will most definitely be utilized even more as people become more comfortable with the medium, and the technology is easier to use and more accessible.

How Do I Learn to Study "Smart"?

I have been studying more than ever, and I know the material really well—at least the material that I've covered in-depth. When the test comes around, there is always material on it that I'm not ready for at all. Then, I start panicking because I feel I'm running out of time—the test will automatically close.

It's frustrating. I do really well on part of the test, but not all. So, as a result, my scores are bad. I'm getting discouraged!

Signed,
Stuck in Stillwater

****

Dear Stuck:

1. Study what you'll be tested over. Be prepared for what you'll really encounter.

2. Branch out from your favorite activities or sections.

3. Fill in the gaps. Identify the holes in your knowledge and skills and work on them.

4. When you get to a part you're not familiar with, don't let it torpedo the entire test. Keep focused on what you do know and can do well.

5. Go into the test with confidence. Don't focus on the clock or the time allotted except to do effective time management.

6. Focus on each question and give each one your full attention while you're answering it. Don't let yourself get distracted.

7. Keep a pad of paper at your side if you can and jot down notes and thoughts to help you organize your knowledge.

8. Don't forget the "whole person." Be sure to have something to drink and perhaps even something to eat (especially if you have blood sugar issues).

9. Mentally rehearse how you'll approach the test before you take it.

10. Take practice tests that replicate the a) form of the test; b) the content; c) the conditions under which you'll take the exam.

I Hate My E-Textbook! What Can I Do?

Help! I hate my e-textbooks!

I know I'm supposed to love them, and that they will make my life easier, but they're not. What can I do?

My college went 100 percent online with its textbooks this term, and I am very frustrated. I was hoping I would be able to download an e-book to my hard drive or to a flash drive, and to use it on any computer that has Adobe Reader.

Alas! Such is not the case. I have to download a special reader that has its own name. I have to download a different reader for each textbook, since each one is published by a different publisher. One publisher even requires me to download the reader every time I access the book, and, I can only download the reader to one computer!

I work with an array of laptops—Windows plus Mac, and I have an iPad, an iTouch, and an iPhone. I was hoping to be able to download the texts and to be able to read them when I'm on a plane, other times when I'm not online and not hooked into "the cloud." Instead, to access the e-book, I have to be online, and I have to have a good connection. I also have to count on their servers being up, and the text being available all the time, which it is NOT.

As a result, I feel I'm at a huge disadvantage. I can't access the textbook when I need it. It won't let me print out my own copy.

What can I do??

Sincerely,
Cloud-Busted

****

Dear Cloud-Busted,

I know it's cold comfort to say this, but I'll do it anyway: The Cloud is great. It's the way to go. Yes, it's frustrating now, but we'll get through this.

We'll look back some day and recognize that in 2011 e-texts were still in a nascent form, and the delivery philosophies evolved quickly and improved over time.

That said, what can you do now?

There are a few strategies that will help maximize your access time and focus you on achieving the learning objectives and demonstrating competence with the outcomes.

1. Download the syllabus for your course and identify the readings and activities from your text, plus key outcomes.

2. Copy and paste core concepts from your e-textbook. If your text will not let you do so, then keep notes. You may wish to put your notes in a file in Notepad and keep it on your computer or on a flash drive. Alternatively you can house them in a note-taking program such as Evernote (**www.evernote.com**).

   Core concepts should include:
   - learning outcomes
   - chapter summaries
   - chapter reviews
   - assigned activities
   - chapter outline, with bullet points of key ideas contained in the chapter(s)

3. Use the "search" feature to move quickly through your e-textbook and pinpoint the topics that you need for the unit you're working on. Highlight them and add them to your notes, either by copying and pasting, or by typing in notes.

4. Find an earlier print edition of the textbook on Amazon market-place. There will be differences, but chances are some of the basic concepts will be the same. With an older print edition, you can annotate the margins, underline, and use the active reading strategies you're accustomed to using. There are some risks associated with using older editions though—they are not complete, the information is different, and they can be in different orders. Be sure to use the print version as a supplement only.

5. Communicate with your fellow students as much as possible and share your doubts, questions, and uncertainties. Chances are, they have the same questions and together you can clear them up.

I'm hoping that in the next year or so, publishers will find a way to allow students to download PDF files they can read from any computer or reader that accommodates PDFs. Ideally, they would make the text available for Kindle and Nook as well. It would be a huge help for everyone if it were not necessary to be connected to the Internet in order to access the textbook, particularly since you're paying so much for it. It would be nice to build a library of texts that you could continue to refer to after the course is over.

I hope that my responses have been helpful, Cloud-busted. Please feel free to share any ideas or suggestions that you might have.

It's Research Paper Time!
Are You Forgetting Government Sources?

As you do web-based research for your online course, you may be over-looking some of the most useful and reliable statistics and reports. Why use a blog post or a website that reports the results of a study when you can find the study directly? Also, why use the statistics from a single year, when you can go back and find historical data? Government websites often contain in-depth statistics, research results, and historical data. Further, they're often free, and you can download the reports in easy-to-transport PDF (rather than having to save the document as website, or to access it only in the cloud by means of a customized reader that you must download on each computer you use to access the data).

Government data, reports, statistics, maps, graphics, and studies are wonderful resources. The main challenge may be determining where to look and how to search for the information you need.

Here is a quick guide, with links and profiles:

Meta-Search: Search Multiple Databases from a Single Site

- **FedStats**
  - ▸ www.fedstats.gov

  Statistics from more than 100 federal agencies are available through this portal, which is organized in different categories including interactive maps, a topic index, statistical reference by geography, and statistical referency by topic. It is very convenient and easy to use. Highly recommended is the search function, located here: *fedstats.gov/search/*

- **Government Printing Office**
  - ▸ www.gpo.gov/fdsys/

  FDSys is the Federal Digital System, which allows users to search government publications at a single site. Featured collections relate to the law and the economy, as well as codes and legislation. This is a very useful site, which helps you sift through agencies, bureaus, and collections that seem to be in a constant state of flux.

- **Forum on Child and Family Statistics (U.S.)**
  - ▸ childstats.gov

  Childstats is a website/portal provided by the Federal Interagency Forum on Child and Family Statistics, a consortium of several U.S. federal agencies. The website allows individuals to search the documents of a number of U.S. government agencies that deal with the well-being of children, families, and communities, namely "family and social environment, economic circumstances, health care, physical environment and safety, behavior, education and health" (childstats.gov, 2011). The annual report: *America's Children: Key National Indicators of Well-Being*, (**childstats.gov/americaschildren/index.asp**) is one of the most useful reports published by the forum.

International and U.S.-Based Organizational Websites

The Economy / Economic Outlook

- **The International Monetary Fund (IMF)**
  - ▸ www.imf.org/external/index.htm
  - Data and Statistics: www.imf.org/external/data.htm

  This is an excellent website for news, facts, and figures relating to the world economy and specific programs designed to stimulate/manage economic health in world regions and individual countries. Some of the key reports include the annual World Economic Outlook.

- **The World Bank**
  - ▸ www.worldbank.org

  The World Bank is an excellent source of a full suite of economic indicators for all the countries of the world. It is an excellent source of information, not just of economic condition, but of socio-demographic information and insight into how people in other countries live. By providing information about employment, economic conditions, as well as economic infrastructure and opportunity, one can also gain insight into the reasons for political unrest and instability triggered by poverty and economic stress.

Demographics and Social Structure

- ### The U.S. Census Bureau
  ▶ www.census.gov

This website provides valuable demographic data covering all U.S. states, counties, and municipalities. Information on employment, race and ethnicity, education levels, household income, and more can provide extremely useful and convincing support in essays and research papers. The reports that are available for download include profiles of households, communities, and states, as well as individuals.

Government/Politics

- ### Congressional Record
  ▶ www.gpo.gov/fdsys/

This will be archive-only after Spring 2011. New documents will be published through the Government Printing Office and the meta-search engine at FDSYS.

- ### C-SPAN Transcripts
  ▶ legacy.c-span.org/special/nmtranscripts.aspx

Not a government website, but a service provided by cable. The transcripts are extremely helpful for providing support for arguments / persuasive papers that involve positions taken by politicians and constituency groups.

- ### Executive Orders / Speeches
  ▶ www.whitehouse.gov/briefing-room/presidential-actions/executive-orders

Are you looking for information on what is happening with the President and his Cabinet members? Are you interested in some of the President's speeches, or some of the Executive Orders? The White House Briefing Room is an excellent source.

Science

- **National Oceanic and Atmospheric Administration (NOAA)**
  ▶ www.noaa.gov

  Thanks to tsunamis, hurricanes, and tornado outbreaks, the information at the NOAA is utterly riveting. The "before and after" satellite photos, along with animations and simulations are quite interesting. You'll find reliable and in-depth reports are very valuable sources of information for courses in many different disciplines.

- **National Science Foundation (NSF)**
  ▶ www.nsf.gov

  NSF is an independent U.S. government agency responsible for promoting science and engineering through research programs and education projects. The website contains access to a number of reports.

- **Smithsonian Museum**
  ▶ www.si.edu
  ▶ www.si.edu/Encyclopedia

  The museum sites contain information on the exhibits as well as historical, cultural, and anthropological information.

- **Department of Energy (DOE)**
  ▶ www.energy.gov

  Energy facts, statistics, and reports for all kinds of energy—renewable and non-renewable.

Culture / History / Anthropology

- **Library of Congress**
  ▶ www.loc.gov

  In addition to articles, reports, and studies, the Library of Congress contains collections of photographs, audio recordings, and videos.

- **Department of Transportation (DOT)**
  ▶ www.dot.gov

  Statistics and logistics information housed here.

- **U.S. Bureau of Economic Analysis (BEA)**
  ▶ www.bea.gov

  U.S. Department of Commerce Bureau of Economic Analysis provides reports, historical statistics, reports, and analysis.

- **Bureau of Labor Statistics (BLS)**
  ▶ www.bls.gov

  In addition to labor and employment, the BLS also gives profiles on careers, together with wage, salary, and outlook information.

Kick-Starting the Returning-to-School Brain

My mom wants to take online courses and to get her degree in psychology. She's worried, though. She's afraid that she's not as sharp as she once was, and she doesn't know what to do to help herself.

I told her to take a lot of Gingko biloba—*I read somewhere that it's a great nutritional supplement. My friend said she should go to her doctor and get a prescription for Adderall. My mom laughed at both suggestions and said she needed something that would really work.*

I'm frustrated. What do you suggest?

Sincerely,
Motivated by Mom's Mind

****

Dear Motivated,

It's great that you and your mom are so close! One of the things I always say is the key to success is family support. There's nothing like "We are THE TEAM" to get people motivated. In fact, statistics support the team approach. The old correspondence courses, where there was no team and very slow feedback, had 10 or 15% completion rates. Yes, it was that bad! Only one out of ten would finish. Very sad.

In contrast, cohort-based groups often achieve 80 and 85% completion rates. That's almost everyone. What that means is that people who avoid isolation and join a group are much   more   likely   to   complete   their course. How exciting!

But—let's be honest. It's not just all about if you've found a "study buddy" or not. You have to believe in yourself. The problem with a lot of returning-to-school adults is that they just don't believe in themselves. They probably had mixed results with high school or college in the first place—and then, when you combine that with the prejudice our society has against aging adults and the individual's own creeping suspicion that there has been serious brain-cell loss over the years (a fallacy, but very much bought into, thanks to the media!), then what you have is a large group of people who are talented and motivated, but who are likely to quit before they even begin. They doubt themselves.

And, it's no wonder! Our society does not help things. With all the stories and reports we read about Alzheimer's and cognitive impairment, it's no wonder your mom is nervous. But if she's worried about her ability to succeed, and she doubts her cognitive abilities, she can relax. She's on the right track. In reality, what she's proposing to do—taking courses—is probably the best thing she could possibly do to improve her cognitive functioning.

And, well, she's right about *Gingko biloba*. There have been a lot of unsubstantiated claims made for "miracle herbs."

As for Adderall—that's for her doctor to decide. It would be odd if he gave it to her though. It's an amphetamine and it's addictive.

Her best bet is to look at the way she studies and the approach she takes toward the tasks she'll be asked to do in class. What I'm going to describe now are a few ways to "kick start" her brain.

Here are a few steps for her to follow. (By the way, these would work for you, too—they're not age-specific tactics by any means!)

1. **Trigger connections.** In *Language and Aging* (2008), Deborah M. Burke reported results of her long-term studies of studies of cognition and aging. What she found is that neural pathways are solid and well-forged in the older adult brain. They don't go away. So, the key is to connect to where the pathways already exist. It's like hitching a ride on a hyper-fast car. Which will get you to your destination sooner? Power walking by yourself? Or keeping the passenger-side warm as your buddy—a nice name for your life,

your prior learning, your experiences—catapult you to race-car status?

2. **Retrieve what you already know.** This is very much like triggering connections, but it's a bit more subtle. As you relate to your courses, be sure to step back and take an inventory of the kinds of knowledge you've mastered that relates to what you're studying. As you start bringing the old knowledge up to the front of your mind—to your working memory—you'll be surprised at how motivated you feel to continue to study. There's something about retrieving prior knowledge that is incredibly life-affirming, and incredibly inspiring. It suddenly kicks in that your life really has meant something, and the more experiences you have, the more insight you have into the human condition.

3. **Leverage your "big picture" vision.** You're experienced. You've seen a lot. Consequently, you have a wonderful "big picture" vision. For example, as you drive to a destination you go to almost every day, chances are, there are places along the way that have changed. The establishments may be transformed—once they were snappy, hip crowd-drawers. Today, they're boarded up. Or, before, they were industrial—almost boarded up. Now, they're hyper-cool watering holes and galleries—and, well, you can see the where and the why when no one else can. That's what makes you special. Don't forget it. Leverage it.

4. **Expand the mental structures you've already built.** What kind of mental structures are the most valuable? Let's think about it. There are hierarchies of knowledge. There are categories. You've already done a lot of the foundational work in preparing yourself for cognitive challenges. You have created file cabinets in your mind, and it's all about keeping them organized, and finding ways to make the knowledge you store in each one easily retrievable.

5. **Pry open your brain networks by considering new ideas.** What? Pry open brain networks?? How scary! Yes, absolutely. But that's the only way to challenge yourself. Get outside your comfort zone. Look at the "what if" scenarios. Look at the ways that other people think. Find the mindset that is the most obnoxious to you, and then role-play it! Pretend you're on a radio talk show interview, and you're defending that position (the one you found loathsome). You'll be amazed at how intense the experience will be. It will reorient your thinking. Just be ready for the ride.

6. **Seek the "disorienting dilemma."** That's what Jack Mezirow said would lead to true change. He was all about transforming the self by means of education. He developed a total transformational learning theory (**www.lifecircles-inc.com/Learningtheories/human ist/mezirow.html**). You may not agree with all of it, but, well, can you imagine the fun of at least trying it out? Talk about adrenaline and euphoria! As you may recall, transformational learning is defined as learning that induces more far-reaching change in the learner than other kinds of learning, especially learning experiences which shape the learner and produce a significant impact, or paradigm shift, which affects the learner's subsequent experiences (Clark, 1993).

Okay, so I've gone through a number of possibilities, dear Motivated. Now, live up to your name and go help your mom. You'll be happy you did!

FURTHER READING

Bandura, A. (1986). *Social Foundations of Thought and Action*. Englewood Cliffs, N.J.: Prentice-Hall.

Burke, D.M. & Shafto, M.A. (2008). "Language and aging." In F.I.M. Craik & T.A. Salthouse (Eds.), *The handbook of aging and cognition* (pp.373-443). New York: Psychology Press.

Burke, D.M., MacKay, D.G., Worthley, J.S., and Wade, E. (1991). "On the tip of the tongue: What causes word finding failures in young and older adults?" *Journal of Memory and Language*, 30, 542-579.

Burke, D.M. & Peters, L. (1986). "Word associations in old age: Evidence for consistency in semantic encoding during adulthood." *Psychology and Aging*, 1, 283-292.

Burke, D.M. & Light, L.L. (1981). "Memory and aging: The role of the retrieval processes." *Psychological Bulletin*, 90, 513-546.

Cena, M. & Mitchell, J. (1998). "Anchored instruction: A model for integrating the language arts through content area study." *Journal of Adolescent & Adult Literacy*, 41, 559-561.

Clark, M. C. (1993). "Transformational learning." *New Directions For Adult And Continuing Education*, (57), 47-56.

Collins, A., Brown, J. S., and Holum A. (1991). "Cognitive Apprenticeship: Making Thinking Visible." *American Educator*, Winter 1991.
▸ www.21learn.org/archive/articles/brown_seely.php

Mezirow, J. D. (1981). "A critical theory of adult learning and education." *Adult Education Quarterly*, 32(1), 3-24.

Mezirow, J. (1991) *Transformative Dimensions of Adult Learning.* San Francisco, CA: Jossey-Bass.

Mezirow, J (1997). "Transformative learning: Theory to practice." *New Directions for Adult and Continuing Education*, 74, 5-12.

Reigeluth, C. R. (n.d.). "What Is the New Paradigm of Instructional Theory?"
▸ it.coe.uga.edu/itforum/paper17/paper17.html

Learning Experiences in an Online Course:
What's Best?

I recently attended an orientation webinar for my new online program. I'm excited about all the ways we can learn, and how many different types of learning experiences that there are online.

I'd love to have your take on this—what do you think are the most effective types of learning experiences in an online course?

Sincerely,
Ready for Experiences in Redding

****

Dear Ready,

You're so right about the kinds of experiences that online learning opens up, especially as you take your learning mobile and interact with other learners and the content in so many different ways.

Edgar Dale (1954) an early researcher in the field of visual learning put together what he called the "Cone of Experience" which links what you see in class with application, either through application or interaction with other learners or the world.

His early cone was really amazing—if you look at the categories, it really seems to anticipate e-learning and social-learning (via m-learning or mobile learning)—50 years ahead of his time!

He ranked the kinds of experience, the bottom of the cone being the most solid and effective, and the top of the cone, less effective. Here's how ranked visual learning experiences (from to most to least effective):

- Direct Purposeful Experiences
- Contrived Experiences
- Dramatized Experiences
- Demonstrations
- Study Trips
- Exhibits
- Educational Television
- Motion Pictures
- Recordings / Radio / Still Pictures
- Visual Symbols
- Verbal Symbols (words on a page)

Dale contends that the most effective ("Direct Purposeful Experiences") are the most effective because more of the senses are engaged, and you can learn through seeing, hearing, touching, smelling, tasting—not just through seeing. He also discusses the effectiveness of engaging the affect and creating a solid, reinforcing emotional responses. In addition, "Direct Purposeful Experience" involves more cognitive functions which allow you to create categories/schema as well as to make connections and engage prior learning.

Over the years, a "Learning Pyramid" has been developed for e-learning which is something of a derivative of Dale's cone, and which establishes a hierarchy of learning strategy effectiveness:

Teach Others / Immediate Use = 90%
Practice by Doing = 75%
Discussion Group = 50%
Demonstration = 30%
Audio-Visual = 20%
Reading = 10%
Lecture = 5%

In e-learning, it's pretty clear that the best approach is to bring together as many experiences as possible.

Thankfully, in the learning environment we have today, it's very easy to do, and we can even track which approaches are most effective.

In addition to the Learning Pyramid approach, we can also take a look at the best ways to learn basic and higher-order skills.

Interactive Multimodal Learning:

Simulations, modeling, real world experiences (typically includes collaboration with peers, but could include interacting with a resource)

» Good for basic skills (around a 10% increase)
» Excellent for higher order skills (around a 35% increase)

Non-Interactive Multimodal Learning:

Includes using text with illustrations, watching and listening to animations, listening to lecture with graphics on devices such as whiteboards, etc. Typically involves individualized learning, or whole-group work that includes listening, observing, or reading, but little to no interaction.

» Very Good for basic skills
» Very Good for higher order skills

We're just at the beginning of the ways in which we can create more experiences in the e-learning space. Here are a few of the emerging e-learning experiences:

- **Wikis:** collaborations through wikis – sharing knowledge, engaging in a dialogue
- **Social Networking:** collaborations through blogging / social networking – expanding the conversation to the visual realm (sharing videos/graphics)
- **Twitter:** quick, high-impact, high-speed mass communication: Twitter, etc. – informs and calls to action
- **Web-conferencing:** share techniques/approaches
- **E-Portfolios:** collaboration on many levels.
- **Web 3.0:** "smart research" (the semantic web) helps you build your research and hone your sources

So, Ready, you've chosen an exciting time to be involved in e-learning!

Levers in Persuasive Writing:
Changing Minds (Your Own and Others)

Chances are, you're going to have to write a number of persuasive papers in any given semester. Even if you're not required to write a paper, you'll probably have to post items in a discussion forum, and you're going to have to be able to defend your position. You'll need to be able to help people change their minds. Further, you may need to change your mind about things you always took for granted. You'll be asked to take another look and to consider things from a different point of view.

For example, you may be taking a sociology course, and you're asked to discuss gender roles, expectations, and behaviors. In one discussion forum, you're asked to comment on a current case in the news where a woman who was jogging in the park at night was attacked and raped. You posted something in the discussion board to the effect that she was "asking for it" and "what did she expect?" To your dismay, your classmates vehemently dispute your assumptions that the woman's dress, behavior, and location made her deserving of attack. Your first instinct is to defend yourself. You are not in a mood to be bullied, you tell yourself. However, your instructor reminds you that the goal of the course is to learn to see things from new lenses, and to gain new perspectives, and then to describe them. So, you step back a moment and analyze what is happening. Why are you starting to be receptive to a different point of view?

Howard Gardner, an educational psychologist and researcher famous for his book, Multiple Intelligences, has discussed the process of cognitive accommodation, which, simply stated, is how we start to change our minds. In *Changing Minds* (2004), Gardner provides examples of how and when minds are changed, and how groups and individuals are persuaded to think in a new way. He looks at certain elements as "levers" that move one from one place to another. Cognitive levers are what help us change our minds.

Reason

Individuals often have a self-concept in which they think of themselves as "reasonable" people. For them, it's important to think of themselves as rational and reasonable. They say that they're reasonable as they're ranting about some sort of political issue, and are verbally condemning everyone who disagrees with them to a ghastly and painful demise. How can such "reasonable" individuals be persuaded? One way is to ask them to consider the pros and cons of certain viewpoints. Chances are, once they've come up with their own list of pros and cons, they can be persuaded.

Research

Another way to persuade your obdurate friend of something they are dead-set against is to present them with clear, incontrovertible evidence. Do the research. Better yet, let them do research and come up with the facts. For example, one might be convinced that measles vaccinations cause measles. If that is their belief, ask them to do research to support their premise. Chances are, the research will support the converse. Measles vaccinations prevent measles. They do not cause the disease.

Resonance

Appeal to your audience's emotions. Or, conversely, find a way to get emotionally connected to the topic at hand. For example, one might assume that a woman jogging in a park at night is "asking for" sexual assault until it happens to their own sister. Then, instead of getting on their moral high horse, they're feeling sadness and anger. Empathy reigns. Suddenly there is a certain resonance when one asks one to have compassion for the individual who was attacked in the park.

Representational Redescriptions

Can you redescribe the problem? Can you put in other words? If you do, chances are you'll disarm your audience, or at least slow them down enough to reconsider the issue and see it from a new point of view. So, the tactic of "representational redescription" can be quite effective.

Resources and Rewards

Carrot and stick. You can try to punish people for their viewpoints, but it is likely that you'll just make them angry and they'll rebel. They'll just become hardened in their mindsets and won't even think of considering your views. So, it's much better to reward them. There are often tangible rewards for adopting a new point of view. You might look at it as "selling out"—or, alternatively, it's just a matter of practical realities. Either way, rewarding people can be a way to encourage them to think of things in a new way.

Real World Events

Sometimes a person's life causes them to stop, check their beliefs, and turn them upside down. For example, someone might be impatient with a person who is getting older and unable to move around in the same way as before. That person might have been even aggressive in their treatment of an elderly person using a walker and having difficulty seeing things. However, something might happen to them and they start to lose their own mobility. Suddenly, real-world circumstances give new meaning to the condition. The person changes her mind about the elderly.

Resistances (Overcoming)

Finally, if you're developing a persuasive paper, or are trying to persuade people of a certain position, then you may have to overcome the person's own resistances. Succinctly put, they've become hardened over the years. How can you overcome the resistances they've developed? You're going to have to do some research into what is going on in their minds and their hearts. What are their beliefs? Their values? Their life experiences? The more you know, the more you'll be able to appeal to your audience.

A Final Thought

Persuasion is often thought as a dark art, something lurking between hypnosis and enchantment. In reality, it's more of a science. If you know exactly how "levers" work, you can move seemingly impossible-to-budge objects, as well as opinions. It just takes persistence, tact, and a calm, well-reasoned approach.

Long-Term Memory and E-Learning

"How am I ever going to remember everything for my timed exam?" asked Renata. She had just completed a practice quiz and had not done very well. For some reason, she just could not seem to put the information she was studying in a coherent form. Everything seemed clear when she read it, but when it came time for the quiz, her mind felt utterly empty. She drew a blank.

"Renata, don't panic. I can help you. I've got a few memory tricks up my sleeve, thanks to my work with individuals with traumatic brain injury and Alzheimer's," said Renata's mother. Renata's mom was a clinical psychologist, and her work often took her in interesting and quite helpful directions.

"Thanks, Mom." Renata opened up her textbook and showed her mom the biology chapter she had been studying. It contained vertebrates and also a food web. "Mom, there's too much to try to remember."

"You probably think so now, dear, but let's work on a few encoding and retrieval tactics. First, let's look at remembering the names of people you meet. How do you do that now, Renata?"

Renata sighed. "Mom. You know I'm horrible with names. I never can remember people's names and it is very embarrassing!"

Renata's mom took out a stack of photographs. They were ones she used with combat veterans who had memory issues.

She went on to explain that there were several ways to remember names, and both were very effective.

1. Remember their salient features.

Renata's mom pointed to a picture of a man with a tattoo of barbed wire around his bicep. "Renata, what is the first thing you notice?"

"The barbed wire tattoo, of course," she said.

"Excellent." She paused. She looked at the card. "Now, if I were to tell you the man's name is Dave, how would you remember?"

Renata sighed again. "I don't know."

"Barbed wire Dave," said Renata's mom. "Repeat it, envision it, think it."

They went through the entire stack of cards—about 20 cards—and developed system. Later, when quizzed, Renata was able to remember 12 of them.

"That's 12 more than you could remember before!" said Renata's mom. "Now I'm going to put this with an even more powerful technique."

2. Create a rhyme that includes their name.

"Wave to Dave!" said Renata's mom.

"What?" asked Renata.

Renata's mom held up the card of Dave and his tattoo. "Wave to Dave!"

Renata waved reluctantly. "I feel like such a child," she said. "But I do see that this will help me remember. I will remember waving and then I'll search my mind for a name that rhymes with 'wave.' Naturally, I'll come up with Dave."

"You've got it!" said Renata's mom. "That will work."

3. Connect the person to an event in your life or prior knowledge.

"Renata, if you're studying for a test and you need to remember information, sometimes a great way to remember is to relate it to prior knowledge. Ideally, it's something that happened in your life. You'll find it will help you."

Renata looked at her mom and thought of the people her mom worked with.

"What if the person you're working with does not want to remember things in the past? What if they can't?" she asked.

"Well, then, this technique will not work as well as it could," she said.

"But, when it comes to an exam, it's much better for me to remember my own experiences with the activity. You're so right about that!"

* * * * * * * * * * * *

As Renata and her mom continued to discuss the issue of long-term memory, they also looked at forgetting. Renata was surprised to learn that things could be forgotten simply by means of "proactive overlay" which is to say that an idea or concept could be generated to interfere with one's authentic experience and memories. It was one way to explain the idea of false memories, particularly as they related to such things as people who claimed to remember being abducted by aliens, or traumatic events early in their lives. "Suggested memory could be a kind of forgetting," said Renata's mom.

"How does that relate to online learning?" asked Renata.

"It relates to discussion forums. If you read something erroneous in the discussion forum, or something erroneous as you're doing online research, you need to make sure that you return to the correct information. Otherwise, it is possible that one memory will be replaced by another."

Renata paused, then looked at her mom. "All the more reason to encode well and when I retrieve the information, be sure to do a reality check."

"That's right," said her mom. "So go out there and ace your test!"

Looking at Literature:
Strategies for Interpreting Texts

I'm taking my second first-year composition course, and we have to analyze literature and write about what we find through our analysis. I've never liked to read literature, and I feel completely in over my head!

What do I do? How do I get started?

Sincerely,
Drowning in Dostoevsky

****

Dear Drowning,

I'm delighted that you're taking a course that requires you to read literature. I'm sorry, though, that you're finding it so daunting.

Here's a flowchart that will help you analyze the work of literature. As you read, jot down notes in response to the questions in the flowchart. Later, you can use the information you've collected to start building your own paper.

Be sure to note the page number and to write down specific passages that you can cite later.

A. Read closely. What is the protagonist doing?

» Traveling?

- » Interacting with people?
- » Making observations?
- » Behaving in a certain way?
- » Making decisions?
- » What do the protagonist's actions tell you?

B. How is the protagonist doing things?

- » With others?
- » Alone?
- » Heroically? Effectively?
- » Bumbling along? Ineffectually?
- » Kindly?
- » Cruelly?
- » Self-defeatingly?
- » Reflectively and thoughtfully?
- » With self-awareness?
- » With self-deception and blindness?

C. What goes in the "space" of the text?

- » A city?
- » A series of rooms?
- » The great outdoors?
- » Home?
- » Work?
- » Hotels? Cafes? Restaurants? Dances?
- » Social settings?

D. What does the "space" do to influence—

- » The protagonist?
- » The behaviors of the people
- » The available options

E. What kind of world do the characters live in?

- » Logical?
- » Illogical?
- » Fair, where causality and reason hold sway?
- » Unfair, where caprice and randomness toss people about and make them actors without agency
- » Fate and predestination determine all
- » No predetermination—all is free will

- » Human self-determination is strong
- » Must be street-smart?
- » Picaresque attitudes help

F. Can you believe everything you read in the text? What does the text suggest about the nature of reality?

- » The world is concrete, and things have true essences
- » Everything is random, chaotic, aleatory
- » Everything always in flux, not reliable
- » In the process of becoming
- » Doomed (must repent—focus on the jeremiad)
- » Didactic—sermons in stone everywhere
- » Smooth/civilizing

G. Repetition in the text has certain functions

- » Inculcates values across the generations
- » Echoes across characters
- » Echoes across the things that exist in the text (values, beliefs, artifacts)

Now that you've collected the information, read over your findings. Take time to ponder, reflect, and take stock. What does it mean? What is the work saying about life? About human institutions (school, religion)? About human relations? About our relation to reality? Does the work say something about women and men in society?

As you decide, you can start drafting up potential thesis statements, and then sketching out a very basic outline of your paper. Be sure to use quotes and to cite using MLA style. You'll be amazed at how helpful it can be to use a flowchart and to develop a systematic approach to analyzing literature.

Managing the Unmanageable:
Dealing with Massive End-of-Term Projects

It's midnight and I am still staring at a blank screen. I'm completely overwhelmed with the research project I have to turn in tomorrow.

I know I should not have procrastinated, and I did not actually procrastinate—I just felt I had no tools to organize the mountains of information I have.

My topic is birth defects, and I was able to find a lot of information, but I don't know how to organize it, and I'm afraid I'm on the wrong track.

What can I do now?

What can I do next time, when I'm faced with another massive research project?

Sincerely,
Paralyzed at Ponte Vedra

****

Dear Paralyzed:

There are a couple of things I'm picking up on in your letter.

First, it seems that you are good at picking out excellent topics that yield a great deal of information. However, be sure to narrow your topic. Perhaps it could be something about how the mother's nutritional deficiencies can lead to birth defects.

Second, I'm detecting a definite "fight or flight" response. It's no wonder you're panicked—the nature of the task is overwhelming. I think that it has been hard for you to break the task down into manageable sub-tasks and action steps. That's something you can do in a "pre-training" phase before you embark on any large project.

Don't panic. If you have very clear steps to follow, you do not have to struggle with how to develop effective procedures each time.

Step One: Identify your core topic.

Step Two: Develop a research strategy. Identify the databases you intend to use. Nail down your search terms.

Step Three: Invent activities to start narrowing your topic. Try mind-mapping/listing/freewriting.

Step Four: Social-network with others on the same topic. Try contacting fellow students, or tweet on the topic if it's something that has to do with a hot, controversial issue.

Step Five: Develop an outline.

Step Six: Narrow your topic; develop a primary thesis.

Step Seven: Slot in your research—which goes where?

Step Eight: Expand your outline. Put bullet points under each body paragraph topic.

Step Nine: Freewrite on each body paragraph/topic. Make sure that each body paragraph flows back to your primary thesis.

Step Ten: Develop a draft from your freewrite. Beef up with quotes and identify where you need more support for your argument and do research.

Paralyzed, I hope this helps. To tell the truth, I felt a bit paralyzed when I read your letter. (I'm only admitting it now). Sometimes the questions necessitate a lengthy, complex response—and, it can be rather daunting to sum up what has to be done in a few clear steps / prescriptive actions.

Mastering the Facts:
Creating Order from Chaos

I'm taking a course in medical coding, and I'm at the end of my wits! I have to learn all about anatomy as well as medical procedures and diagnoses.

I don't know how to keep anything straight, and I'm not sure how I'll ever be able to accurately build codes so I can fill out forms for medical reimbursement.

Is there any way I can get my head around this amazing, swirling tornado of information?

Sincerely,
Code Red in South Dakota

****

Dear Code Red:

Without a mental model, facts and information are fated to be just what you've discovered: a violent, chaotic tornado! And, just like a tornado, random, disorganized facts and information can be destructive.

The most basic element in the content of e-learning is factual information. Consider facts as building blocks of knowledge. In Bloom's taxonomy, facts often involve cognitive activities such as "identify" or "list."

Clearly it is necessary to organize the facts in some way, and the way you organize them can make all the difference in the world when it comes to succeeding in your courses. You need to learn how to organize the knowledge you are acquiring into categories, and to build meaningful mental models or schema (in the U.K., they are known as "schemata").

A schema is a mental file cabinet that you label and then attach to something familiar so that your working memory is triggered and you're able to retrieve and process the information.

So, for example, if you're involved in learning about medical procedures and also anatomy, it's important to find a way for you to create schema that facilitate the information transfer process.

I'd recommend developing your own schema that flow along with the ones in the official manuals you'll be using (ICD-10-DM and ICD-10-PCS). That will allow you to work through the tables with confidence.

The worst thing you could do would be to try to develop a schema that does not align with the materials/databases you'll be using in real life. For example, it does not make sense to organize them alphabetically.

Keep in mind that schema are often developed culturally and are valid within a community. For e-learning, that would indicate a learning community which will start to develop a kind of short-cut or code language in order to express thoughts and to add to or transfer knowledge.

Your medical coding community may have, for example, special schema for mastering the new seven-character codes. It may be a schema built around exceptions. Or it could be aligned around the most common codes in your specialty.

You may work in a dermatologist's office. If that's the case, you may develop a few convenient schema for dealing with the most common diagnoses and hospital procedures that affect your client base / patients. One of the best ways to fast-track communal schemata is to participate in groups and social networks that share tips and techniques, as well as experiences.

I hope that these ideas and thoughts have been helpful. As you "tame the tornado" of undifferentiated, unorganized data and facts, consider these classic lines:

> Facts are simple and facts are straight
> Facts are lazy and facts are late

Facts all come with points of view
Facts don't do what I want them to
Facts just twist the truth around
Facts are living turned inside out
Facts are getting the best of them
Facts are nothing on the face of things
Facts don't stain the furniture
Facts go out and slam the door
Facts are written all over your face
Facts continue to change their shape

—Talking Heads, "Crosseyed and Painless."
Remain in Light. Sire, 1980.

As the lyrics suggest, facts can change meanings, depending on their context and how they're used.

So, it's doubly important to nail them down and keep the meanings somewhat static (and easily retrievable) by developing great schema and mental models.

Think of your schema as "required equipment for living" as well as a way to tame the tornado.

Math Phobia, Anyone?

I'm thrilled that you've started answering e-learning questions, and are willing to give excellent tips that will help me succeed. I appreciate it because I'm terrified.

I have been avoiding math as long as I can, but, as they say, "You can run, but you can't hide." I need to take and pass (this is the key consideration!) Beginning Algebra.

Help! I have math phobia. To make it worse, I've successfully avoided math for many years, and I've forgotten anything I ever knew.

What can I do? I'm doubly afraid because I'm taking the course online. How will I ask questions? How can I get in a study group?

Signed,
Numbers Give Me Nightmares

****

Dear Numbers,

Don't worry—you're in luck! Do you realize that by signing up for an on-line Beginning Algebra course, you'll have probably ten times the resources that you'd have in a traditional class?

Also, you'll have the opportunity to form a study group or have a study buddy, and you'll be able to communicate with them 24-7. That's a lot better than meeting after class or trying to figure out everyone's schedules so you can meet, isn't it?

Real World Applications

Even the most basic math concepts begin with real-world applications. You'll automatically ask yourself questions: How do I solve this? How do I do this?

Teaching math has changed a great deal over the last few years. You're going to be introduced to concepts as they appear as applications in real life so the entire process makes sense. For example, you might be faced with a real estate problem. How do you figure out how much commission your real estate agent will make? How much will you have to bring to closing? Wouldn't it be nice to be able to check the numbers that you've been given by the title company? Chances are, you're already thinking about how you'd make the calculations.

If so, you're on your way. You're involved in what is called "situated learning"—the problem is located or situated in a specific time, place, and it's a comfortable, practical way to approach abstract concepts.

What happens if you get stuck? The nice thing about online learning is that you'll have a chance to work with other people, and you can share steps in the process.

Tag Team Algebra

Solve problems together. Each member of the team breaks problems into steps. Then, in the discussion board area, or in a special collaborative space online, each member of the team will post his or her part of the problem. You'll have a chance to comment on it and to see how they arrived at their approach.

Videos with Step-by-Step Guide

You might have trouble getting started and would like someone to lead you through the process, step by step. You're embarrassed to ask your professor, and you don't quite understand the explanations that your fellow students provide. Plus, you may not have a lot of confidence in them. After all, they're learning, too!

This is where videos in which a professor explains each step are great. Usually, the professor works with a whiteboard or a computer tablet that records his or her moves, but sometimes the professor is even writing on a chalkboard and someone is filming while as he or she works the problems out on the board, and he explains each step. The nice thing about video is that you can replay it as many times as you need, and you can practice alongside him or her—just take out a piece of paper and a pen/pencil and get to work.

Write down the problem. Start to solve it. Then play the video and see if you're doing the same thing. Then stop the video, and continue solving the problem. Play the video again and check. You'll be amazed at how it feels just like having a mentor. The nice thing is that your mentor or tutor is infinitely patient, will repeat things a thousand times if necessary, and is utterly free. ☺

Collaborative Learning

Answer questions collectively. Teams and study buddies are great. If your instructor does not have a thread in the discussion board where you can ask questions, and then respond to each other, please ask her to add one right away. Also, the "virtual student lounge" concept can be great for facilitating team learning.

Online Quizzes and Practice Problems

Your online course will come with a number of resources. They may be a part of your textbook. Alternatively, there may be links to online resources—quizzes, review, and interactive practice items. They help you practice solving the problems in a way that will help you prepare for a testing situation.

Taking online quizzes and solving practice problems in a format similar to your tests will help you gain confidence, and will help you conquer performance anxiety.

Online Mentors and Tutoring Services

Do you need a live person to guide you through the problems? There are many online tutoring services—you can find them online and even in multi-user virtual worlds such as Second Life. Here's a cautionary note, though—you may find yourself deviating a bit from your course textbook, course problems, and even the material you'll be assessed on. You'll learn a lot, but it may not be what you'll be tested over. So it may better to focus on your course, your course outcomes and the learning objectives, along with the specific texts, practices, and more.

MATH SIMULATIONS

Mathworks Matlab
▸ www.mathworks.com

Instrument Control Software (for electricians)
▸ www.mathworks.com/products/instrument/?s_cid=HP_FP_ML_instrument

Demos
▸ www.mathworks.com/products/instrument/demos.html

Webinars
▸ www.mathworks.com/products/instrument/demos.html?show=recorded

Simulink 2007
▸ www.mathworks.com/company/events/worldtour/simulink07/agenda.html
It's possible to download the lectures and also simulations.

Test Measurement
▸ www.mathworks.com/test-measurement

Design and Simulate Complex Communication Systems
▸ www.mathworks.com/communications-systems/

Mind Mapping Your Way to a Term Paper

Have you ever been stuck while writing a term paper? It happens to all of us. You try making lists, you attempt a few "free-writes," and you even try discussing the topic with peers in the discussion board. But still the thoughts are not flowing, and there is no depth to the topics you're working on in your body paragraphs.

Try mind mapping!

Mind mapping is a graphical approach that engages different parts of your brain to see relationships and to trigger thoughts. By putting a together a mind map, you can easily associate ideas and initiate chains of related thoughts and ideas.

Mind mapping is effective if you are working alone, and can be dynamic if you're working in a group with other people. For example, if you are using web conferencing software such as Adobe Connect or Elluminate, you can collaborate with other people in creating a mind map. Each person can draw on the whiteboard and add his or her ideas or insights.

The technique works for writing, math, creative problem solving, and in developing creativity. For example, a study conducted with engineering students (Zampetakis & Tsironis, 2007) found that mind mapping was an effective strategy for explaining in detail all the possible applications of an engineering design or problem, particularly in team assignments.

What is a mind map?

Essentially, a mind map is a diagram on a piece of paper. It is a freeform space where you can put topics and then attach what comes to mind to them. Remember that you can use graphics as well as words. So, for example, if you're writing about pit bulls, you can put a picture of a pit bull in your map as well as words. As thoughts occur to you, you can put words or images next to them, and draw lines to denote relationships.

How does a mind map work?

Mind maps are extraordinarily effective because they minimize the cognitive overhead required in processing text on a page. Your mind does not have to decode all the words and the concepts. It can go straight to the work of generating ideas, associating words and concepts, and triggering chains of related thoughts.

You are doing semi-structured knowledge modeling, and in doing so, you are enabling your mind to represent structures from various information tools (Volkel & Haller, 2009).

In mind mapping, you are creating a form that employs the following:

- Spatial layout
- Freeform layout and structure
- Nesting of ideas
- Zooming and telescoping
- Non-related free associations
- Clusters of same-category ideas, concepts, examples
- Blend of abstract and concrete knowledge

Tony Buzan, who has written extensively about mind mapping, is an advocate because he points out it is an excellent way to use both sides of your brain. His book, *Use Both Sides of Your Brain* (1991), points out how our brains use different hemispheres to process different types of information, and if you have techniques for harnessing both sides, your thinking processes will be enhanced. Later, Buzan came to be regarded as the originator of a certain approach to mind-mapping that seeks to trigger both sides of the brain. His book, *The Mind Map Book*, has been widely adopted, and Buzan's approach has influenced instructional strategies in many parts of the world.

There are many ways to do mind mapping. The key is to remember that mind maps are spatial, and they are intended to be freeform. You're trying to engage both sides of your brain, and you should welcome any of the associations that the words, images, or spatial arrangement trigger. Here is a step-by-step approach:

Step 1: Draw a circle in the middle of the page, then write your topic in the circle.

Step 2: Draw a few lines coming out from the circle, and label them with ideas about your topic.

Step 3: Analyze the lines. Which ones can you develop further? Draw more lines as you see relationships, and place labels on them. Write details when they seem appropriate.

Step 4: Repeat the process until you run out of ideas. If you see a cluster of ideas developing, circle it. Discuss whether or not that would be something you can write about.

After you complete the steps of mind mapping, you can then focus on a cluster and use that as the basis of a paper, or a body paragraph. The mind map can be utilized in conjunction with your thesis statement, your outline, and your "free-writes" to add information and depth to your argument. You can also use it to critique your argument, your supporting evidence, and the logic used in constructing your case.

In all cases, the mind map is a powerful (and surprisingly fun!) tool to use in your online learning endeavors—alone or with a group.

REFERENCES

Buzan, T. (1991). *Use Both Sides of Your Brain*. New York: Plume Books.

Buzan, T., and B. Buzan. (1997). *The Mind Map Book*. London: BBC Books.

Steyn, T., and A. De Boer. (1998). "Mind mapping as a study tool for underprepared students in mathematics and science." *South African Journal of Ethnology*. 21.3 (Sept 1998): 125-138.

Volkel, M., and H. Haller. (2009). "Conceptual data structures for personal knowledge management." *Online Information Review*. 33.2: 298-315.

Zampetakis, L., and L. Tsironis. (2007). "Creativity development in engineering education: the case of mind mapping." *Journal of Management Development*. Vol 26 No 4: 370-380.

New Time Management Tactics

I'm having a terrible time making my deadlines, and preparing well for quizzes and exams. I am trying everything—I try to study all the time, and I do as much as I can with my BlackBerry, I share ideas and drafts with classmates, and I do practice exams with my BlackBerry, too.

But when it comes time for the real thing, I freeze. I run out of time. I also can't seem to focus on the real exam or quiz, even when I do a great job on the practice one.

What am I doing wrong?

Help!
Time-Tied in Tulsa

****

Dear Time-Tied:

Don't worry—you're not alone with your challenges. In fact, you might be surprised how many people suffer from the same problem. They're using all the new social networking applications with their smartphones and netbooks.

You may be overdoing the social networking. Instead of "ubiquitous learning," you may be feeling ubiquitous chaos!

The key is to reintroduce order into the chaos.

From "anytime/anywhere" to "right time/right place"

Be sure to do practice exams and quizzes in conditions that replicate the conditions you'll be in when you do the actual work. Otherwise, you're not really preparing your whole mind for optimal performance. So, if you're using your handheld to do a quiz, then be sure to try to recreate the conditions of the exam. If you tend to be nervous and have exam anxiety, be sure to incorporate that as well.

From "multi-task" to "mono-task"

Have you asked yourself the tough question: When does multitasking harm rather than help me? As you look into that question, you may find that the things you're doing as you multitask with Twitter, Facebook, YouTube, etc. are not as productive as you may have thought. In fact, they may be time-wasters. Be honest with yourself and cut out the time-wasters, or at least save them as rewards for after you've finished a task you've been dreading.

Make a list of tasks you do when you're multi-tasking:

- **Which are time-wasters?** Here are a few: checking celebrity sites, checking your stocks, checking the weather, sending tweets, updating Facebook with trivial stuff, shopping online, browsing auctions on e-Bay, browsing Amazon.com, etc.
- **Which are time-savers?** Here are a few: clarifying assignments by posting questions on the discussion board; sharing drafts and outlines with fellow students, downloading movies/presentations to watch on your handheld when you have a bit of downtime.

Try doing the tasks sequentially, rather interspersed with everything else.

- ✓ Dedicate blocks of time to email rather than letting it interrupt everything.
- ✓ Do not try to read course material, engage in presentations while involved in unrelated tasks.

Cognitive Reinforcement While "Mono-Tasking"

As you read your work online, or watch a movie or presentation, be sure

to take notes. You can take notes on a piece of paper, or you can maintain them in a handy web-based notebook, using Evernote (www.evernote.com) or Google Docs, both of which are sharable.

Develop a calendar that is independent of the course calendar.

Enter the due dates; create your own due dates / targets.

Correlate subtasks to time required.

Small blocks of time should map to tasks that do not take much time or concentration (some discussion board posts, downloading readings/activities, etc.) Longer, more complex tasks that take more time should be done when you have more uninterrupted time.

Identify productive social networking.

- Facebook course updates for class members (create special group)
- Twitter to individuals in your class
- RSS feeds or automatic email updates for important updates (team member postings, etc.)
- Blog entries / posts for portfolio
- GPS / Google Map posts for field projects / demographics
- Social bookmarking for research projects library

Identify non-productive social networking.

- Tweets and posts
- Non-school-related Twitter/Facebook, etc. posting
- Instant responses, rather than waiting to do them later

There is a lot to learn about yourself when it comes to time management. It's not easy, and the best approach is to keep an open mind, but also learn how to eliminate distractions, and to supercharge your productive time.

I hope that these tips and ideas help you get started and help you transform your study experience.

Overcoming Anxiety: Self-Regulatory Strategies Are Critical for Online Students

What is the best way to overcome anxiety that e-learners might feel about their courses? Researchers (Warr and Downing, 2000) have suggested that self-regulatory learning strategies are the most effective for students suffering from learning anxiety. When self-regulation (control of emotions, etc) is combined with behavioral and cognitive learning strategies, the result can be a very powerful approach.

Motivation: Intrinsic motivation can be channeled by maintaining connections to the individual's goals and aspirations. Alleviating boredom and maintaining interest by building in rewards and positive reinforcement are quite effective in an online environment.

Motivation can also be bulwarked by interaction and responsiveness. The learner who is suffering from anxiety may feel motivated to persist in the studies if the instructor provides prompt and meaningful feedback, group activities help provide a sense of connection and community, and the course content is clearly relevant to the learner's academic, life, and personal goals.

Learning communities / social networking: Learner anxiety is augmented by frustration. Frustration can result from technical difficulties, connectivity, unclear interfaces and instructions, and ambiguous performance expectations. A responsive help desk is important, as well as a robust Frequently Asked Questions page. In addition, if possible, establish an onsite mentor or team leader if several individuals who are taking the course are in the same place of employment or military unit.

Facilitate support: Make sure that your help desk or support is provided in a way that emphasizes the human aspect of the individual. Anxiety can be exacerbated by seeking help from a faceless entity known only through the design on a computer screen. Personalizing help-seeking helps assuage anxiety. Using live chat, and including a webcam with Internet telephony (example, Skype) can help.

Situated Learning / practical application: Learning strategies that situate the content and make connections between the content and the individual learner's lived experience are highly effective. This utilizes a constructivist epistemology and may require a rethinking and recasting of learning activities and assessment. Further, a cognitive epistemology comes into play when the individual learner makes connections, and then begins to form categories and to organize the knowledge in systems useful to the learner. Retrieval and application of information are facilitated, and the function is fluid, seamless, and meaningful when the learner can apply the knowledge to a real-life situation or to solve a problem perceived by the learner to be urgent and relevant.

One useful benefit of using practical application as a learning strategy for students suffering from learning anxiety (whether situational or performance-related), is that the learner can employ the new learning model to other aspects of his or her life. It is more than self-regulation, and more of an eclectic approach to learning and life.

REFERENCES

Kuhl, J. (1992). "A theory of self-regulation: Action versus state orientation, self-discrimination, and some applications." *Applied Psychology: An International Review.* 41, 97-129.

Mueller, J. H. (1992). "Anxiety and performance." In A. P. Smith and D. M. Jones (Eds.), *Handbook of human performance.* Vol 3, pp. 127-160. London : Academic Press.

Warr, P., and Downing, J. (2000). "Learning strategies, learning anxiety, and knowledge acquisition." *British Journal of Psychology.* 91, 311-333.

Overlooking the Obvious?
It Might Be Inattentional Blindness

A very strange thing has been happening to me in my online courses. I'm doing really well with the discussion board activities, and I'm downloading and working through all the instructional materials.

Somehow, though, I'm missing all the announcements. I'm not sure why that is happening.

They slip right by me, and I never even notice that they've been posted, or that there are new announcements. It's as though I'm blind to them. This is not good... it is affecting my grade.

What do you think is causing this? Is there anything I can do?

Sincerely,
Focused in Fairfax

****

Dear Focused,

What you are experiencing is something psychologists have been studying for years as they have attempted to find a way to explain why people do not always notice things happening right before their eyes.

The online course environment is largely a visual environment, so it's important to understand how and when the eye tends to not notice rather major changes and elements.

You're probably familiar with the following situations:

You're at a basketball game, and you are looking for an open seat. You scan the stands and you finally see one. As you make your way, you hear someone shout your name. You turn to see your good friends who say, "Didn't you see us? We've been waving at you."

You're surprised—you were looking closely for a seat, but you totally missed them. You had eyes only for what you were looking for.

An even more revealing example of how people seems to see only what they want to see has to do with an experiment conducted by psychologists Simons and Chabris in 1998. They asked a group of people to focus on passing a basketball to each other and remembering elements of the basketball-passing task. The individuals in the group were so focused on what they were doing that they did not notice people wandering their midst—even a person dressed up in a gorilla suit.

So, amazingly enough, people were blind to the gorilla. Their experience echoed what a researcher found out more than 100 years ago. Pioneering cognitive psychologist Rezco Balint noted in 1907: "… focusing our attention on a certain object may happen to such an extent that we cannot perceive other objects placed in the peripheral parts of our visual field…" (Balint, 1907, translated in Husain and Stein, 1988, p. 91).

Here's what can be done in online courses to make sure that you're catching everything you need to pay attention to:

1. **Move** announcements from your peripheral field to the middle of the visual field.

2. **Find** a way to receive announcements in more than one location. For example, have announcements automatically emailed to you.

3. **Change** the focus of your attention, and look again at the page or visual field.

4. **Practice** reconfiguring perception. Perhaps you don't have to go as far as to buy a set of "Where's Waldo" books, but at the same time, train your brain to pick up the unexpected, and to see "everything."

Don't forget, however, that you've learned to focus for a reason. It's often very important to be able to tune out distractors, just as it's important to be able to manage intrusive thoughts. So, after you've practiced looking for the gorillas (thinking back to the work done by Simon and Chabris), try blocking out the gorillas.

Stay focused, and then, stay alert. Your mental agility will serve you well in your online courses.

REFERENCES

Husain, M., and Stein, J. (1988). "Rezso Balint and His Most Celebrated Case." *Archives of Neurology*. (45) 89-93.

Simons, D. J., and Chabris, C. F. (1999). "Gorillas in our Midst: Sustained Inattentional Blindness for Dynamic Events." *Perception*. (28): 1059-1074.

Peer Review: Benefit or Bear Trap?

Are you frustrated with the peer review process in your online composition courses? Are the comments superficial and relatively meaningless? When you have to write a critique, do you find yourself oscillating between being too lightweight or heavy-handed?

It's never easy to critique a fellow student's paper. There are social norms that constrain one in both a face-to-face environment and online. The truth is, as human beings, we have a need to be liked and accepted. Dishing out criticism and negative commentary is one of the fastest ways imaginable to a rather vexed if not openly hostile relationship with your peers.

However, peer reviews are often a fairly significant part of your grade. So, you're faced with a dilemma—what is the best way to do a peer review, and what's the best way to get the most from your results?

The first step is to look at the guidelines that your instructor has provided. Map out the due dates and also the expectations. Then, as you follow the instructions, make sure you follow additional steps:

1. Establish a positive tone at the outset with all your communications.

2. Identify the rhetorical situation. What is the goal of the assignment? Who are the readers/audience likely to be? What is the outcome that you desire?

3. Read your fellow student's work from beginning to end without passing judgment. Think about the work as a whole. What are its strong points? What is it doing? Can you identify its goals? Its primary thesis? The support for the argument?

   Make a list and then point out the strengths, and then where the author might expand or clarify.

4. Look at the introduction. Is it engaging? Does it relate well to the rest of the essay?

5. How is the flow? Transitions? Are the body paragraphs balanced? Do they tie to the primary thesis? Offer suggestions for expansions and clarification. Be sure to mention your favorite passages, and what seemed to be particularly effective.

6. Finally, look at mechanics. Save spelling, grammar and syntax for the end. It's tempting to focus on those elements at the beginning, but it's actually more effective to clean up everything in a final round of copy-editing.

Once you start to feel comfortable with peer review, you'll start to incorporate it into your writing process even when it's not required! You'll look for study buddies or simply an individual in your class with whom you feel a special rapport and a sense of trust. As you start to work through the process, you'll find it becomes increasingly intuitive and automatic. In the meantime, your writing will improve and you'll feel more confident and self-assured.

Peer review is one big step in the right direction toward developing strategies that will serve you well for success in your undergraduate classes, and then later in your graduate program.

Proposal Writing Checklist

A proposal may be one of the most valuable documents you'll ever learn to write. After all, writing a successful proposal could change your life in a very positive way. You could be awarded a grant or a contract, or you could travel to distant places to involve yourself in research or field investigations.

WHAT IS A PROPOSAL?

A proposal is a plan of action offered for acceptance or rejection. The proposal may be informal or formal, and its form may range from a letter to a formal document written in response to an RFP (request for proposal).

YOUR RHETORICAL GOALS AND REASONS FOR WRITING

What is the rhetorical situation? In other words, what is the exigency (the urgent need)? Who is your audience, and what are their values, beliefs, and needs? What are the rhetorical constraints? What are the situational elements or the context that may limit or constrain your ability to persuade or spur the reader to action?

FLOWCHART APPROACH

As you develop your proposal, it is useful to use a flowchart approach and respond to the questions that appear below.

What kind of proposal are you writing? What is the rhetorical situation and the reason for writing it?

If it is a formal proposal, which of the following elements do you need to be sure to include?

- » Title page
- » Table of contents
- » Executive summary
- » Introduction
- » Background
- » Discussion
- » Project organization with timetable
- » Budget
- » Qualifications and experience of personnel
- » Summary
- » Appendix

Who is your prospective client? What are the goals of the project they want to have done? Do you know anything about budget constraints or their financial situation? What are their most urgent needs?

How can you fit your ideas and abilities into your client's needs?

How can you solve the technical needs in a way that shows your understanding of the client's critical needs?

What are the critical factors that evaluators use in assessing proposals? Make a list.

Does your proposal address every element mentioned in the RFP? Make an RFP checklist at the front of your proposal and let the reader know where in the proposal each RFP element has been addressed.

Are you using graphics and visuals to illustrate your points?

Make a list of the documents you will need (representations, certifications, letters, affidavits, etc.) and put them together in a folder.

Have you prepared an outline of your proposal?

Are you using headers in order to highlight every important point in your proposal?

THE SEQUENCE

In general, the best approach to writing a proposal is to create the document using the following sequence:

1. Identify the urgent need—the exigency—and identify/address it.

2. Develop a broad understanding of the needs the person or entity you are addressing the proposal to.

3. Pinpoint the desired results; then map the best and most likely way to achieve your goals or obtain the desired results.

4. Develop a set of steps to start building the elements of the proposal that will match your audience's needs with the desired action.

5. Remember that your document is, in many ways, a sales document, and you must persuade your audience that your approach is the most effective.

Individuals who know how to write successful proposals are deeply respected and valued in their organizations. So, even though you may be writing a proposal in order to satisfy the requirements of a course, do not forget that the experience could be quite practical.

Regaining and Maintaining Focus
in Your Online Course

I'm having problems with concentration when I'm working on my online course. It's really frustrating, and I'm totally losing my confidence.

Here are a few things that happen to me:

1. *I click on the wrong buttons or links, or can't find the files I need. I start to feel lost. I lose my focus.*

2. *I can't concentrate when after getting a poor quiz score.*

3. *I'm missing easy questions when I take a quiz because I get distracted.*

4. *I blow early assignments or quizzes because I lack focus at the start of the course.*

Help! I'm starting to get very nervous.

Sincerely,
Frazzled in Fredonia

****

Dear Frazzled,

I totally understand your frustration! You'd be amazed how many e-learners have had the same experiences.

Let's take a look at the situations you've described. You may not realize it, but you have something in common with other e-learners.

All of them erroneously assume that a lack of focus is to blame for their mental mistakes while they're taking an online course. They think it's all about focus or concentration, but the true reality is a bit more complex.

The reality is that they're committing all kinds of errors as they take their courses and there are numerous contributing factors. Many times, the mental errors are tied into self-regulation and self-concept. Let's dig a bit deeper and see what's going on.

1. Frustration causes a lack of focus because you are upset with something that just happened and can't focus on the present.

   If you're busy thinking about the bad grade you just received, or you are busy grousing about how difficult the site is to navigate, you're thinking about the past and not the present.

   Take charge of your thoughts and put them squarely in the present while you're studying.

2. Lack of motivation or intensity can cause you to lose your focus because you're simply not at your peak level of desire and drive. You've got to care about what you're doing, and you need to want the outcome.

   Start thinking about the pay-offs and the reward and get yourself in an "up" mental state.

3. Tension, self-doubt, fear, or anxiety can wreak havoc on your ability to focus on the tasks you have to do in the course before you've a good sense of self-confidence, and before you're convinced that you can perform well in the class.

4. A lack of trust in your abilities may lead to missing easy questions, getting caught in a digression or tangent, and to start to focus on the things that are pleasant, but which do not contribute to the grade.

In order to keep focused, it is useful to keep a brief checklist of "Back on Track" questions:

1. What's the task I'm trying to perform now? Identify it. Stick with it.

2. Why am I taking this course? What's my end goal? Renew your desire to achieve your goal.

3. Trust your training. Let go. Flow. You've been writing, doing math problems, studying for tests for years. If you're stuck, free-write. Get unstuck.

Rehearsal and Repetition:
When Can It Work for You?

Rehearsal and repetition, when used in conjunction with online and mobile learning, can be a good way to master the basics of a course, and to feel comfortable with identification, definition, and description of concepts and specific content. However, if you're an e-learner, and you are not able to keep distractions at bay, then the strategy of rehearsal and repetition may not work for you. This is the conclusion reached by several learning specialists and educational psychologists who studied why students perform poorly even after adhering closely to the "practice makes perfect" traditional cognitive learning strategies of rehearsal, organization, and elaboration.

In order to make sure that rehearsal and repetition help you organize your knowledge, and then elaborate/describe/apply the concepts learned, you need to be sure to create ideal conditions for learning.

What are the typical learning activities that involve rehearsal and repetition?

- **Flash cards:** Digital, on both your laptop and used with your handheld mobile device such as your smartphone.

- **Vocabulary and Pronunciation Drills:** These can utilize voice recognition software in the case of learning a language, and pronunciation.

- **Identification and Familiarization of Items and Processes:** Can incorporate graphics, as well as audio and video, in order to familiarize an audience with processes and procedures.

There are other applications for the rehearsal and repetition technique, and all can be effective when applied when conditions for learning exist.

Here is a quick checklist of what to do to create a good learning environment that favors rehearsal and repetition:

- **Foster an environment that encourages focus.** Concentration is required for rehearsal and repetition. According to some educational psychologists (Kuhl, 1992), people have finite resources for cognitive and information processing. If too much capacity is dedicated to quelling one's anxiety by self-reassurance and relaxation techniques, there is little capacity left for the actual task at hand.

  Further, if the learning situation or setting creates distractions, more cognitive resources will be required to maintain focus. Finally, if an individual is suffering from post-traumatic stress disorder or there are work or family conflicts, unwanted intrusive thoughts may create even more problems with concentration, and require the marshalling of cognitive resources.

- **Make sure you have good connectivity.** Online rehearsal and repetition often take the form of automated, interactive forms, requiring good online access and time online. Many online courses rely heavily on automated, online quizzes and "skill and drill" activities.

  While these are considered effective by some, particularly if the test is in the same format, there are questions about the efficacy of skill-and-drill in the attainment of deeper learning. Nevertheless, this is a moot point for an individual learner who cannot access the quizzes or review materials because he or she has limited access to the Internet, and may be accessing the learning activities through a very slow dial-up connection or Wi-Fi node. Needless to say, the frustration involved when one cannot access the material contributes to learner anxiety.

- **Keep the content interesting and engaging.** Motivational control lacking as boredom sets in. Motivation is an important factor in success, and anxiety acts as a huge demotivator. Further, learners may find that rehearsal and repetition—particularly in isolation, is extremely boring. Educational psychologists (Pintrich and DeGroot, 1990), have traced connections between motivation and learning strategies. Make sure the content relates to real live. Material must be made relevant, and reconnected to real life. Further, if repetition and rehearsal are used as learning strategies, it must be made clear to the learner that the content forms a foundational underpinning for situated learning to come in the future.

- **Employ learning communities.** Effective rehearsal and repetition occurs in groups, where immediate support is available. It might be useful to examine if rehearsal, organization, and elaboration are most effective in study groups and informal communities of practice. In distance settings, collaborative strategies rarely involve the cognitive strategies, but instead tend to stress practical application focused around a set of clearly defined outcomes.

USEFUL RESOURCES

Driskell, J. E., Copper, C., and Moran, A. (1994). "Does mental practice enhance performance?" *Journal of Applied Psychology*. 78, 805-814.

Ferguson-Hessler, M. G. M., and de Jong, T. (1990). "Studying physics texts: Differences in study processes between good and poor performers." *Cognition and Instruction*. 7, 41-54.

Karabenick, S. A., and Knapp, J. R. (1991). "Relationship of academic help seeking to the use of learning strategies and other instrumental achievement behaviors in college students." *Journal of Educational Psychology*. 16. 117-138.

Pintrich, P. R., and De Groot, E. V. (1990). "Motivational and self-regulated learning components of classroom academic performance." *Journal of Educational Psychology*. 82, 33-40.

Seipp, B. (1991). "Anxiety and academic performance. A meta-analysis of findings." *Anxiety Research*. 4, 27-41.

Snow, R. E. and Swanson, J. (1992). "Instructional psychology: Aptitude, adaptation, and assessment." *Annual Review of Psychology*. 43, 49.

Weinstein, C. E., and Mayer, R. E. (1986). "The teaching of learning strategies." In M. C. Wittrock (Ed.), *Handbook of Research on Teaching* (3 rd ed. pp. 315-327). New York, Macmillan.

Report Writing Checklist

If you are taking a technical course that requires you to learn about differ-

ent types of equipments, procedures, or technologies, chances are, you'll have to write a technical report. In order to be effective, it is a good idea to develop a checklist of the elements you need to be sure to include in your report.

WHAT IS A TECHNICAL REPORT?

A technical report documents the results of your work. It is an important product because it presents information resulting from weeks, even months of work. The work is evaluated on the basis of the report, and so the report needs to be clear, well-organized, and to contain the depth of information needed and required.

UNDERSTANDING THE REASON FOR WRITING THE RE-PORT AND WHAT YOU WANT TO ACCOMPLISH

What is the rhetorical situation? (Your audience? Their expectations? The context? Background or history of this document and what you're trying to accomplish?)

What is the primary exigency? (What makes this urgent? What need are you addressing? If there are desired action steps, what are they?)

What kind of report are you writing? Select the type from the following list:

- **Annual or quarterly report:** Financial or progress reports that are created and disseminated on a regular basis, at predetermined times. In addition to formal financial reporting, other reports may include production statistics, bank statements.

- **Progress report:** This is a summary of the activities accomplished in a specific period of time, recorded and compared with timelines. It identifies milestones and discusses places of deviation from stated goals.

- **Research report:** This report summarizes the results of studies, research, experiments, or data-gathering. The work may have been done in a lab or in the field.

- **Field/Operations report:** Information gathered during reconnaissance investigations, inspections of installations or equipments, or plants (pilot plants, turnarounds, etc).

- **Recommendation report:** Information submitted to management in order to make a request for action, or form the basis of a decision. Purposes may include funding decisions on research programs, projects, land acquisition, or capital investment, or acquisitions/divestitures.

- **Feasibility report:** A document that presents information that relates to the potential feasibility or viability of a project, venture, commitment, or activity. The report includes comparisons, analyses, discussions of costs and benefits, presentation of alternatives, and preliminary budget estimates.

What kinds of sections should you include in your report?

1. Cover and title page
2. Abstract
3. Table of Contents
4. Executive Summary
   - Goals and objectives
   - Main activities
   - Main results
   - Recommendations
5. Introduction – a brief overview
   - Scope of problem

- Why important
- Discuss previous work
- Research method
- Key results

6. Body
   - The reasons for the work
   - Primary research question
   - Theories/literature review
   - Research method
   - Equipment
   - Research procedures

7. Results
   - The experimental data
   - Observations analysis/algorithms/methods of analyzing the data
   - Discussion of the potential significance of results
   - Discussion of the potential problems in the analytical approach
   - Comparison with other similar investigations generalizations
   - Potential problems

8. Conclusions and recommendations – be sure to relate these to the abstract and the primary purpose for writing your report.

9. Nomenclature – not necessary unless specialized nomenclature is used.

10. References/Works Cited/Bibliography – use the appropriate style guide (Chicago, ABA, etc.)

11. Appendices – better to include data here than in the body of the report.

The technical report is a document that lends itself to outlining and good planning. You will benefit from developing a checklist and being sure to follow it carefully.

Research Sources to Avoid
in Your Term Paper

I am at my wits' end. I am taking a first-year composition course and I had to write a research paper. I did research, quoted the material, cited my sources, and got an F! I asked my professor what happened, and she told me that I used Wikipedia, and that my block quotes were too long.

I totally lost confidence, so I decided to go online and find a paper I could buy or "borrow."

At Termpapers.com, I found a great paper (I thought). I was going to use it as a guide, but I ran out of time (and confidence). I turned it in. I got a failing grade on it, too. I am not surprised, but I am very embarrassed.

Now I'm in real trouble. My professor is giving me one last chance to write a research paper.

Where do I start?

Sincerely,
Frazzled Fledgling E-Learner

****

Dear Frazzled Fledgling E-Learner,

You've been given another chance, which is a good thing. But, don't let this "teachable moment" slip away just because you're feeling like skulking away in shame. Hold your head up high and get back into that research paper! You can do it!

Wikipedia and most other wikis:

For most people, Wikipedia is the first "go-to" source. After all, Wikipedia is what usually comes up first in Google searches. Many times, Wikipedia is a great place to start. The entries provide fairly reliable results, and there are links to other sites which allow one to investigate further. Comparisons between Wikipedia and traditional encyclopedias have pointed out that Wikipedia is often more complete, and the information is more up-to-date. So, what is so bad about Wikipedia? The problem lies in the fact that it is a wiki, and that anyone can add information to the entry. While in theory this means that there is a system of checks and balances, in operation, it has made Wikipedia the site of mischief and deliberate misinformation. Don't let yourself be unwittingly drawn into someone else's lack of complete knowledge, agenda, malicious play, or warped sense of humor. There is nothing wrong with using Wikipedia as a first step, but always be sure to double check the information and to use other information.

Second-order research results:

You're doing an online search and you find an article in the *New York Times* that reports the results of a recent research project. The topic is perfect, and they've selected the statistics that are perfectly aligned with your needs. You cheerfully incorporate the material from the *New York Times*, and you cite your source. You are happy. At least, you're happy until you happen upon another newspaper article-this one from the *Chicago Tribune*—that is reporting the same results. The numbers are different, and what is worse: there are findings that the *New York Times* article did not include, due to space. It turns out that the *New York Times* article contained typographical errors, as well as significant omissions. You wish you had cited the *Chicago Tribune* article instead of the one from the *New York Times* article. But would that have helped? Chances are, the *Chicago Tribune* article omitted other information that might have been useful to you but not to their general readers. What is the best approach? In this case, the best is to look for the original paper published to report the results of the research. It is not as hard to do as it sounds—the key is to look at the article, write down the citations, and then to look them up. Often the results are from a prominent journal, or a government study, both of which are fairly easy to locate. If you're feeling bad about your research skills at this point, don't worry. Almost everyone makes this mistake when writing research papers.

Here is a quick list of other sites to avoid:

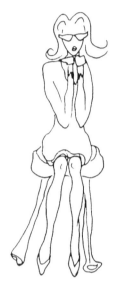

- **Op-Ed "rant-sites":** Many newspapers have online editorial pages that may or may not be reliable. They are extremely biased, which is sometimes good if you're writing a paper that discusses bias, but can be problematic if you're trying to promote other things.

- **Unreliable blogs:** Some blogs are considered even more reliable than traditional news sources. Most are not. In fact, they can include pure disinformation or lies, and yet sometimes they get picked up by Google, to the point that the lies become so commonly believed that they become urban legends.

- **Some online encyclopedias:** Encyclopedias sound good. They can be very incomplete. Use them, but be careful.

- **E-mails (unless part of an interview):** Generally speaking, emails are unreliable unless they are used in very specific ways, such as being a part of an interview.

- **Tweets (unless directly related to the topic of your paper):** That said, using Twitter is a great way to share information.

- **Term papers posted on the Internet**

- **Student papers for sale or made available**

- **Out-of-date statistics**

At any rate, Frazzled Fledgling, don't give up. Please rewrite your paper and use your own thoughts and use reliable sources, in moderation. Keep in mind that your paper should be about your thesis statement, and not just data.

Mainly though, write about what you care about. Gain confidence through your own interests. Express yourself and your interests.

Revision Flowchart
for Essays And Term Papers

How many times have you received your essay or term paper from your instructor with the comment: "Needs further revision"? How many times have you decided to revise your paper, only to find that all you can think of to do is to run spell check and look for obvious grammatical mistakes? How often have you been asked to conduct a peer review of a fellow classmate's paper only to realize, to your dismay, that you're not quite sure of what you're looking for?

Revision is not as easy or transparent as it might seem. It's not just about paring down and fixing spelling and typographical errors. To revise effectively, you need to have a good sense of what your paper is about, and you need to be able to describe what you want your audience to do. What do you want to accomplish with your essay?

Once you have your topic and your goals clearly in mind, you're in a better position to start editing and revising. Here's an eight-step process that may help you enormously as you start the revision process.

EIGHT-STEP REVISION PROCESS

1. **Thesis statement clarification.**

   After you've written your first draft of your paper, you may find that your primary thesis and focus have changed a bit. This often happens when the data you find to support your thesis is not as clear-cut as you had hoped or, when doing your research for the paper, you were able to narrow or tighten your focus. So, the body of your paper may no longer fit the primary thesis. If that's the case, identify it. Underline or highlight your old thesis, and then start hunting for a replacement. How do you do that? Making a list of possible thesis statements is very effective. Brainstorm, and don't self-censor. After you have a list, you can select the one that fits best.

2. **Definition section revision.**

If you're writing an essay or term paper, there will be a moment in time when you'll need to let your audience have a clear picture of what you're talking about. For example, if you're writing a paper on hydraulic fracturing in shale gas reservoirs, you'll need to dedicate a bit of time to defining the key terms and concepts. Granted, your audience may be very specialized and you can safely assume that they're experts in the field. This is a time when knowing your audience makes a difference. Be sure to provide information on the level that they need. If you are writing for a general audience, you'll need to provide definitions and explanations that are on the level of basic knowledge. If your audience consists of technical specialists, you'll need to make sure it is written at the level that your audience needs, wants, and expects.

3. **Evidence / Body paragraphs.**

The topic sentence for every body paragraph should tie in with the primary thesis. Your paragraphs should flow from the primary argument and should provide support, either in the manner of evidence/details, or in explanations. With that in mind, make sure that the body paragraphs are organized in a way that makes sense, and be sure they are balanced in terms of content and complexity. Avoid having imbalanced paragraphs.

4. **Case studies and examples.**

For many of your papers, case studies and examples are excellent ways to provide support for your primary thesis. Be sure to provide sufficient information for the reader to see how the example ties into the primary thesis, and be sure to clearly cite your sources. Avoid making your case study such a large part of the paper that it starts to be a digression rather than a supporting piece of evidence. When possible, include statistics and details. If it is appropriate to include graphics, figures, and photos, be sure to do so.

5. **Strengthening the theoretical foundations.**

There is no better way to legitimize your argument than to place it within a context and to place it within a theoretical framework that allows your reader to see the bigger issues at work. For example, if you're writing about how wards of the state are often financially, physically, sexually and psychologically abused by their guardians, provide information about what other researchers have found and what they've had to say on the subject. If your focus is the legal side, then be sure to provide information about the seminal thinkers and ethical issues. If you're focusing on human rights, discuss the ethical issues and provide theoretical underpinnings for the work done be activists and advocacy groups.

6. **Adding needed details and statistics.**

Facts are persuasive. When you need to persuade your audience of a certain perspective or point of view, be sure to incorporate appropri-ate details in terms of facts, figures, and statistics. It is often very helpful to cite findings from studies or research. Here's a cautionary note, however. Be sure to cite from the original, and not from a synopsis that might appear in another article, news item, or blog. Also, be sure that your statistics are relevant, up-to-date, and well sourced and cited. Be wary and do not trust everything you read on the Internet. Be sure you're using facts and figures that are reliable and relevant.

7. **Cutting tangents and superfluous details.**

As you wrote your first draft, you might have let yourself go a bit far afield, particularly as you explore a compelling side story or case. It is also easy to go overboard with statistics and details. For example, on a paper on the impact of obesity on school children's sense of identity and performance in school, it is common for authors to go into detail on adult obesity statistics, and to bemoan the nutritional content of fast food. However interesting the information in the digression, the fact of the matter is that it detracts from the primary thesis. Be sure to stay focused and use information that directly relates to your thesis.

8. **Revising and copy-editing for clarity.**

    As you re-read your paper, you may find that it loses focus and is not as clear as it could be. The reasons are often fairly easy to identify: repetition and redundancy, poor organization, weak or sloppy introduction, and a conclusion that simply restates the primary thesis. As you revise, be sure to identify where there are redundancies and misplaced paragraphs. At the same time, be sure to step back and ask yourself which paragraphs are underdeveloped. One method for doing so is to use headings and sub-headings. Once you have your essay demarcated in a way that is clear, it's fairly easy to see where the content imbalances lie. Then, the next step—fleshing it out—is much easier to do.

As you follow the Eight-Step Revision Process, keep in mind that it is very useful to use it in conjunction with peer reviews. In fact, a peer review process can be formed around the Eight-Step Revision Process, individuals can use the eight points as a checklist. It is a great way to keep everyone on the same page.

At any rate, the bottom line is this: don't fear revision. Learn to enjoy it, embrace it, even make it your best friend. You'll develop your analytical skills and your creative problem solving abilities. You'll learn to think with clarity, and you'll enjoy a new-found freedom from worry about your academic writing.

Saving the Sinking Online Student

Help! I am so overwhelmed. I don't even know where to start to describe my e-learning situation. What can I do? I have two midterms this week, and I feel totally confused and lost.

I've even started snapping at my family members. I think they are secretly wishing for me to fail. It makes me angry.

Demoralized in Des Moines

****

Dear Demoralized:

You may need an e-learning intervention. Take a look at the following 11 interventions and see which one might work for you. I feel confident one will help.

1. **Writing Help**

   It is amazing how many people point to writing as the one thing that stops them in their academic tracks. Don't let a fear of writing stop you. Get help now. Your college may offer a writing lab. If it does not, there are many places to obtain tutoring help, all at a very affordable price. Smart Thinking and other tutor systems can help.

2. **Math Help**

   You may not be dismayed by writing term papers and essay exams, but the fact you have to take math and to well may be looming over you and discouraging you. If you're a nursing major, you know that you're going to have to do well in math. There is a lot riding on your grade. So look for math help. You may wish to find "study buddies" in your math course. Also, find math tutors.

3. **Chunk Your Time**

   Time management used to be one of the big student-success items to consider. The problem used to be that people wasted time and did not organize their time effectively. If anything, now people organize their time too effectively and are used to accomplishing things in small burst that take 10 or 15 minutes at a time. For an online course, you're going to need to develop the ability to stay focused for an hour or so. So, build in a chunk of time in which you focus on your online course. Ideally, it should be an hour or an hour and a half at a time because that replicates the amount of time you're generally given for online tests. When you start working on your course, don't let anything get in the way. Stay on task. It will be difficult at first, but do whatever you have to in order to keep your mind into your game. The best approach may be to turn off your cell, play mellow tunes on your iPod, and develop flow.

4. **Tweet-Free Zone**

   Twitter is great. So are text messages and automatic feeds from your friends' and colleagues' Facebook accounts. However, they constitute a huge distraction. After all, isn't it easier and more immediately rewarding to post a comment about your friend's post about the antics of her wayward cat? The key to starting to feel in control about your courses, and not so overwhelmed is to get a handle on the information flowing into you. Avoid distractions. Keep your mind clear for the task at hand.

5. **Self-Determination**

   What is your major? Did you select your course of study or are you doing it because it sounds like the right thing to do?

6. **Need for Affiliation**

   The online world can be a solitary place if you're new to something. It can also be a place where you feel very vulnerable and exposed. It's hard to defend yourself if someone decides to say something cruel, or to make fun of you for being a newbie. Keep in mind that instructional designers know this well and have worked hard to make online courses a safe zone—a warm, fuzzy place where you can count on the support of your instructor and your fellow students. In a well-designed course, your feelings of isolation will soon be replaced by a feeling of acceptance and warmth. You're a part of a group. You're in a community. You're accepted, and your success matters. So, don't delay. Jump into the discussion boards and start posting and reinforcing yourself, your work, your goals.

7. **Self-Doubt Elimination / Self-Efficacy Building**
Do you know anyone with an "I'm going to fail" attitude? Not only are they in danger of creating a self-fulfilling prophecy, they're also running the risk of destroying their belief in themselves. Actively counter the bad attitude with an "I can do it!" attitude. Easier said than done? One positive approach is to do realistic goal-setting. Set small, achievable goals and reward yourself. Remind yourself that you're doing a great job and you're accomplishing your goals.

8. **Financial Worry-Free Zone**
While it's true that it's more difficult to obtain private student loans, the government is opening up loans for college and making them more available. For example, Pell Grant limits are being increased, as are low-interest federally guaranteed loans. So, don't be lazy. Do something. Be proactive and apply for your financial aid early. Having the acceptance letters early will relieve anxiety and will allow you to do effective planning.

9. **Stop Multitasking, At Least for the Moment**
We live in a multi-tasking world. For example, as you read this, how many tasks are you simultaneously doing? Technology has blessed us with the ability to do a lot of things at the same time, but it has also made it possible to do a lot of things halfway and never quite bring them to fruition. It has also made it possible for us to become self-gratification junkies who can't go 15 minutes without a "fix" of Facebook or LinkedIn. If you want to be able to do well with courses that require focus and tasks, stop multi-tasking and try doing one task at a time. It will feel uncomfortable at first, but once you get a feel for it, you'll be glad you did.

10. **Care about Your Topics**
Incorporate experiential learning, prior knowledge, and your own interests and goals. Ask your professor to write about things you want to write about. Having a choice will make a huge difference. You will be amazed at how motivating it is. Deci and Ryan have said that what

you're doing is a part of self-determination theory, and that you'll be amazed at how relevant it will feel.

11. **Replace "Overwhelmed" with "In Control"**

    Think about what is going on in your life. Does everything pour over you in a flood of details, unrelated tasks, and garbled text and voices? No, you're not schizophrenic. You're in the online world, and you're overwhelmed. Don't worry—it's normal! How do you regain control? One effective way is to start organizing tasks. It does not have to be complicated. Jot down what you need to do on a piece of paper, or make a note to yourself. Even better, you can text yourself or send an email to yourself. Then, put the basic  things on a calendar. Don't go overboard on the calendar, however. If you do, you run the risk of taking too much time organizing your calendar. Relax. Prioritize your tasks. Map them. Then start working down the list—most important things first, then move to the less important tasks. Granted, the less important tasks will be more fun, but hang in there. You'll make it!

So, dear Demoralized, I feel very confident that you'll find a good approach—don't be hesitant to try more than one intervention strategy.

Schemas and Other Memory Structures
You Need to Know for Effective Micro-Learning

I've been reading a lot about how our memories are constantly changing. From what I can tell, memory melts down, reforms, and melts down all over again. That seems to apply to autobiographical memory,

Does this mean we can create false memories? Does it mean that we have to be careful about what we put in our minds since we're apparently charging/re-charging our memories, and the new information could be supplanting the old?

I'm worried. I am a busy working mom student who needs a degree. I have to study in fits and starts—in 20 and 30 minute chunks—and I need to make sure I'm studying correctly. I can't afford to be melting down and rebuilding my memory in a bad way. What do you suggest?

Sincerely,
Cognitively Compromised

****

Dear Cognitively,

What you've described is something we should all take very seriously. You're not wrong. Researchers are constantly showing us the mind's plasticity. Our brains are amazing, and we've only scratched the surface.

It is a very good idea to approach your limited study time with extreme circumspection.

You're right. If you're not careful, you'll rebuild your memories/cognition with incorrect data. It will rewrite, if you will, certain aspects/sectors. If you're going to work on something, keep this as a rule of thumb: repeat/review the correct information 5 times for every time you do a practice test.

That bears repeating:

For every practice test, make sure that you've gone through 5 repetitions/reviews of the information you need to be able to present. This also applies to skills and abilities.

For every skill or activity you need to master, make sure you've gone through at least 5 practice runs; 10 would be ideal.

Let's take a look at meta-memory issues. For example, there are issues of the classification systems that help organize and—even more importantly—retrieve information.

What do you do when you're taking a sociology test and you can't remember any of the theorists and their relation to various basic concepts. What do you do?

The best approach is to sit down and change your studying strategies.

First, be aggressive as you approach your course. Start making a list of categories that make sense. Use them as a kind of mental filing system, and then develop easy-to-remember memory schemes.

Trust in your personal filing system. Trust in your personal schemas (categories / organizing systems), and don't allow anyone to destroy your confidence.

Then, repeat, reinforce, repeat, repeat, repeat, then CONNECT.

What do I mean by that? Repeat the information for the course. Then, reinforce it by connecting it to a classification/schema system. Think of schema as flash cards or index cards. Think of them as file cabinets back in the day when people actually kept paper files.

Then, repeat the basic concepts. After you've done that, be sure to look at the connections.

Connect to your prior knowledge. Connect to your lived experience.

By doing so, you'll be working out that muscle we call memory—and you'll be giving it a workout in many different ways.

Finally, after you've explored and expanded your core, elemental knowledge of what you're studying, look within. Introspect. Find what you have left behind. Find what you still are lacking and make your knowledge and understanding complete by making a connection to your personal experience.

Empathy built by seeing the relationship between your own personal (and even painful) experiences and the relation of others will serve you well. Feel, think, and then feel again. What do I mean by that? Dredge up your deepest memories by invoking the emotional tie to memory. Then, connect it to your rational side—science, business, ethics, relationships with others. After you've made that connection, make a connection again to what you see as your future—think of how to relate your knowledge to dreams, hopes, and desires.

I hope this has been helpful. As I bid fare-thee-well, I would like to share a few nice "knowledge nuggets"—

★ Embrace Schema ★

A schema is knowledge.

A schema is general, and it does not encode information about one particular situation, but rather about a particular type of situation.

A schema is structured—it includes how the facts are related.

A scheme is used in comprehension. The structure of the schema is such that it includes how the knowledge is related in this type of situation but it does not include information about any exact situation.

I hope this has been helpful. Your questions and thoughts were very energizing for me to contemplate, and I'd like to let you know how grateful I am for that.

Have a successful semester. I have faith in you!

Short-Term Memory & E-Learning

When Renata decided to enroll in an online certificate program, she realized for the first time how many logins she would have and how many computer processes she would need to remember.

"How can I possibly remember all of these passwords, codes, and procedures?" she asked her mom.

Her mom, a clinical psychologist who worked with individuals with memory and cognition issues, including Alzheimer's patients, was a bit unsympathetic. "I guess you'll just have to improve your short-term memory," she said. "The best way to keep your mental abilities sharp is to exercise them."

"But how?" asked Renata. "I'm not supposed to write them down."

"Well, one way is to repeat the code over and over to yourself," said Renata's mom. "That way you keep the information active and available in your short-term memory. It's what psychologists also call 'primary memory.'"

Renata paused for a moment. She realized for the first time that taking an online course—with all the links and places to go—could potentially help her develop her short-term memory. It was an interesting bonus for taking the course.

"But… what exactly is short-term memory?" asked Renata.

Renata's mom explained that short-term memory is the part of the memory function that keeps things fresh, and keeps information available for further processing.

"Renata, here's a test for you. Take 20 seconds and repeat the following four words over and over to yourself: cat, road, brick, boot."

Renata paused, rehearsed the words a few times, and the repeated them perfectly. "Hah. That was easy, Mom."

"Yes, of course it was," replied Renata's mom. "You're doing what's referred to as 'maintenance rehearsal.' However, it's not something that is sustainable."

She went on to explain that there are two things that often interfere with short-term memory and maintenance rehearsal: 1) interruption of the rehearsal (which leads to forgetting); 2) an explicitly interfering activity. Interruptions will often disrupt the rehearsal and make it impossible to hold the items in short-term memory.

Short-term Memory Boosts

Strategies for holding more items in short-term memory involve coding, avoiding distractors, and chunking:

- **Coding:** Coding allows you to recode items into a different form. For example, you can recode written information to acoustic codes, through verbal rehearsal. So, explaining what you're doing to someone or finding a way to put it into verbal form and rehearse, can be very helpful.

- **Avoiding Distractors:** What's the best way to forget something? Interruptions and distractions are probably the most destructive elements to short-term memory. So, if you're trying to remember something, do not let anything interrupt you as you rehearse.

- **Chunking:** Storing easy-to-remember groups of information rather than every single individual item is called "chunking" and it is extremely helpful when it is necessary to remember details.

Working Memory

It's one thing to discuss how to store information in short-term memory. However, what is most important is how to use the information.

"To understand how the mind makes use of short-term memory, we have to look at 'working memory,'" explained Renata's mom.

The working memory manages information. It is assumed to consist of a central executive and two subsystems—phonological loop (verbal) and visuospatial (visual). The central executive helps coordinate the two subsystems, and makes it possible to both access and use information from memory.

Being able to work actively with one's short-term memory, or working memory, are both vital in online courses, particularly in the daily navigation of the interface.

* * * * * * * * * * * *

Renata looked at her mom. "Do you think it's possible to do well with in an online course if something happens to your short-term memory?" she asked.

Her mom said, "Frankly, I think you'd have a very difficult time if your short-term memory is constantly being interfered with, and you're always distracted. For that reason, I advocate studying in a quiet, distraction-free environment."

"No tweeting while I'm studying online?" asked Renata

"That's right. Save Twitter for another day." Her mom smiled. "I'm all for you getting an education, and I want to help you in every way I can."

"Thanks, Mom," said Renata. "You're great. I couldn't do it without you! It's great to think I have a support team as I take online courses."

Specification Writing Checklist

If you are taking engineering courses or technical classes that correspond to the new "green jobs" or "green energy" careers, chances are, you'll have to write a specification, or "spec," about a piece of equipment, a system, or a product or building.

WHAT IS A TECHNICAL SPECIFICATION?

A specification is a description of work to be done. Your specification can be for equipment, a building, or a system. When you write a precise specification, you will be helping the creation of a product, building, system, or piece of equipment that will do what it should do.

FLOWCHART/CHECKLIST APPROACH

As you develop your specification, it is useful to use a flowchart or checklist approach and respond to the questions that appear below.

What kind of specification are you writing? What is the rhetorical situation, and the reason for writing it?

What is the problem that will be addressed?

What are your customer's or client's requirements?

What are the basic functions of the piece of equipment or system? What can you do to break them down into things that you can measure?

How can you best expand on the requirements?

Are you using clear, technical language?

Are your descriptions precise and concise?

Are you thorough (but not too detailed)?

As you review the specifications, is it clear how the equipment—

- » responds to the client's needs?
- » has different parts that relate to each other?
- » functions to efficiently do what the client needs it to do?

AN INTEGRATED APPROACH TO FUNCTIONAL WRITING

Technical writing does not have to be intimidating. Keep in mind that you are engaged in "functional writing" which serves a specific purpose, and which will allow individuals to function more effectively in their jobs. The focus is on the function, and clearly providing the elements to make sure that the core objectives are accomplished. While it may seem to be a bit tedious or mechanical to construct and follow a checklist, the practice will serve you well, particularly as you begin to internalize the process, and become more analytical and precise.

Strategies for Avoiding the "Filter Bubble" That Can Harpoon Your E-Research for Essays and Term Papers

You're in a bubble, thanks to all the web filters programmed into your search and browsing experiences. It's dangerous. Without your knowing it, the tight information bubble you're living in could be narrowing your intellectual scope, and sabotaging your academic research.

You may not be aware of what is happening when you do searches and browse the Internet, and the results seem strangely familiar. After all, it's nice to have more information about the things you know and care about.

How does it work? You've probably noticed that when you search on Google that the results that are displayed are informed by your previous searches. In the past, it may have seemed that only the Google ads on the side were determined by your searches and preferences. The same information sources will tend to come up, to the point that you'll start to develop reliable "go-to" places.

But are they giving you the variety of information and perspective that you need to advance? Is the quality of the information sufficient to be successful in your academic writing? You may be introducing bias and a narrow, flawed argument without realizing it.

Is there any way to transcend the progressive filtering of information that occurs in the most popular "smart" search engines such as Google, Yahoo, and Bing? In the past, your results were often corrupted by the insertion of sites that had paid a fee for visibility. Today, your results are corrupted by your own proclivities—your habits, patterns, and tastes—at least those of right now and the immediate past—are shaping what you'll see tomorrow.

Where can you go for unfiltered information? One approach might be to go to databases and repositories that are limited by their topic and scope. Within those databases, you'll probably have more variety of results. For example, your library online databases can bring you interesting and perhaps unexpected results which will show several different points of view and perspectives. For academic writing, they have the advantage of being peer reviewed.

Some of the repositories that your library may have include EBSCO, Gale, Wilson, JSTORE, LexusNexus, Project Muse, Geoscience World, Elsevier, and others. Although you can save searches, and your customized searches may yield specific information, they are not likely to apply the progressive filtering. The reason is that they do not sell advertising directly; they tend to rely on sales of subscriptions and single document downloads.

Other good places to search include government databases and repositories. They tend to not incorporate "smart" or "affinity" search algorithms.

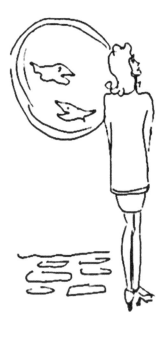

The practice of filtering the information that is delivered to you based on your own inputs and site visits was pioneered by Amazon and the "long tail" marketing approaches. It's also a cornerstone strategy for building the number of friends/connections in popular social networking sites, especially Facebook and LinkedIn. It's also utilized in more specialized sites that target special interests (book reviews, sports, etc).

Case in point—Facebook employs algorithms that track your clicks and searches. For example, the ads that appear as well as recommended sites that pop up will tend to correspond to key words and the other Facebook pages you have visited, as well as those you've friended.

While it's a comforting and convenient encounter with outside information, but your internet experience is not really giving you much of a sense of the potential of the worldwide web. Instead, you're in a little bubble world that has been constructed. Rather than opening your world, it constricts it.

Social networking is a clear example of a bubble world that, while seeming vast because of the number of contacts you may be accumulating, is in some ways a hall of mirrors infinitely repeating, reflecting and replicating the same thing—in essence, yourself as you are right now, or were a moment ago. In such an environment, is truth growth possible? It is possible if you consider growth to be that of "all the same, but bigger."

If you consider growth something that takes you out of your comfort zone and challenges you, the time has come to be proactive and use different types of search techniques, repositories, and philosophies.

The Cognitive Domain and E-Learning Success: Active Learning for Structuring and Managing Knowledge

It is always useful to know what is going through the minds of the instructional designers who are creating the online courses you're taking. A standard approach is for course designers to follow Bloom's Taxonomy—ever since his book was first published more than fifty years ago, it has become the gold standard to use when developing educational objectives.

Granted, in the last several years, there have been additions and expansions but, by and large, the framework has remained intact.

Basically, there are six levels of cognition that range from the most basic (simple recall/recognition of facts) to the most complex, highest order, which is evaluation.

How does knowing Bloom's Taxonomy help you, the e-learner?

The key is active learning. As you approach your reading, your activities, and your participation, think of how you can perform tasks in accordance with Bloom's Taxonomy.

Further, if you understand the approach that is being taken, you can more effectively practice the activities that demonstrate your knowledge. For example, if you understand which verbs correspond to categories in Bloom's Taxonomy, you'll understand the assessment strategy.

Level 6 (highest level):	Evaluation
Level 5:	Synthesis

Level 4:	Analysis
Level 3:	Application
Level 2:	Comprehension
Level 1 (lowest level):	Knowledge

What are you being asked to do? Look at the verb.

Instructional designers adhere to the way that verbs correspond to levels within the cognitive domain, and when they design assessment tools, they are careful to select the words that will elicit the appropriate behavior or activity.

So, let's take a look at the verbs, with an end to decoding the way you're being assessed.

Verbs for Level 6 (Evaluation): Appraise, argue, assess, attach, choose, compare, defend, estimate, judge, predict, rate, core, select, support, value, evaluate.

If you see any of the verbs listed above, keep in mind that you're being asked to show your skills in evaluating the subject matter of the course.

Verbs for Level 5 (Synthesis): Arrange, assemble, collect, compose, construct, create, design, develop, formulate, manage, organize, plan, prepare, propose, set up, write.

If you see any of the verbs listed above, keep in mind that you're being asked to show your skills in synthesizing the subject matter of the course.

Verbs for Level 4 (Analysis): Analyze, appraise, calculate, categorize, compare, contrast, criticize, differentiate, discriminate, distinguish, examine, experiment, question, test.

If you see any of the verbs listed above, keep in mind that you're being asked to show your skills in analyzing the subject matter of the course.

Verbs for Level 3 (Application): Apply, choose, demonstrate, dramatize, employ, illustrate, interpret, operate, practice, schedule, sketch, solve, use, write.

If you see any of the verbs listed above, keep in mind that you're being asked to show your skills in applying the subject matter of the course.

Verbs for Level 2 (Comprehension): Classify, describe, discuss, explain, express, identify, indicate, locate, recognize, report, restate, review, select, translate.

If you see any of the verbs listed above, keep in mind that you're being asked to show your skills in comprehending the subject matter of the course.

Verbs for Level 1 (Knowledge/Recall): Arrange, define, duplicate, label, list, memorize, name, order, recognize, relate, recall, repeat, reproduce, state.

If you see any of the verbs listed above, keep in mind that you're being asked to show your skills in recalling the subject matter of the course.

You've probably noticed that some of the verbs are used in more than one level of the cognitive domain. There is definitely a bit of overlap. Don't worry—the verbs are meant to be guidelines and tools, rather than absolutes.

Keep in mind that the goal is not to test your ability to Pavlovianly perform a set routine of gestures in response to triggering verbs. Instead, the verbs and the categories are meant to be guidelines that help you have a more robust structure into which to organize your knowledge, and to have more power, flexibility, and freedom to work with your knowledge.

Expanding Bloom's Taxonomy:
Organizing and Classifying Knowledge

Knowledge Types: It is very useful to have a framework for classifying the knowledge that you're acquiring. Having an effective classification scheme allows you to integrate knowledge with activities.

A final note as you start using your new knowledge of how instructional designers design courses, learning activities, and assessments: practice active learning. Take your course content and work with it.

The process will require you to move forward and to look at how to dissect the pieces of what you're learning, and to make a judgment about what it is that you're dealing with.

The Pre-Training Principle:
Why You Should Never Skip
the Orientation Session

I've signed up for a few online courses, and I've noticed that I'm supposed to go through a Blackboard orientation before I do anything else. Is this really necessary? I like to learn things as I use them, and I hate going through tutorials.

What's your view on this? Am I right? Am I wrong?

Sincerely,
Restless and Ready in Reno

****

Dear Restless,

Oh no! I'm worried that your eagerness to jump right into your course may result in a very negative outcome.

I know that it might seem that going through "pre-training" is a waste of time and that you'd prefer to learn the LMS (in this case, Blackboard) on your own. However, it's definitely worth the time and effort to go through the training on the interface.

The pre-training principle suggests that as you get started, it's good to have a diagram that you can mouse over, which discusses the function of each of the element.

For example, with Blackboard, as you go through an orientation session, you should be able to mouse over the icons and learn what their functionality is.

An orientation session pointing out the framework of a system used in a classroom setting or in e-learning before segmented instruction is helpful.

Do you remember when you first started building spreadsheets? It is possible that you went through a guided lesson (online or a webinar) where an instructor could point out all the icons in MS Excel and define their uses at the beginning of a lesson before moving on to the construction basic and more complex formulas.

Research supports pre-training as an effective learning technique.

One of the ways you'll see immediate benefit is learning how to best to use the practice tests and exams and where the interactive graphics can help your performance in outcomes assessments.

E-learning students who can click on parts of a system to reveal names and functions perform better on tests (Mayer, et al., 2002, 147-154). Showing how individual components work before showing how an overall system works has a clear advantage (Pollock, E., et al., 2002, 61-86).

How much time should be devoted to pre-training is not clear, but labeling components and defining their characteristics reduces the processing time for learning a greater system.

Other areas that are useful are in the navigation of the course. Be sure to click on all the links and to go into the nested links. This will help you familiarize yourself with the course content, the exams and quizzes, and the basic functionality of the interface itself.

The more time you spend on learning how to negotiate the ins and outs of Blackboard, or whatever learning management system you're using (Moodle, D2L, eCollege, etc.), the less time you'll have to waste worrying about if you're doing things correctly, such as uploading your files to Dropbox.

Also, you will feel more confident about the content and the requirements, and you're less likely to overlook a key assignment.

REFERENCES

Mayer, R.E., Mathias, A., & Wetzell, K. (2002). "Fostering understanding of multimedia messages through pre-training: Evidence for a two-stage theory of mental model construction." *Journal of Experimental Psychology: Applied*, 8, 147-154.

Pollock, E., Chandler, P., & Sweller, J. (2002). *Assimilating complex information. Learning and Instruction*, 12, 61-86.

Try Micro-Learning
for Quick Bursts of Learning

I'm having a hard time finding 2- to 3-hour blocks of time for my online course. I can spend 2 to 3 hours per day on it, but I hardly ever have more than 20 minutes at a time.

Am I in a hopeless situation? What can I do?

Sincerely,
Time-Blocked in Buffalo

****

Dear Time-Blocked,

While it's true that it is usually good to have a solid block of time for many of the tasks that face you, such as drafting and writing essays and term papers, there are many learning activities you can engage in that take between 2 and 20 minutes.

In fact, many are ones you can do on the go—short videos you can download to your mobile device, mini-lectures to listen to on your mp3 player, maps and graphics you can study on your handheld.

If you've got 15 minutes, you can take a few moments to read posts by your classmates and do you own post on the discussion board.

You can also contemplate a case study or current events in your course and connect them to your own experience. You can jot down your thoughts on your digital notepad or post them to cloud computing-based note service such as Evernote.

You can also do brief online research if you've got 10 to 15 minutes. You can do a web search, or a brief search for articles on your libraries data-based.

Learners engaged in micro-learning are engaged in the following activities, among others:

- Finding and reviewing instructional materials (often accessing learning object repositories supplied by the institution).
- Reading posts in a discussion forum, and responding by posting text, images, audio, video.
- Sharing ideas in real-time via tweets, text-message, email, chat.
- Building and sharing reaction pieces: video reaction to a video, posted on YouTube; a reaction in PowerPoint to another PowerPoint, posted in a forum designed to accommodate portfolios.

This approach to learning is called "micro-learning" by instructional psychologists, and it can be highly effective because it ties to learning theories:

Self-directed learning, a concept expounded upon by Knowles (1975) as he developed the notion of "andragogy"—people-based learning.

Situated learning, which ties the content of your course to a concrete setting or situation, is developed by Lave and Wenger (1995), and it explores how the mind makes meaning through connections to one's active experience, either past or present.

Community based learning is also incorporated in micro-learning. Community-based learning, as explained by Wenger (1991), is effective because it encourages people who have similar interests and learning goals to share information and provide meaningful feedback.

Process-oriented media creation and sharing can form a part of micro-learning, especially if you respond to a video by creating and posting your own video or audio.

Micro-learning is effective in a formal setting, such as an online course, but it's also effective in self-study and informal learning. You can use micro-learning if you're following Open Courseware. You can also use it as you work on a research project for your own knowledge, or to help you with work.

I hope that this has helped you! Please let me know if you have any questions, and prepare to experience high-adrenaline bursts of knowledge as you try micro-learning!

REFERENCES

Davenport, G., Barry, B., Kelliher, A., & Nemirovsky, P. (2004). "Media Fabric : A Process-oriented Approach to Media Creation and Exchange." *BT Technology Journal.* 22 (4).

Knowles, M. (1975). *Self-Directed Learning: A Guide for Learners and Teachers.* New York: Association Press.

Lave, J. & Wenger, E. (1991). *Situated Learning: Legitimate Peripheral Participation.* New York: Cambridge University Press.

Wenger, W. (1998). "Communities of Practice: Learning as a Social System." *The Systems Thinker.* 9 (5).

Understanding and Harnessing Creativity

Understanding the nature of creativity and then developing your own creativity will help you not only in your online courses, but also in a world that is changing extremely quickly. Now more than ever, it is important to maximize your creativity in order to be able to perceive the true nature of the changes that are occurring around us, and also the ways to take advantage of opportunities.

You may think of creativity as a magical force, or a gift that only a special few are lucky enough to be endowed with. In reality, creativity is more prosaic. Cognitive psychologists have conducted research and have determined that creativity often consists of a series of mental processes, and the facility by which one learns to manage the processes and the steps determines how effectively one develops one's own creativity.

The first step in understanding creativity is to stop thinking of it as "magic" or an innate gift or attribute. Instead, think of it as a skill, or, better yet, a muscle that you must constantly exercise. Your creativity muscle will atrophy if you don't use it. Likewise, if you make sure to exercise it every day, you'll do well.

Creativity as Incremental Problem-Solving

Many researchers have tied creativity to problem solving, to the point that they say that creativity almost requires a problem in order to fully flower. As one starts to try to solve a problem, there will always be obstacles, and it is necessary to propose solutions.

In this model, creativity involves a step-wise process, in which each step builds on the other. According to Weisberg (1986), creativity is something that occurs by incrementally building on earlier ideas or thoughts. Each time an idea or a thought is modified, expanded, or elaborated, an incremental change takes place.

The solutions to the problem are not static. Instead, they evolve and develop as the problem-solver continues to tease out the solutions, and to modify approaches. In this case, it is often useful to map out one's approach to the problem, and to list one's processes and steps in order to make them visible. The free association of thoughts in conjunction with the step-wise increments will often lead to more refinements and changes.

The Best Ideas Self-Select Over Time

The cognitive psychologists Weber and Dixon (1989) studied creativity by looking at inventions and inventors. They found that inventions do not appear overnight. They take time, and the process is often one that requires a great deal of time. Also, inventions flow from a process of winnowing out the bad ideas and letting the others come to the surface. The best ideas stay in the mix, while the ones that are less useful fall to the wayside.

Where is the creativity in this process? In this case, the decision-making process is the heart of the creative process, and the way that options are weighed and deliberated determines the effectiveness of the solution. One thing to keep in mind in this case is that because the process is an evolutionary one that takes place over a great deal of time, it is often collaborative.

Creativity as Problem Finding

Despite what people often think, creativity is not just a solution that appears in a flash of genius. Instead, the process requires mental work on both sides—the origin of the problem as well as the solution.

Sometimes a solution is not forthcoming because the problem has not been identified. The real problem may be obscured by superfluous details or distracting "noise"—too much information. Researchers have looked into the process of identifying the problem and discovered that the process of finding the "real" problem involves complex and challenging cognitive operations. Being able to find the real problem involves a creative process. Further, selecting the problem to tackle can help create ideal conditions for creativity to operate.

Getzels and Csikszentmihalyi (1976) found an analogue in the creative process of painting. After studying painters and other artists, they found that the ones who had the most positive outcomes—the best paintings—were often the ones who spent the most time in selecting objects to represent. In other words, they dedicated a great deal of mental energy in identifying the "real" problem. Another way to look at it is that successful problem-solvers and creative people engage in an extensive exploration of options, problems, and possibilities before they embark on the problem-solving activity.

Multiple Cognitive Approaches Flowing Together

As you look at your own development of creativity, it's important to keep in mind that creativity is the result of many different cognitive approaches working together. For example, if you consider creativity as an aspect of problem solving, then you'll see clearly that processes include identifying, sorting, developing rankings/hierarchies, decision-making, comparing and contrasting, and proposing causal relationships.

The processes used to create creative thought are the same as those used to create non-creative thoughts, and the way you approach the process is often different if you're working alone vs. working with a group or team. Further, how you work with the team also makes a difference. If you're in a face-to-face setting, your ideas will be more often mediated by group pressure than if you're working in a distributed setting and communicating via the Internet or wireless technologies.

Use Wikis to Speed Up Writing Term Papers, Team Projects, Peer Reviews

Although Wikipedia can be incomplete and sometimes unreliable, it is often a first choice when looking for information on a new topic. It's a collaborate work in progress, and at any given moment, thousands of individuals are contributing to the entries in Wikipedia.

The fact that Wikipedia's collaborative approach is efficient is part of what reinforces the "wiki" concept. "Wiki" which means "fast" in Hawaiian, is an approach to knowledge development that can pay off, when harnessed correctly.

Unfortunately, even with the existence of free wiki hosting and the widespread of Web 2.0 collaborative software, many online learners are not familiar with the way that a wiki can help one speed up the development of a term paper, team project, or multiple person peer review of documents.

Many online learners may have investigated wikis when they first became available. In the early days, they were a bit cumbersome and individuals were uncomfortable with adding or potentially deleting the work of others. Also, it was difficult to share documents and to engage in a threaded discussion.

Since the early days, wiki software has expanded its functionality, which means that it has more features for collaboration and sharing. Some wiki hosting services also incorporate social networking elements such as micro-blogging, wiki workspaces, and spreadsheets, which can facilitate the collaborative activities.

Where can wikis help?

- Collaborate on a single paper—put edits in a single place
- Share drafts
- Review drafts
- Build/revise papers
- Make comments and ideas in discussion board
- Share resources (upload file in discussion board)
- Proofreading and formatting workflows

Before engaging in collaborative writing activities, it is important to keep a few cautionary thoughts in mind:

- Be sure to save often; practice good version control.
- Before making significant changes, post the ideas/drafts in the discussion board area.
- Be respectful of team members and their contributions.
- Stay on task and be goal oriented.
- Share outside resources by posting links, citations, annotated bibliographies, and copies of the articles/summaries when and where helpful.

Wikis are often an overlooked collaboration tool, even though many learning managements systems incorporate them, and wiki providers offer free space on the Internet, particularly for educational use. For e-learners wishing to harness the power of collaboration, or wishing to assure high quality work in collaborative activities or portfolios, it is worthwhile to investigate using a wiki.

Free wikis for individual users, which can be used for collaboration:

Wikia
▶ www.wikia.com

Wikispaces
▶ www.wikispaces.com

Wiki workspaces in Socialtext.com
▶ www.socialtext.com

Video Game Addiction
and Your Online Courses

I'm very worried. I haven't really told anyone, but the truth is, I'm addicted to video games. I know that if I told anyone, they'd scoff at me—after all I'm not a 16-year-old kid, but a 38-year-old network administrator. I hate telling people that I spend all weekend gaming—mainly World of Warcraft, but I can also get really deep into a new game for my Xbox. It just depends on what it is.

I've been able to enjoy gaming along with working, but now that I need to be studying at nights and on weekends, I'm a mess!

Soon I'll be hopelessly behind in my courses, and I'm not having much luck making up the "Incompletes" I received last term.

What can I do?

Sincerely,
Gamed Out

****

Dear Gamed,

I'll never forget my first semester teaching first-year composition. It was 1994 and I was in the Ph.D. program at the University of Oklahoma, where I was required to teach at least two sections of composition as a requirement for the doctorate. I really enjoyed see how students explore topics and the kinds of ideas they expressed in their papers. One student seemed especially sensitive and insightful. He was tall, thin, and quite pale. He dressed in a rather nondescript way—generally jeans and some sort of sports-themed sweatshirt and a T-shirt. He was quiet and did not participate in class discussions except when in a small group. He kept a small leather-bound diary on the top of his stack of books. In one of his papers, he explained that his leather-bound diary was where he kept his ideas for characters, stories, and settings for video games.

About halfway through the course, he stopped coming to class. I was surprised, since he had received high A's on his first two assignments.

Several weeks later, after he had missed a few assignments, he showed up after class. I noticed he was thinner than before and his hair was disheveled. I did not think much of it—you could say the same for most of the students as they negotiated their way through their first semester away from home.

He explained to me that he had gotten caught up in a MUD, which, he explained was a "Multi-User Dungeon," a online role-playing game. Looking back, I think it must have been the forebear of MMORGs, which are massively multiplayer online role playing games. He said he hated to stop playing—and he played for 41-hours straight.

"Have you thought about cutting back?" I remember asking him. I guess it wasn't that easy. He turned in one more paper—hand-written, half-scribbled collection of notes—and then I never saw him again.

I'm not one of those people who demonizes video games, and I don't think that people have to worry about instant, helpless addiction, or that the game will take over your mind and cause you go zombie and do to things you would not ordinarily do.

I have to say that I get annoyed when I see people who come on talk shows to talk about the evils of video games. I'm not a fan of violent video games, and I recognize the fact that people emulate what they see (as in the famous Bo-Bo doll experiments that Albert Bandura conducted in the 1960s).

Obviously, video games—especially the role-playing ones—can provide an escape while triggering pleasure centers. They can also provide one with the feeling that they're actually participating in a social network, even if it's one in which no one has any idea of one's real identity or location. It's easy to lose oneself in virtual worlds and simulations as well.

There's definitely an "addiction industry" out there, and there are programs to help people who have different kinds of dependencies as well as obsessive-compulsive disorders. I don't want to make light of those who are suffering. But still, I like to think of the educational potential, and the opportunity for those who are adept at gaming to transfer their interests and skills into game-based education, when available.

It's also good to think of the connection between role-playing games and serious games. I don't know if you've visited them, but they're quite interesting. What's your major? Chances are, you'll find something there that resonates with your interests and career goals. For example, let's go to Serious Games. There are a number of games in "Games for Change" that might appeal to you. One that captured my imagination was "At Risk" which helps people identify mental disorders and their impact.

Learning is continuous, which is to say that whatever we're doing involves learning—and we just have be mindful that what we're learning is what we need and desire. If you're spending too much time with video games, look within. What are you avoiding? What are your beliefs about yourself? Why do you have to turn to externally-generated approval and positive feelings?

If what is going on is a deeper issue, please think about finding a counselor you can talk to you. In the meantime, please consider taking online courses that include more dynamic interaction—simulations, role-playing, etc. Also, look for courses that require portfolios. The key word here is "agency"—you need to take courses that make you feel as though you have the power and the ability to change your own life.

Well, Gamed, I hope that has helped. Let me know which serious games you find that appeal to you.

What Went Wrong?
Why Did I Crash at the End of the Term?

I was off to a great start this last term, but something happened, and I totally crashed. It is weird, because I love online courses and working toward a degree.

It is strange. I still don't know what happened. I lost steam, became frustrated, and couldn't seem to organize my thoughts or my activities. I started to think of myself as a complete failure and I started to wonder if it was a good idea to take courses. All my reasons for getting an online degree seemed to fade or to seem foolish.

When I got a bit of distance from it, though, I still knew why getting a degree is so important for my own career and my family.

What can I do to get myself together?

Sincerely,
Crashing in Texarkana

****

Dear Crashing,

It is my firm belief that we often forget that a huge part of academic success has to do with what psychologists call "self-regulation." It is the part of the learning process that has to do with how your brain processes knowledge and how that relates to how you feel emotionally. Self-regulation is the subject of a great deal of research and investigation by cognitive and educational psychologists.

Let's look at ten specific areas that will yield positive results for you:

1. **Self-evaluation.** Be sure to constantly evaluate the way you are studying and relate it to what you will be expected to do at the end of the course.

2. **Organization.** You may feel you have too much to study and to master. How can you manage all of it? The key is to look at how you're organizing your knowledge and information. Are you leaving out big sections? Are you ignoring some of the outcomes because they are less interesting to you? Be sure to cover everything.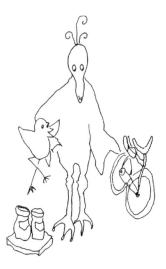

3. **Goal-setting.** Instead of trying to do everything in one massive chunk, break down your tasks in small, manageable sub-tasks. You can schedule the subtasks. More importantly, you will be building a mental map of what you need to do.

4. **Seek information.** Mystified and puzzled by what you're expected to do? Before you panic and self-paralyze, seek information. Get the facts. Find out what you're expected to do. If you're supposed to do online research, do it before you start outlining your paper. Why? You'll be amazed at how the research process will help you with your invention and pre-writing processes.

5. **Keeping records and monitoring.** Do you remember getting smiley-faces, stars, and happy sunshine stickers when you made your bed, put up your toys, cleaned your hamster's cage, brushed your teeth for three minutes, and said nice things to your little sister? If you lived in a household or went to a school that visually rewarded such behavior, you know the value of positive visual affirmation. It's not a bad idea to start doing that again.

6. **Environmental structuring.** How do you like to study? Some people like to bring their laptops to their local coffee shop and to study there without the distractions of home. Others prefer being at home, and keeping an environment that is quiet and soothing. Other people like to mix it up. It's all about what you need to keep focused. It's also

important to do your practice quizzes in the same environment as your testing environment.

7. **Gap Analysis.** You may think that you're covering everything, but when you take tests, you find your assumptions were rather flawed. How can you prepare yourself? Be sure to conduct a "gap analysis" which allows you to pinpoint where you're skipping content. What's the best way? Take practice exams.

8. **Rehearsing the key elements.** As you study, be sure to build a strong, clear structure upon which you can hang your course content.

9. **Seek social assistance from peers, teachers, advisors.** Don't go it alone. Be sure to reach out to your fellow students and your instructor.

10. **Review your course material.** Be sure to organize and take notes on your course content—presentations, texts, audio, and video.

USEFUL READINGS:

Zimmerman, B. J. (1989). "A social cognitive view of self-regulated academic learning." *Journal of Educational Psychology*, 81(3), p. 329-339.

Zimmerman, B. J. (1998). "Academic studying and the development of personal skill: a self-regulatory perspective." *Educational Psychologist*, 33(2/3), p.73-86.

Zimmerman, B. J., & Martinez-Pons, M. (1988). "Construct validation of a strategy model of student self-regulated learning." *Journal of Educational Psychology*, 80, p. 284-290.

What Your Professor May Not Tell You about Writing and Term Papers

I love my online writing class. It's clear, it's well-organized, and I know exactly what I'm supposed to do and when I'm supposed to turn it in.

I also really like my instructor. She's easy to work with, and she responds quickly.

Still, I'm nervous. Is there anything I'm missing? Are there any hard-and-fast pointers that apply across the board to all composition courses, and to all courses that require a term paper?

I would love to have an idea of how things look from the other side. Do you have any pointers?

Sincerely,
Hopeful in Helena

****

Dear Hopeful,

Your question is excellent. I'm delighted that you asked it, because I think it helps you develop insight and better focus your papers. It's always good to know your audience.

It is probably no surprise to find out that writing professors love what they do and there is nothing better for them than to find an interesting, engaging, and engaged paper written by a person who obviously cares about the topic.

Conversely, it can be disappointing to plow through papers that are simply loose paraphrases of information from published reports or blogs. Even worse are the lame derivatives of papers culled from places like termpapers.com or helium.com.

So, as you embark on your paper, look at the subject. Select one you like and then take ownership of the whole process. In the meantime, here are a few tips to keep in mind.

1. A Broad Topic Is a Boring Topic: Narrow It, Focus It

A potentially fruitful topic can be rendered very boring when it's too general. How many times have you looked a list of topics such as substance abuse or domestic violence. While these are good topics, one could write an entire library and still never exhaust the topic. The best approach would be to narrow it down to something such as a subset of it. It might be useful to look certain aspects: "The Physical Effects of Methamphetamine Abuse" or "Meth Labs in America."

2. Avoid Footnotes: Cite Sources with In-Text Citations

Getting students to use the proper citation style is always a big challenge. It's amazingly frustrating for the instructor to see half-hearted attempts to replicate APA or MLA style that sometimes consist of nothing more than a URL copied and pasted at the end of the document. Footnotes are a different issue. While the intent was good, it's often misguided. Footnotes are generally used only in very special and specific circumstances, and it's not really a good idea to used them. True, some journals do prefer footnotes, but they're in the minority. The best approach is to use in-text citations, direct quotes, block quotes, and an end-of-the paper "references" or "works cited" section.

3. The 15-Percent Rule for Block Quotes

Some students are so nervous about their own thoughts and ideas that they prefer not to produce any at all. Instead, their paper becomes a patchwork quilt of block quotes and paraphrases stitched together. While the ideas may be perfectly sound, the problem with this approach is that it violates academic integrity policies. You should try to keep your use of direct and block quotes under 15 percent of the total word count.

4. Don't End on a Quote

You're not likely to find this pointer in any composition textbooks. Nevertheless, it's a good one. Don't end a paragraph or your paper with a quote. Instead, follow up with more insight, analysis, and discussion. You'll be surprised how helpful this approach is because you'll automatically be adding depth, flow, and insight to your work. So, don't avoid quotes, just use them as an opportunity to expound and elaborate.

5. Use Multiple Types of Evidence

Some writers fall in the trap of using only kind of evidence to support their primary thesis/claims. They may like using statistics, or examples from current contemporary events. However, be sure to provide a good blend of statistics, examples, case studies, and theoretical foundations.

6. If You Use Examples, Don't Use Just One

Even if your example is a great one, and it's fairly complex, you're much better off if you use at least three examples. Ideally, the examples illustrate different aspects of the primary thesis and the point you're trying to make.

7. Avoid Second-Hand/Derivative Stats: Find the Primary Sources

It doesn't happen often, but it does happen. There may be a typographical error in the press release picked up by a major news outlet, and it's then picked up by everyone's blog, newspaper, and online journal. What is even more common is for bias or spin to be carried down from one media outlet to others. Avoid the problem altogether by going to the primary source, which is usually referred to in the secondary source (new outlet or blog).

8. Write About Something You Care About— Don't Second-Guess Your Prof's Interests

Writing about things you care about is motivating. You discover more about something you're intrinsically interested in, and the thoughts just flow. Forcing yourself to write about something that bores you or worse, makes you feel pressured and confused, is a nightmare. So, try to select a paper topic that interests you, and then clear it with your professor.

9. The Rhetorical Situation: Learn It, Heed It

The rhetorical situation is—succinctly stated—the reason, the motive, the ultimate goal for writing. You're in a situation and you're attempting to communicate in such a way that changes minds, precipitates action, and inspires responses. In order to be effective, you need to have a very good grasp of your audience's views, ideas, and proclivities.

10. Balance the Structure: Avoid One Long Paragraph or Small, Choppy Sections

As you go in and do your final revision, be sure to smooth out the structure. Don't be afraid to expand the short sections and paragraphs, and to break long ones into shorter, clearer ones. Above all, avoid paper that consists of one long paragraph. If you turn that in, it will look like you've turned in your preliminary draft. So, show that you've put time, effort, thought, and care into your paper.

Finally, let yourself enjoy your paper!

When You Have to Write a Paper
over an Ethical Dilemma: Success Strategies

Your first-year composition course often requires you to write persuasive papers, and more often than not, you'll be required to look at controversial issues. Many of them involve profound ethical dilemmas, which may leave you frustrated and wondering how to start your paper. Can't you simply announce what you believe is the right approach, and then explain why you believe what you believe?

Unfortunately, if you simply state what you believe, and then go into a passionate defense of your beliefs, it is likely that you'll earn a poor grade. Your instructor might say something about avoiding creating a rant or launching into a diatribe.

What went wrong?

The key is to look at what you're doing as defending a claim by using reason. You'll have to look at more than one side of the issue, and you'll need to provide evidence.

> **POOR APPROACH:** "I believe that poverty can never be eliminated" or "My view is that poverty is and always be a part of our world."

Why is this a poor approach? It's not that you're wrong. It's that you're not engaging in a reasoned defense of your claim. You're simply stating your position and leaving it at that. Let's look at a few ways to take that initially poor approach and turn it into a good approach.

GOOD APPROACH: "My view is that poverty can never be eliminated, and I believe this because… (add two or three reasons here)."

GOOD APPROACH: "I find that the following ideas about poverty such as (list them), provide a compelling argument for the notion that poverty is and always will be a part of our world, despite efforts of governments, families, groups, and individuals."

You've created a solid thesis statement which opens the door to creating a very nice structure for your paper. Each reason can be a part of a topic sentence for body paragraphs.

Now that you have an idea of what a good approach looks like, you also have a solid idea of what a good thesis looks like. Before you begin to write, be sure to incorporate the following necessary elements for your persuasive paper and answer the following questions:

1. What is your position or opinion on the topic or question you have chosen?
2. How can you best explain your position in a clear manner?
3. What is the most compelling argument you can think of for your position? What would someone who disagrees with you likely to say?
4. How can you support your position with examples, statistics, or published articles? Where would you look?

As you start to develop an idea of your paper, here are a few things to be sure to remember to include:

1. Clear thesis statement that includes your claim and points of defense.
2. Reasons to believe or accept your thesis.
3. Counter examples that help your readers understand other points of view, and which help them reject the counter examples.
4. A criticism of poor arguments, or positions that are flawed and do not hold up to scrutiny. Be sure to explain why.
5. A strategy for defending your point of view against the view of another person.

6. What are the strengths and weaknesses of two opposing views of the argument?
7. What consequences would there be if your thesis were true?

As you search for a topic, be sure to avoid over-used topics, or ones that do not allow for any subtlety in the arguments or counter-arguments. It is difficult for your instructor to evaluate your argument if you invoke ultimate moral authority, or by taking a satirical approach.

Here are a few possible thesis statements that could be used in a persuasive paper that involves an ethical dilemma:

1. "My view is physician-assisted suicide is likely to increase as our population ages, and demographic shifts occur in our society. I believe this because… (add two or three reasons here)."

2. "In my opinion, it is wrong to import dangerous or venomous animals and to sell them to collectors as pets because (list reasons.)"

3. "I find the following ideas about religious cults (list them) create a compelling argument that our society is all too ready to judge and condemn behavior that does not seem to fit the norm."

4. "In my opinion, performance-enhancing drugs are very detrimental to sports, as well as to individual athletes. I believe this because of what has happened in the cases of Barry Bonds, Lyle Alzado, (list more), and the concept of fair play (and other ideas)."

As you start to craft your paper, make sure that you enjoy your topic, and that you let yourself follow the areas that interest you. A paper that bores you is likely to bore your reader as well. If your argument seems hollow to you, it is most likely pretty empty to your reader as well. Just let yourself go with your topic and go with the flow. You'll find that, before you know it, you actually enjoy writing.

Why Do Good Students
Underperform on Tests?

I do really well on all my projects and in my discussion board posts. But I blow it on the quizzes and tests. What should I do to succeed? I'm willing to study as much as necessary.

Sincerely,
Desperate in Delaware

****

Dear Desperate,

You might not perform as well as you could because:

1. You want to get a perfect score, try too hard, and focus too much on results rather than the questions you're answering.

2. You are afraid to fail and so you tighten up, exert extreme caution, and reread/over-control your answers.

3. You are too concerned with others' opinions or not disappointing others.

4. You lack academic self-confidence in tests and have too much self-doubt.

5. Your high expectations cause you to feel frustrated quickly after errors or a difficult question that you could not answer well.

6. You focus too much on writing perfect sentences and paragraphs, and using the perfect word, and thus limit your ability.

7. The pressure of a timed assessment causes you to become anxious or tighten up.

To reach your potential when you have to take tests or perform in assessments, you must first understand how your mindset limits your performance. In order to do so, it is often a good idea to step back and to answer the following questions:

1. What are your top five distractions during a test or quiz? This applies to essay exams as well as short answers and multiple choice.

2. What are your top five distractions while you're studying for a test or quiz?

3. How are the distractions different during the actual performance vs. when you're studying? Which ones have to do with lack of confidence and fear? Which ones preoccupy themselves with avoidance? (Thinking about what you're going to do after you finish the test, rather than focusing on the task at hand and answering the question, vs. thinking about what your mother will say when you tell her about your grades.)

At this point, you might be beating yourself up for not being able to focus all the time, and for being less than perfect. Don't worry. Everyone suffers from focus problems, even the best, most experienced students. What they've learned, however, is what you may need to practice. Learn the Three R's:

1. Recognize: Be aware that you've gotten distracted and are not focused in the moment.

2. Regroup: Tell yourself to stop and to get back to the task. If you're studying, put your iPhone or BlackBerry in another room, and refuse to open another browser window to surf the web instead of focusing.

3. Refocus: Become intensely focused on the task at hand. Immerse yourself and concentrate deeply on the single task that you're performing, and do it with all your mind, and give it your undivided attention. Tell yourself, "I'm giving this my undivided attention," and then remind yourself that you have studied.

If you practice these techniques, there is a good chance that you'll see immediate improvement. If you do not, don't give up. Keep the faith, and keep working as hard as you can.

Winter Demotivation Blues:
Any Suggestions for Me—
Wacky or Otherwise? Please?

We've had horrible weather this last month, and I've been snowbound. You'd think that would perfect—time off work, with lots of time for my online courses.

I got caught up in all my courses. In fact, I even worked ahead.

But instead of feeling confident and good about things, I feel lonely, isolated, and depressed. I'm having a hard time believing in myself, and I want to give up. I'm on track to graduate in a year, but that seems to be a very long time from now.

In the meantime, it's snowing again.

Help! How do I regain my sense of confidence and beat these winter blues?

Yours truly,
Snowed Under

****

Dear Snowed,

You worked ahead. That's great! What did you do to reward yourself? I would bet that you did absolutely nothing.

As you looked at your long-term goal, did you see any short-term goals along the way?

Chances are, you're not setting small, short-term goals, and also, you're not building in a reward system.

If you do not reward yourself for achieving your small goals, it means that you're probably not meeting your need for recognition and accomplishment. What kinds of rewards are best in this situation?

It's customary to reward a dog or cat with a treat. I do not recommend that—you're probably already rewarding yourself with tasty, greasy treats, and it's not working as hoped.

So, I'd try rewarding yourself with a satisfying set of words, or sound. As you finish an assignment, and if you're alone, let out a big yelp and clap your hands. Be sure to smile as you do this. You can even find clickers or noisemakers, or something that makes a satisfying rattle. Finish your work, then stand up and make a nice sound—sand blocks, marimbas, clickers—all are good!

You're snowbound right now. Are you cut off from friends and family? If so, you are well aware that you're isolated and alone. So, what does that do or mean in motivational terms? It means you're not meeting your need for affiliation. In an online course, it sometimes helps to go to the discussion board and interact with other people.

Do you have Wimba or video chat capabilities built into your school's learning management system? It's often a great idea to go ahead and turn on your webcam and let the world see your smiling face. It's a kind of contact that will help motivate you because you can encourage each other as you work on your courses. It's often useful to find people who are in the same major; start a group for your fellow majors in Facebook or Linked In. If you're feeling overexposed on Facebook or LinkedIn, try other social networking sites.

Another option would be to invite people to meet at one of the open islands in Second Life. If you're in a health field, how about the CDC Island? You can attend lectures with your buddies, and even start a club—Respiratory Therapists Club—for example. This is another way to meet your need for affiliation. You can also relax and let the power of the group propel you toward your goal.

Finally, how much "play" did you do when you worked on your assignments? Did you have the chance to select your own topic? Did you have any autonomy?

Some people are motivated by the need for autonomy, and they have a high need for self-determination. If that's the case, you're likely to be pretty frustrated by assignments that do not give you any latitude at all with respect to choosing your topics, etc.

Finally, if you're snowbound, what are you doing for your physical self? Remember that when your exercise, your body generates building blocks for a healthy brain. You may not enjoy *Sweatin' to the Oldies*, but you may enjoy Wii Tennis or simply improvising dance moves.

Invent a new dance to your favorite new group. Here's one to get started—try inventing crazy cat moves to Ratatat's "Wildcat." It's fun! If you feel confident enough, you can even video yourself and post a reaction video to Ratatat's YouTube videos. I'd recommend disabling comments though. And perhaps wear a mask.

So, Snowed, please take all my suggestions with a grain of salt, and feel free to pick and choose. The bottom line is that you need affiliation, autonomy, and affiliation. Work on building in ways to meet those needs, and you'll be amazed at the results.

Writing an Outstanding Cause-and-Effect Essay

I've drafted my cause-and-effect essay, but I'm worried that it's not what my professor wants. It is on how schools got violent when principals stopped having the authority to administer corporal punishment. Spanking kept us safe.

I think I've got an airtight cause and effect relationship between violence and the lack of discipline.

I let a friend read it and she thought I was way off base. What do I do?

Sincerely,
Whipped in Whitcomb

****

Dear Whipped,

I haven't read your essay, but it might not be a bad idea to take a look at the essay and see if you're guilty of the most common errors in the cause-and-effect essay.

Top Errors in the Cause-and-Effect Essay

1. Oversimplification.
2. Bias—politically or ideologically motivated set of underlying assumptions.

3. Lack of effective evidence or support.

4. Failure to consider multiple possible causal chains and to evaluate them objectively.

5. Stacking the deck—considering only the evidence that supports your claim.

6. Relying on magic or the supernatural.

Best Things to Remember in Your Cause-and-Effect Essay

1. A Manageable Topic

2. Causal Explanations that You Can Support with Reliable Evidence

3. Examples and Case Studies that Illustrate Your Points

4. Effects that Are Reasonable and Logical

5. Alternative Explanations

After you've drafted your paper, be sure to let someone read it. Have your reader or your peer answer a few simple "reality test" questions.

Cause-and-Effect Essay "Reality Test" Peer Review

1. Does the main topic or cause-effect relationship seem reasonable to you?

2. How does the essay make you feel? When do you find yourself agreeing or disagreeing with the points in the essay?

3. When does the logic start to break down? When does it seem the essay is overreaching, and does not have the evidence to back up the claims?

If approached well, you will find that the cause-and-effect essay is probably one of the most satisfying you'll do. It establishes order in an often chaotic world, and it reinforces the idea that there are rewards for careful observation of our world, and for positing and testing possible causal relationships.

Writing Readiness

I am getting ready to start an online program, but I'm worried about my writing skills. I don't know if I'm ready for college. Do I need to take a remediation course? A developmental course?

Is there a way that I can prepare for a placement exam? What kinds of things do I need to know in order to do well in writing for college?

Sincerely,
Phobic Felicia in Rye, Rhode Island

****

Dear Phobic,

Don't worry—you're not alone! You might be surprised to find out how many people have self-doubt about their writing skills. I'll go even further with that statement: they not only doubt themselves, they're afraid.

Fear is something you can eliminate with a little bit of knowledge and planning. Just familiarize yourself with the kinds of things you're going to have to do.

It's always good to think about what you'll need to do in order to succeed in college. The following points are adopted from several different assessments, including ACT Writing Test that helps determine your college readiness.

1. Using Language

Your use of language should clearly communicate ideas. Be sure to demonstrate effective use of grammar and properly use punctuation, capitalization, and other mechanics. Use a precise and varied vocabulary, and vary your sentence structure to maintain an engaging pace and to reinforce meaning.

2. Organizing Ideas

Your essay should demonstrate unity and coherence, and the ideas need to progress logically. You should use transitions well, and develop a structure that helps the reader understand the logical relationships between ideas. The paper should have a good, engaging introduction and a clear thesis statement. Each body paragraph should contain a topic sentence that ties to the thesis statement. The conclusion should be well developed.

3. Expressing Judgments

Your essay should be persuasive and you should take a position and express it in your essay from several points of view. Be sure to evaluate implications and complications of your position, and acknowledge the counter-arguments. Then look at evidence and discuss how and where the evidence supports your point.

4. Focusing on the Topic

Your essay should keep a clear focus and maintain it throughout the essay. Be sure to have a clear topic sentence in each of your body paragraphs, but avoid repetition and redundancy. Keep your focus and use unique support, evidence, and examples in your paragraphs.

5. Developing a Position

Your essay should contain several ideas that are fully developed, and they should contain very solid support, with rationale, details, examples, and case studies. Be sure to use good transitions, and to provide the kind of background and contexts you need in order to have a coherent essay.

One of the best ways to prepare for a placement exam or for the kinds of writing you'll have to do in college is to practice. It's not just a matter of practicing writing. It's also a good idea to practice reading academic essays and analyzing how they're achieving the specific writing goals of the rhetorical situation. If you learn to express yourself quickly and in a structure that is clear and coherent, you can show what you know in no time!

Chapter 3

E-Learning Technology

Adding Audio and Video:
Step-By-Step "How To"

I'm in a course that requires a portfolio. I want to add audio and video to my portfolio. How do I do it?

We're putting everything together in a blog so that everyone has access and can comment easily. I know I can link to YouTube videos and podcasts, but I want to create my own.

Sincerely,
Media-Happy in Mississippi

****

Dear Media-Happy,

You've asked a great question. It's great that you want to create your own audio and video files, and while you're at it, you can build a nice library of your own photos. Thanks to blogs and social networking, it's easier than ever to build the media. Here's how to get started:

VIDEO

- Record your video using your smartphone or camera.
- Download it to your camera in a special file or archive.
- Open it using Windows Movie Maker (which comes with Windows).

- Be sure to optimize it when you save the file.
- Then, upload it to YouTube. (You'll need to open an account to do so).
- To share the video with your classmates or to present it in an e-portfolio in a blog, you'll need to:
    a. create a link to the YouTube site, then
    b. embed the video in your blog by copying and pasting the HTML into the HTML of the website.

AUDIO

If you're using a Mac, it's very easy to create an MP3 file with Garageband. Just record using a microphone with your computer.

There used to be a number of free services that allowed you to call a number and record an MP3 file that you could then download from the Internet. They were a great idea, but I suppose it was ultimately not sustainable—like so many "free" web services, they disappeared. What happened? My guess is that they were sold to a larger entity, or that they morphed into a site that offers a suite of services that require a monthly fee.

That said, it's probably best to go with open-source freeware. Audacity (audacity.sourceforge.net) can be a bit confusing at the outset, but it's fairly powerful and it has a surprising array of functions. Be sure to download the LAME encoder so you can convert the recordings to MP3 files.

You may wonder what you're supposed to do with the recordings once you have them. The best approach is to upload them to a server space that you might have. I'd recommend going to Tripod or Yahoo, and getting some server space where you can host your audio files. Tripod (www.tripod.lycos.com) still offers great free website space and support.

PHOTOS

No portfolio project is complete without photos. Snapping images is very easy, and it's not difficult to download them to your computer. The problem is that they can be huge (6 MB is not uncommon!) and completely unwieldy. The following software programs can help you:

- **Flickr**

Upload your documents directly to Flickr.com and create albums which are called "sets." You can then link to them, or embed them in your blog. You can also edit your photos using piknik.com. There are a few annoying quirks in Flickr though. For example, be sure to set the time/date on your camera and/or phone—whatever date is set will show up as the date of the photo, and it will be organized accordingly. There is nothing you can do to change this. I found out the hard way. I inadvertently set the year to 2004 and did not notice it until the photo was posted. I labeled the photo with its date of April 2011, but the little tag to the side clearly said January 2004!

- **Picasa**

Download the program, which will allow you to easily modify your image, and optimize it. You can then upload the images (after you've cleaned them up and optimized them) to a place like Flickr, or to a webspace you've obtained through Tripod, Yahoo, or other free hosting programs (which, sadly enough, are not as plentiful as they once were). Once you have taken, processed, and uploaded/hosted the image, then you're in the position to incorporate them in your blog. You can do it by uploading the image directly (as JPG) or by embedding HTML, or providing a link.

- **GIMP**

There are a lot of GIMP fans out there who swear by this powerful open-source photo editing software. I am one of them, sort of. It's powerful and will do many of the things that Photoshop will do. However, there is a fairly steep learning curve.

- **Zamzar**

Do you need to change formats, save a file to PDF, but do not have Adobe Professional? Zamzar.com is quick, high-quality, and free. I use it often. Word of warning—PDF to word conversions can be slow, and about as random as an OCR (optical character reader) scanning approach.

• JUST DO IT •

If you're reading my descriptions of what you can do, chances are, you're feeling a bit overwhelmed and fearful. It's normal to feel anxiety when you try something new. Don't worry! This is a very easy-to-conquer set of skills/tasks. Invest a bit of time to learn how to create video, audio, and images and then to upload/embed them in a way that allows you to create an e-portfolio.

Do it, and you'll be amazed how simple it is, especially after you've created and uploaded videos, audio, and photos a few times.

Can I Tweet My Way to an A?

I am totally hooked on Twitter. In my opinion, it's the best way ever to get the word out and to let people know what's going on.

I wish I could use it with my online class. Do you know of any ways it's being used?

I love online courses, but sometimes they frustrate me because I feel I have to be online to communicate with my classmates.

Couldn't we just "tweet" each other?

Signed,
Tweetness and Light in Texas

****

Dear Tweetness,

I'm very happy to hear you're excited by Twitter. You're not alone. It's just amazing how many people use it to communicate to groups. It's a lot more efficient and immediate than text messaging. In many ways, it's even better than RSS feeds because they're so easy to use with your cellphone.

Twitter is addicting! Yes, I follow several users on Twitter—and, yes, I admit, I follow a few celebrities and also news feeds.

You're right. Twitter can be perfect for e-learning. Instructors can set up a

Twitter feed for the class, which has all the class members in it, and it's easy to follow. The instructor can send tweets, and students can "tweet" each other.

Tweets, with their short-burst 140-character limit, and the ability to achieve ubiquitous, spontaneous messaging to a potentially massive number of recipients, can be an excellent way to maintain a high level of communication, openness, and motivation.

So, let's take a look at what we can do with Twitter in the e-learning space. First, let's start with instructors.

Instructor Tweets

- **Due dates:** Weekly reminders of key due dates are very helpful. In fact, they're key for good time management.
- **Critical concepts:** Worried that you're missing the major points in the unit or the lesson? Ask the instructor to send out tweets that list the critical/key concepts. They will make mental organizers. You'll be able to start developing a schema for yourself, which will help you create clusters and groups of knowledge. It will be easy to retrieve them.
- **Key questions:** Sometimes it's a great idea to have a little "Twitter Fest" your instructor can send out a good question for you to answer (in 140 words or less!) and all the members of your course can tweet a response. It's a wonderful conversation that can take place anytime, anywhere.
- **Links to Flickr, YouTube:** You may not be able to stream a video or retrieve graphics from a web-based image repository such as Flickr. However, you might be able to send a tweet with a link. You can email the link to yourself and then go to the website once you have a Wi-Fi connection and enough bandwidth to download or stream the media files. Alternatively, you can upload your own photos or video and send out a link to the file. It's a great approach if you're taking, say, a biology class, and you're looking for things in the field. For example, you could take pictures of environmental problems - erosion, a pond overrun with algae and pond scum. Your only limits are those of your own imagination. Explore, express, share!

Student Tweets

Here are a few things you might tweet with your fellow students:

- Questions for professor
- General comments about course content
- Responses to questions
- Notes and observation from the field
- Collaborations

Administrative Tweets

Having the ability to contact many people simultaneously is a huge benefit for college administrators who need to get the word out quickly, especially when immediate action is called for, such as enrollment deadlines, scholarship announcements, and more.

- Announcements
- Directions
- Bulletins
- Alerts

Before you start using Twitter in your studies:

- Can too many tweets constitute a distraction?
- Make sure the tweets are relevant.
- Connect tweets to learning objectives.

Can I Use Wikipedia, About.com, Ask.com, Yahoo Answers for My Term Papers?

As you prepare to do your online research, you probably turn to Google, where you promptly type in a search term or research question. Chances are, the information that will pop up will be from a few of the more well-known resources, starting with Wikipedia, and also including online information repositories, such as Ask.com, About.com, and Yahoo Answers.

If you have used Wikipedia, at least to get started with a topic, you're not alone. But, how ubiquitous is it?

To give one an idea, here's an experiment. Conduct a search on Google for each of the following terms: impressionism, pit bull, surfactant, Bolshevik, and "Mr. Mom." You'll find that the Wikipedia entry will be number one for each one, except for "Mr. Mom," where it comes in as number four.

Wikipedia seems to be the obvious source of information, and it's quite popular. If you cite the source correctly, what's wrong with using it?

Here's the problem: As opposed to peer-reviewed or corporate-author online reference sources, where the contributors' credentials have been reviewed, Wikipedia is collaborative venue where anyone who is willing to register a name with their contribution can instantly modify the entry. The names of the contributors, by the way, do not show up on the Wikipedia entry. Most learners who are writing papers have not the slightest idea that the material they are citing could be biased, incomplete, or just flat out wrong.

- **Wikipedia**

  Because Wikipedia is an open forum that anyone can contribute to, it's easy to see how misinformation and errors could occur. This is not to say that Wikipedia is not a useful and valuable source of information. Also, it's not to say that wikis and other collaborative efforts are not without merit. Certainly, refereed journals and peer-review are not without flaws and bias.

- **Ask.com**

  Ask.com started as Ask Jeeves in 1996, and was renamed to Ask.com in 2005. The method of determining responses and how answers/information is validated is not detailed on their website. However, Ask.com is not a community-based, non-profit endeavor. Instead, it's a part of a larger cluster of knowledge subsidiaries of IAC, a public company listed on the Nasdaq as IACI.

- **About.com**

  About.com is a company that hires acknowledged experts to write columns and to provide resources/references on topics. As such, it's more of an encyclopedia than Ask.com. Further, the format tends to be fairly standardized, which is different than the free-wheeling, open format of Wikipedia. About.com tends to be a source of very basic, entry-level information. Further research is needed for most research questions, but for basic familiarization, About.com is fairly reliable. That said, some About.com entries clearly express the bias/opinions of their authors. Since the authors receive bylines, this is not quite the problem it could be—if nothing else, one acknowledge that some information provided at About.com can wander into Op Ed territory.

- **Yahoo Answers**

  If you plan to use information you glean from Yahoo Answers in an academic essay, think twice! Your decision could be disastrous! Anyone can contribute to Yahoo Answers, and the answers are often provided in order to entertain, persuade, or to provoke— not to simply provide information. It's fun to read, but ultimately, you need to reality-check the information. To ask a question on Yahoo Answers, you have to have a Yahoo account. You can ask up to five questions per day, unless you earn credit by answering questions.

Once you ask a question on Yahoo Answers, be prepared for potentially wacky free-for-all, as people answer questions, not with their real names, but with their Yahoo usernames. If you ask something like "What is Islam?" you're likely to get all kinds of spurious answers along with more legitimate and mainstream responses (histories, cultural background, etc.).

Try all of them—you'll learn as you explore (informal learning). While you may end up not finding anything official or reliable enough to use in a term paper, the experience of reading through the various answers to your research question can be very informative and enjoyable. You'll be participating in informal learning, and you'll be surprised at how much information you retain.

Developing Workplace 2020 Skills
& Media Literacy Now:
Effective Graphics and Presentations

Media literacy is one of the "must-have" skills for the workplace of 2020. It is quickly becoming evident that media literacy is extremely important for academic success as well. After all, you're increasingly required to create presentations which involve PowerPoint, graphics, charts, maps, and photos, and they must be robust enough to communicate the message you need to get across.

In order to be effective, you need to know how the mind processes graphical information, especially when you're using graphics, text, video and audio.

Here are a few key concepts that will help you develop effective presentations and media materials:

- **Temporal Contiguity Principle:** Present words with pictures, rather than words after the pictures. So, if can put a caption with graphics, it is best.

- **Coherence Principle:** Avoid extraneous words, pictures, and sounds. If you include too many additional/extraneous words, you will create distraction and your audience will miss the message.

- **Modality Principle:** If at all possible, include audio with animation, so that you have narration that flows with the animation. It's more difficult to process if your audience has to read on-screen text with the animation, or captions.

- **Redundancy Principle:** Try to avoid too much repetition and redundancy across the media. For example, if you're creating a script to record as an audio narration to go with your images, or text, be sure that you are not simply repeating/reading what your audience is seeing on the screen.

- **Individual Differences Principle:** The design of your presentation is very important. It's especially critical for people who are not familiar with the topic, and who do not have a great deal of working knowledge of it. So, if you're building a presentation that has new or complex information for people who are not familiar with it, please be sure to keep the design clear, and free of distractions. As you develop your design, keep in mind that high-spatial learners are more dramatic than for low-spatial learners.

- **Direct Manipulation Principle:** Be sure to look at the complexity of materials, and keep in mind that if you have the ability to manipulate the learning materials with respect to animation and pacing, work with it carefully. You may need to slow the pace of information delivery as the complexity of the content increases.

As you build your 21st-century academic and workforce skills, the ability to develop effective graphics and presentations will be more important than ever as you start to work collaboratively with web-conferencing in globally distributed teams.

The concepts you learn and the skills you practice in making presentations and creating portfolios for your online courses will help you in the workplace as well.

Google Docs
for Your iPad and Your Online Course

When Google Docs first opened up, I was very excited about it, and thought I had a great opportunity to have "anytime/anywhere" access with a document stored in the cloud, which would be very easy to share.

I used to use Yahoo notepad, but it went away, and it was not very friendly for multiple users. I also found that using Wikispaces seemed okay, but ultimately was pretty unwieldy because each user had to set up a separate account, and I had to register them. What a headache!

The nice thing about Google Docs is that I can easily register users to have access to the documents, and it's especially easy if they have a Gmail account.

Google Docs is not perfect, though. Sometimes it seems "sticky" and it's also not really clear which user is adding comments/changes. I'm not sure how important that is, but it would be nice to have something akin to "track changes" and "comments" in MS-Word.

The other problem I'm encountering is that Google Docs does not always work well with my iPad. Sure, the mobile version works quite well, but it lacks almost all the features of the desktop version.

Plus, it's really quirky when it comes to things like building a table of contents. I'm able to assemble a table of contents if I use Chrome, but not with Firefox or Internet Explorer. Why is that? Is it because Google products do not play nicely with Microsoft?

At any rate, my question is this: What do you think will be the future of Google Docs?

Should I continue to use it in conjunction with my tablet? Should I use it for collaborating and creating a shared document or portfolio?

Sincerely,
Google.Doc Fan

****

Dear Google.Doc:

I really like the points you've made about the pros and cons of Google Docs.

I've encountered the same things—although I think it's gotten a lot better in the last year. Here are some of the things I really like about Google Docs.

1. Updates constantly. There is no need to hit "Save"—it automatically saves.
2. Saves in the cloud. Cloud-based docs are backed up often, and are more secure than your handy flash drive.
3. Can copy and paste into a Word document to create a local backup.
4. Can collaborate easily.
5. Can save easily to a website for public viewing.
6. Integrates nicely with Blogger for making a more "open" document.
7. Encourages portfolio development and other multimedia incorporation.
8. Can use easily in conjunction with a web conference or even phone conference in which each person is able see the same screen and to add to the "living" document.

That said, there are a few downsides. Google Docs can be a bit unwieldy and the formatting not very friendly if you want to turn it into an HTML document, or to format it for publication as a book or e-book.

The collaborations themselves can be a bit "sticky" and there can be annoying lag times. It's also hard to tell who did which edit unless you are disciplined and use a specific color for your own edits.

To answer the core question about whether or not Google Docs will be around in the future, I believe it will expand. I do think that it will become much more iPad-friendly, particularly as HMTL5 starts to be adopted across the board.

Thank you very much for your questions and your desire to collaborate "live" with others via Google documents.

Google Maps Mashups:
Great for Term Papers, Projects, and Portfolios

If you're taking a course that requires you to develop a presentation or put together graphics that bring together historical events and geographical places, you may find that using an integrated web application, commonly referred to as a mashup, will save you time and headaches.

There are a number of effective mashups that you can use which allow you to embed the code in HTML, if you're using a website, blog, wiki, or online portfolio space to display your information. If you're building a report or presentation in PowerPoint, MS-Word, or Excel, you can often save the shots as graphics (JPEG) and copy and paste them into the file. You can then save the file as a PDF in order to preserve the formatting.

Here are a few examples of reports, term papers, or projects in which a Google Map mashup would be ideal:

» *Tracking the Gulf Oil Spill and Clean-Up:* Develop a series of maps that show the progress of the oil. You can put in balloons and text call-outs in order to provide more information.

» *Tracking the Real Estate Bubble "Pop":* Connect photos (using Flickr) of "for sale" homes in bust-afflicted cities (Las Vegas, Phoenix, and Tampa, FL come to mind).

» *Migration of the Monarch Butterfly and the Scissortail Flycatcher:* Connect notes and photos to show the migratory pathways of various species.

» *Memoir and Creative Writing:* Link to stories that tie to locations on the map; also connect thumbnails that are clickable for larger views.

Annotated Maps

Use Google Maps to create annotated maps. You can put in annotations, pushpins, polygons, and balloons. You can embed images in the balloons, as well.

- earth.google.com/outreach/tutorial_annotate.html
- www.google.com/intl/en_us/help/maps/tour/#business

Illustrated Maps

Use Google Maps to embed html code that will allow you to display photos and other images next to locations on a Google map. There are several programs that you can use to integrate photos / photo albums such as Flickr with Google Maps.

- **Earthalbum.com** (www.earthalbum.com)

  This is a very easy-to-use mashup – fun to experiment with.

- **Flickr2map** (www.robogeo.com/home/Flickr2Map.asp)

  Here's a script to use that links your Flickr to Google maps using geo-tagging.

- **Trippermap.com** (www.trippermap.com)

  It is a flash-based world map on your own website or blog. Trippermap automatically searches at Flickr for location information and plots the photos on your a customized Trippermap, on your own website. Trippermap also supports photos that have been geotagged or photos that have location data encoded in their EXIF properties. Trippermap also supports Flickr's new mapping tools so you can drag your photos onto the map at Flickr and have them show up on your Trippermap and then see them using Google Earth.

Social Networking with Tagged Google Maps

iMapFlickr (imapflickr.com)

This is a way to create custom Google Maps from geotagged Flickr Photos. You can embed in your website or blog, or for send them to Facebook, Twitter, and other social networking sites.

Image Hosting

- **Imageshack.com**
  - ▸ imageshack.us

- **Imagehosting.com**
  - ▸ www.imagehosting.com

  No limit, automatically makes thumbnails, can link & embed html to display images and thumbnails.

- **Tinypic.com**
  - ▸ tinypic.com

  Works for vidoes and images, scripts that can be uploaded/embedded in other programs, including Facebook and eBay.

- **Supload.com**
  - ▸ www.supload.com

  Image hosting, video hosting, audio and ringtone hosting.

Mashup Makers

- **Yahoo! Pipes**
  - ▸ pipes.yahoo.com/pipes/

- **QEDWiki**
  - ▸ www.icewalkers.com/Linux/Software/526780/QEDWiki.html

- **Intel Mash Maker**
  - ▸ software.intel.com/en-us/articles/what-is-intel-mash-maker/?wapkw=(mash+maker)

HVAC Training:
Innovative Uses of Technology

Many career colleges are being very proactive in innovative uses of technology to allow students to pull in the content they need. Their view reflects idea that it is preferable for learners to pull content on demand rather than having the institution "push" it. They are also taking it a step beyond the "anytime/anywhere" concept and moving to a philosophy that is more social networking based, and has as its goal to foster collaboration and to develop a learning community.

The videos and other innovative technologies do not replace lectures and laboratories. They provide case studies, examples, and allow students to relate and share their own experiences via discussions, group projects, or individual projects. They also help learners see the "big picture" and to maintain a sense of engagement.

Videos/Diagrams from Manufacturers

For students to be able to retrieve specifications and mechanical information about the systems, it is very important to be able to know where to find it. Although diagrams, samples, and photos are good, they can be out of date. Being able to access information from the manufacturers allows learners to stay up to date.

Videos and Slide Shows from Trade Associations

The National Association for State Community Services Programs (NASCSP) has made a series of videos available in conjunction with their overall mission to help prevent and reduce poverty, in part by helping train individuals how to weatherize residential buildings.

- Furnace Testing
  - ▶ www.youtube.com/nascsp#p/u/18/DTATClgPpek

- Weatherization Works (slide show)
  - ▶ www.youtube.com/nascsp#p/a/u/1/hdXkCqyDjGg

- Air Conditioner Replacement
  - ▶ www.youtube.com/nascsp#p/a/u/2/dh7ouZQAhXU

- Furnace Replacement Demonstration - Weatherization
  - ▶ www.youtube.com/nascsp#p/a/u/5/UX0BvLxEk00

- Use of Infrared Camera During Energy Efficiency Audit
  - ▶ www.youtube.com/nascsp#p/u/21/FNw1l-_LMfM

- Furnace and Draft Tests
  - ▶ www.youtube.com/nascsp#p/u/25/t5kebIgZqx8

- Health and Safety
  - ▶ www.youtube.com/nascsp#p/u/24/CgbrMwFyKoM

- Blower Door and Infrared Camera
  - ▶ www.youtube.com/nascsp#p/u/31/yEKXKZhIkKs

Virtual Tours of LEED-Certified Green Buildings

Owners of buildings that have received Leadership in Energy and Environmental Design (LEED) Certification from the U.S. Green Building Council (**www.usgbc.org**) often provide virtual tours of their buildings. These are extremely helpful for learners who wish to put the things they are learning into a context, and to engage as far as they can in situated learning.

Here are a few examples:

- Tri-North Builders Gold LEED Certified Headquarters in Fitchberg, WI which uses highly efficient climate control and water heating.
  - ▶ www.youtube.com/watch?v=IKHYMNksJN0

- Tour of a Platinum-rated LEED Sustainable Building: The Morris Arboretum (University of Pennsylvania)
    - www.youtube.com/watch?v=GutUg3FU2ak

- Great River Energy Corporate HQ: LEED Platinum Summary
    - youtu.be/2TYCkBiG85U

- Bentley Building Mechanical Systems - Overview
    - youtu.be/p21tFBHXuOM

- How to Get LEED Certified
    - youtu.be/cWZ3JjPZNfO

Webinars and "Live Feed" with Learner Participation Virtual Classrooms

As web conferencing software has become more common, many institutions offer synchronous (or "live") training via a webinar. What differentiates the webinar of today from the old streaming media of the past is the ability of the participant to interact. Today's webinars all learners to ask questions, to take polls online, to share documents, and to chat with the instructor as well as other participants. It's a dynamic, friendly place that can be archived and returned to if the learner would like to repeat certain sections.

For HVAC training, synchronous web conferencing is most effective when there are procedures and processes that should be demonstrated, and where there may be questions, as well as opportunities for collaborative learning.

Virtual Worlds (HVAC in Second Life)

While some have found the virtual world, Second Life, to have a bit too steep a learning curve for students (it takes awhile to be able to walk, sit, fly, communicate, and travel from island to island), others love the immersive environment.

There is no doubt that it can be extremely helpful for helping students gain a good idea of the kind of equipment they will be working with, and the 3D environment give a better representation of the equipment than flat graphics.

The College of North West London's gas and heating lecturer Martin Biron bought an island and installed a house with an interactive central heating system for plumbing, gas, heating and ventilation students at the College of North West London to study.

More than 600 HVAC students at the college in became the first UK students to be given a Second Life education.

The island is open to visitors, and Biron has created resources that individuals may download while they're on the island. For example, he made a copy of *Heating and Ventilating Review* available, and visitors may obtain a copy as they also get a tour of the site's facilities.

Speaking with a copy of *Heating and Ventilating Review* on his desk, Biron says HVR readers are welcome anytime to drop by the virtual college to see him and get a tour of the site's facilities (**www.secondlife.com**).

Multi-Device, Multi-Modal Learning: Integrate All Your Devices for Power Learning

Chances are, you're walking around right now with at least four separate digital devices through which you access information and communicate with others. You've got a smartphone, a laptop or two, perhaps a dedicated e-reader such as a Kindle, an iPod or other media storage and playback device, and an iPad or other tablet. It's bulky, but when all the devices are fully charged and Wi-Fied, you're amazing—at least when it comes to communicating with friends and family. With your online courses... well... not so much.

When you communicate with friends and family, chances are, you're using your devices in a seamless, integrated way, and you know exactly how to leverage the capabilities of each one in order to do what you want to do.

When it comes to your online course, you may be in a different situation, and your situation may be a bit chaotic.

Some people are advocating finding a single device that makes it unnecessary to carry around so many devices. How likely is that? Frankly, it's not likely at all. After all, your devices all serve different forms, functions, and services.

Let's take a look at one specific example of how you can best integrate your devices.

Multi-Modal Learning Through Multiple Devices: Case Study

- **Learning Management System:** Blackboard

- **Textbook:** e-text with Cengage CourseSmart
- **Communication with Professor:** email, discussion board, chat
- **Communication with other students:** email, discussion board, Wimba (video)
- **Additional Instructional Materials:** videos/websites
- **Assignments:** quizzes, short papers, web research, portfolio

Needless to say, you'll need to start by positioning yourself in a location that has electrical outlets and a good wireless connection to the Internet. I'd recommend adding a power strip in your kitbag of necessary digital items, tucked away next to the cellphone chargers and the headphones. If you travel to Europe or South America often, you'll need at least one adapter for the U.K. and one for Europe / South America plugs.

Toting a power strip along with you definitely obviates the need for multiple plug adaptors. You can purchase a Belkin 6-plug power strip for about 10 dollars. The only problem is that at any given time, you can probably only plug in four devices, thanks to their space-hogging, clunky designs. I'd recommend going with a 12-outlet "pivot plug" design by Belkin, which also has a solid surge protector. You'll actually be able to plug in your cellphone chargers, your DVD players, and various device plugs. It's a more expensive option—lists for $50 (but available for $25)—but you'll be an instant friend to anyone waiting in the departure lounge at the gate at the airport.

Now that you've got all your devices up and running, how do you orchestrate them?

Best uses of multiple devices:

- **Cellphone/smartphone:** Use it for texting & taking photos/movies and posting (good for discussions, communication with professors, developing material for your papers and portfolio). You can post the videos and images to Flickr or YouTube, and then embed them and provide a link within your ePortfolio project.

- **iPad and/or e-Reader:** Use it for your digital textbook. It's a good option because there is no real need to have it open on your laptop (with your learning management system) because you're not allowed to copy and paste much text (even if you wanted to, or there was a need to do so). You can use your iPad for collaborative learning / social learning in a very graphics-rich, emotionally-rewarding way.

- **Laptop:** Use this for your learning management system where you need a robust operating system and large screen to be effective with the discussion board, embedded materials, quizzes, gradebook, and more. Also, use your laptop for producing documents and presentations, and for editing audio and video presentations. Your laptop is also effective for updating websites, accessing ftp sites with robust information and zipped files, and for uploading information.

- **iPod:** With Cloud storage, you can access the same material simultaneously with multiple devices. So, if you need to watch a video or listen to an audio podcast, you can download it for immediate or future viewing/listening (even if you don't have connectivity). It's a great approach because you can save time, and also not worry with having to flip back and forth between screens.

An integrated multi-device, multi-modal approach de-clutters your mind.

One of the biggest advantages of a multi-device, multi-modal approach is that you're not spending a lot of time and mental energy flipping between screens and losing control of the information flow.

This approach enables you to multitask in a way that is not really multitasking as much as it is providing "reinforcement learning." You're able to turn to the information you need exactly when you need it, and you're able to pinpoint where the information is, and then achieve a state of deep focus. You're able to apply your knowledge more quickly and effectively by using multiple devices, and you can collaborate in ways that are productive and lead to substantive results.

Online Reference Resources: 2010 Update

Online resources change. Links change. It is always good to revisit online references resources fairly regularly to review what they contain, and which ones might have merged with others. Here is a list of online references sources that you can use in your online courses as you conduct online research and participate in collaborative projects. Keep in mind that this list is by no means exhaustive, and it focuses on open-text, full-text articles that are available free of charge, even though some of the portals do incorporate free PDFs (without the free article), or may simply include a snippet for free.

ONLINE ENCYCLOPEDIAS

- **Encyclopedia Britannica**
  - ▶ www.britannica.com

- **Encyclopedia.com**
  - ▶ www.encyclopedia.com

  A portal to a number of different reference resources, including dictionaries, encyclopedias, databases of articles from newspapers and magazines, plus databases of peer-reviewed journals.

- **Wikipedia.com**
  - ▶ www.wikipedia.com

  Everyone's favorite wiki, a good starting point, but sometimes unreliable, incomplete, and biased. This is not to say that others are not biased, but as a volunteer effort, and a collaborative effort of users, the quality can be less than uniform.

- **Columbia Encyclopedia** (available via Questia)
  - ▶ www.questia.com/library/encyclopedia/

- **Encarta**
  - ▶ encarta.msn.com/encnet/features/dictionary/dictionaryhome.asp

  Limited version is free, expanded version available for subscribers. Also includes a thesaurus and a word-translator to and from various languages.

NEWSPAPERS AND MAGAZINES

- **Pathfinder** – Portal to Time-Warner publications
  - ▶ www.pathfinder.com/pathfinder/index.html

- **Magportal**
  - ▶ www.magportal.com

  The search engine brings articles from different online journals and magazines, including Salon.com, Wired.com, and more.

- **IPL.org**
  - ▶ www.ipl.org

  Created through a merger, this database helps you find journals, magazines, and newspapers on topics and in regions. Links to the publications.

- **Highbeam**
  - ▶ www.highbeam.com

  Some full-text free, some articles require a trial subscription.

PEER-REVIEWED ARTICLES

- **Directory of Open-Access Journals**
  - ▶ www.doaj.org

  Peer-reviewed journals, with open content, where readers can read, download, copy, distribute, print, search, or link to the full texts of these articles.

- **EBSCO**
  - ▶ www.ebsco.com

  The summaries and abstracts are free, full content is not.

- **BNET**
  - ▶ www.bnet.com

  Business management articles, full-text.

- **Search and Discovery**
  - ▶ www.searchanddiscovery.net

  Full-text of geoscience articles, with a petroleum exploration and production focus.

- **Google Scholar**
  - ▶ scholar.google.com

  Some full-text articles are available, others simply provide links in order to purchase the articles.

GEOGRAPHY / POLITICAL INFORMATION

- **CIA World Factbook**
  - ▶ www.cia.gov/library/publications/the-world-factbook/

  Extremely useful source of information for world countries and regions, which includes demographic, geographic, political, and economic data.

- **International Monetary Fund publications**
  - ▶ www.imf.org/external/pubind.htm

  Useful statistics on economic growth and development across the world.

- **International Governmental Organization Full-text publications portal**
  - ▶ www.lib.berkeley.edu/doemoff/govinfo/intl/gov_intlfulltxt.html

  Excellent set of links and descriptions.

GOVERNMENT PUBLICATIONS AND STATISTICS

- **FedStats**
  - ▶ www.fedstats.gov

  Sources of useful information (search block allows you to search federal agencies' publications); "one-stop shopping" for government statistics, etc.

- **Library of Congress Reading Room**
  - ▸ www.loc.gov/rr/news/extgovd.html

  Extensive portal to information links

- **ChildStats**
  - ▸ www.childstats.gov

  Forum on child and family statistics and reports; links to very helpful reports and statistics on child welfare (government sources).

FULL-TEXT PUBLICATIONS

- **Project Gutenberg**
  - ▸ www.gutenberg.org

- **Bartleby**
  - ▸ www.bartleby.org

- **Online Literature Network**
  - ▸ www.online-literature.com/author_index.php

  Full-text of many articles. The numerous ads are a bit annoying.

- **Google Books**
  - ▸ books.google.com/books

  Some full-text is available, and some with limited previews and snippets.

TWITTER POSTS

- **Hashtag Directory**
  - ▸ twitter.com/hashdir

  Find topics and start following the twitter accounts that resonate with your own interests.

Reality Show-Inspired Portfolios

With Ustream and the ability to blend together different applications, there is no reason to repeat the same old approaches to presentation and collaboration. Along with social networking (Facebook, Twitter) and presentation software and graphics (Flickr, etc.), creating live feeds is easier than ever and very dynamic.

There are many uses:

- Portfolio for course
- Collaborative project for course
- The course itself—students and/or professor can be streamed as well as archived. The course content and the "lectures" would be much more spontaneous and would have a feeling authenticity and unscriptedness (although there would be a bit of direction, although not direct scripting).

This would be a 40-minute show (with commercial breaks, if you can find sponsors and advertisers) with 8 minutes per segment: the goal is to look at what people are doing and in-depthly explore what happens when one goes with the flow rather than hanging tough and enforcing an aggressively egalitarian view of competence and inclusion (essentially a meritocracy).

1. **Twitter-licious:** This spot follows an employee who is tasked with generating tweets to send out over the next month to promote your new products and specials.

   Our heroine must come up with an inventory of 140-character (or less) tweets with key words and hash tags to maximize exposure.

She will then post them, asking all the branches and managers to retweet. So, in addition to writing the tweets, she needs to develop a way to keep track. She can develop a database to keep track—something as easy to manage as a spreadsheet. Or, alternatively, she can use customer relationship management (CRM) software.

You might say that it does not sound very interesting to watch a person send tweets. However, perhaps one set of tweets could revolve around getting a flash mob to do something orchestrated, a crazy collaboration—a virtual picnic (who brings the ants?).

2. **Facebook Play-offs:** Live streaming of a discussion by two people who have been in competition to find ten sports team pages (or fansite). They will rank them—best and worst—then start designing their own. They will use the best attributes of both.

    Poor grammar, inadequate communication skills; some Facebook presences are a liability rather than an asset. Intriguing links, special information, up-to-date information. Some Facebook pages contain hidden treasure.

3. **Geographical Netherlands:** We try to go global, but it's not good when our employees think that Ecuador is in Africa.

    Follow the discussions of two people who go around the globe virtually to collect information about different countries and develop a presentation.

    For each episode, they debate each other—try to convince the other to move to the country.

    - Name of capital
    - Name of the neighbors
    - Climate
    - Main economic activity
    - Population
    - Religion, groups
    - Loveliest flowers, trees, plant
    - Any dangerous reptiles?
    - Any unforgettable landmarks?

4. **Math Phobia Is No Longer Cool:** A live feed of employees caught in painful math gaffes.

    Perhaps it's better to focus on the positive rather than the negative. However, it's always fun to see absurd scenarios and situations—and what better fun than to see goofy gaffes and absurd miscalculations when it comes to applied math. Think of a few situations that you yourself have experienced, and then enact them.

    This is a portfolio project that has the potential to go viral.

5. **The Leaderless Organization: Enlightened, Evolved, or Utterly Foolish?**

    This could tie into the concept of self-managed teams ("bossless teams"). Follow the team as they are faced with really extreme challenges—becoming event planners for high-stakes events, such as receptions for dignitaries, and places where crazed, over-the-top fans will congregate in order to transcend their own conceptions of self, and merge with some sort of collective unconscious that takes them either really high or really low. It's volatile, and you're not anywhere near being comfortable about it. So, the reality television elements start putting pressure on the "pain points"—they elicit defensive and/or aggressive reactions, which then feed into the audience's sense of reality, a balanced world, and life itself.

    If you've decided to take this path for your portfolio project, you might need to talk to your team members and let them review the videos you plan to upload and make public.

Smartphone M-Learning:
Virtual Personal Trainer

I'm getting a degree in sports leadership, which is perfect for me because I want to be a coach and eventually an assistant manager or manager at a sports club—hopefully, a racquet club.

I played tennis as a junior and also for the small college I attended in Texas. I did not graduate, so the program I'm in is just perfect for my needs.

The program is amazing and I'm loving it. One of the most interesting elements is the fact that we have to design programs that incorporate social networking.

My first assignment? Develop a "coach-on-the-go"" smartphone-based approach to helping athletes build their confidence when competing.

My second assignment? Develop a "personal trainer" approach to strength and conditioning; include plyometrics, diet, weights, stretching, yoga.

So here's my question: I love what I'm doing, and it's fun. But is it sound? A good idea? What are other programs doing?

Sincerely,
Totally Tennis in Tulsa

****

Dear Totally Tennis:

Wow! You have found a great, cutting-edge program! Yes, absolutely, the activities that are required will help you achieve your goals.

Let's look at what progressive online programs are incorporating. I'm including the ones that you described because they're right on track with what the future holds. Courses that incorporate new technology and new approaches will help you land a job—and will help you be amazing at what you can offer your employer. You'll be a hit with your employer because the clients—the athletes, families, club members—will see immediate results in their performance as well as in efficiencies and cost-savings.

1. "Coach on the Go"
2. "Smartphone Personal Trainer"
3. "24-7 Diet and Exercise Buddy"
4. "Tiger Blood Virtual Clinic: UStream Live Streaming Court Time"
5. Tiger's Milk? What my mother made me eat vs. what our society sees as utterly normative.

These are just a few ideas that you can use—either for a final project, a portfolio or as a "live journal" sort of concept that helps you modify your behavior.

Life has gotten a lot more interesting with the advent of automated tweeting and scheduled texting. It is perfect for a number of academic activities that can later be leveraged and expanded to help you with cognitive therapy, behavior modification, and life coaching.

Using this approach means shifting one's perspectives a bit.

Don't worry. It's all good.

The technology is the light that stays on, unwavering, through the darkest stretch of night.

The "Works Cited" Challenge:
Tools to Make Your Life Easier

You spend hours and hours finding just the right articles in your online library's database of refereed journals, and you find the perfect quote to support your argument. But then you're stuck. You can't figure out how to format your paper.

It's frustrating! No one likes to lose points because they've failed to follow the correct formatting for their sources, but sometimes it seems unavoidable. Reading through APA, MLA, Chicago, and Turabian style manuals can be maddening. Isn't there some other way?

The key to success is to feel confident in your ability to create a bibliographic record in whatever style is required.

One quick way to achieve that is to take advantage of bibliographic tools, many of which are free.

Here is a list and description of time-saving tools which can help you increase the precision and accuracy of your citations, and which may help you avoid losing points on your papers and research projects.

EasyBib.com
▶ www.easybib.com

EasyBib bills itself as a free automatic bibliography and citation maker with a twist: it can help you develop virtual note cards and what they refer to as "dynamic outlining." They cover APA, Chicago/Turabian, and MLA styles, and they work with both footnote and parenthetical (in-text) citations.

Bibme.org

▶ www.bibme.org

Bibme.org is a fully automatic bibliography maker that auto-fills and quickly builds a works-cited page. With BibMe, it is possible to save bibliographies and also to refer to an in-site citation guide. Bibme.org incorporates guidelines from the following:

MLA: *MLA Handbook for Writers of Research Papers*, 7th edition

APA: *Publication Manual of the American Psychological Association*, 5th edition

Chicago: *The Chicago Manual of Style*, 15th edition

Turabian: *A Manual for Writers of Research Papers, Theses, and Dissertations*, 7th edition

KnightCite

▶ www.calvin.edu/library/knightcite

KnightCite is an online citation generator service provided by the Hekman Library of Calvin College. This service simplifies the often tedious task of compiling an accurate bibliography in the appropriate style by formatting the given data on a source into a reliable citation, eliminating the need to memorize minute details of style for multiple kinds of sources. The service is provided free of charge by the college, and is available to members both within and outside of the Calvin community.

NoodleTools.com

Not free, but requires a monthly fee. NoodleTools has an interesting advantage over other bibliography makers in that it provides ways to use unique search engines.

INTUTE
▶ www.intute.ac.uk/search.html

INFOMINE
▶ infomine.ucr.edu

SURFWAX
▶ lookahead.surfwax.com/index-2011.html

SWEETSEARCH
- ▸ lookahead.surfwax.com/index-2011.html
  (organizes search engines in categories)

OPENJ-GATE
- ▸ www.openjgate.org
  (searches open journals)

DIRECTORY OF OPEN ACCESS JOURNALS
- ▸ www.doaj.org

Noodletools, also contains a nice guide for finding Government Information:
- ▸ www.usa.gov
- ▸ www.fedstats.gov
- ▸ www.childstats.gov
- ▸ www.direct.gov.uk

One unique aspect of NoodleTools is the fact that it incorporates excellent search tools (the world beyond Google and Wikipedia!)
- ▸ www.noodletools.com/debbie/literacies/information/5locate/adviceengine.html

Zotero
- ▸ www.zotero.org

Zotero [zoh-TAIR-oh] is a free, easy-to-use tool to help you collect, organize, cite, and share your research sources. It lives right where you do your work—in the web browser itself.

Bibomatic.com
- ▸ www.bibomatic.com

Need the ISBN to generate the citations. I tried it, and *The Adventures of Tinguely Querer* came up as *Tale of Murasaki*. I'm sure that Bibomatic.org is largely accurate—but I think I'll test it out a bit before I bank on it.

I hope that these resources have been helpful. To tell the truth, it's sort of the tip of the iceberg—there are many, many sites and tools that offer to help you develop bibliographies. So, it's worth your while to check them out and find the one that best meets your needs. Plunge in and enjoy!

The Expanding World of E-Learning:
Apps for Electricians (and a Few Others)

Colleges and universities are incorporating applications for iPod/iPhone/iTouch/iPad to make their e-learning programs very flexible, and to be able to use materials on all the devices that learners are using. The pace of change is rapid, and keeping pace means tapping into the energy and innovation of the app-developer world. Many interactive programs are being converted to applications.

Here are just a few examples of the programs that are available, many of which are provided by not-for-profits, professional associations, and government agencies, and thus are high-quality, reliable sources which then can be incorporated in e-learning, and specifically m-learning (mobile learning).

Keep in mind that textbook publishers often bundle high-quality videos and apps with their digital textbooks, and some publishers even have assessments/review quizzes that can help you prepare for certification. The descriptions below are ones that were provided by the app provider.

ELECTRICIANS

MikeHolt.com

▸ www.scribd.com/doc/7255890/Basic-Math-for-Electricians

Basic Math for Electricians

▸ www.mikeholt.com/free-exams-menu.php

Online electricians review quizzes and exams (Journeyman, etc.)

iTunes / Smith Chart 2.0.1
▶ www.apple.com/downloads/macosx/math_science/smithchart.html

This is an automated Smith chart, which allows the RF and Microwave circuit designer to choose among several component elements to match an electronic load to a source for maximum power transfer.

iTunes / Seafoid 3.1
▶ www.apple.com/downloads/macosx/math_science/seafoid.html

Wide variety of electronics-related calculation tasks, for example:

- Getting resistor values from their color bands.
- Calculating LED dropping resistors
- Ohm's Law – Heat sink thermal resistance calculation
- Inductances of air-cored coils
- NE555 circuit calculation.

iTunes / Solve Elec 2.5
▶ www.apple.com/downloads/macosx/math_science/solveelec.html

An educational electricity and electronics software for circuit analysis and resolution.

Niranjan Kumar / Electrical Toolkit iPod App
▶ itunes.apple.com/us/app/electrical-toolkit/id301308656?mt=8

iTunes / RF Toolkit iPod App
▶ www.apple.com/downloads/macosx/math_science/rftoolbox.html

David Ullian Larson / ElectricianMath.com
▶ www.electricianmath.com

iTunes / LBT – Light 9.2
▶ www.apple.com/downloads/macosx/math_science/ltblight.html

Permits natural and artificial lighting calculation with a color radiosity method applied to a finite elements plan. LTB-Light runs under Apple Macintosh and implements OpenGL. Data management take places through an internal powerful CAD system, directly in a perspective view. It is possible to introduce flatten surfaces with colored glazing, furniture, curved surfaces like cylinders, cones, ellipsoids, hyperboloids and complex objects like cross vaults.

HEALTH OCCUPATIONS

iTunes / Guardian 1.2.4
▶ www.apple.com/downloads/macosx/math_science/
guardian.html

In the framework of promoting the prevention of cardiovascular disease, the World Health Organization (WHO) has produced new guidelines (1) for the assessment and management of cardiovascular risk. The present software is named GUARDIAN, that stands for: GUidelines for cARDIovasculAr risk implemeNted through an interactive computerized access.

Stillinger's Dosage Calculator 5.1.2
▶ www.apple.com/downloads/macosx/math_science/
stillingersdosagecalculator.html

Using 11 calculators, SDC calculates virtually every drug found in the modern veterinary hospital or ECC. SDC consolidates drug dosage information you find in the vast array of reference material. SDC DOES NOT come with a prefabricated formulary. Building the formulary is left to the end user which allows for complete customization.

kSpectra Toolkit 2.25
▶ www.apple.com/downloads/macosx/math_science/kspectratoolkit.html

A set of advanced tools for spectral estimation, decomposing of time series into trend, oscillatory components and noise with sophisticated statistical tests, cross-spectrum and coherence estimation, data compression, as well as reconstruction and prediction. KSpectra Toolkit takes full advantage of latest Max OS X technologies to provide the best user experience and performance. It includes examples in finance, economics, geophysics, and biomedical sciences.

GRAPHIC COMMUNICATIONS

Nonio C 10.0
▶ www.apple.com/downloads/macosx/math_science/nonioc.html

A program for modeling large topographic and cartographic surveys using triangles, contour lines, slope charts, color shading, sections, and three-dimensional views.

DRAFTING AND CAD

McCad Schematics Plus 5.2.0

▸ www.apple.com/downloads/macosx/math_science/mccadschematicsplus.
html

A powerful professional CAD software tool that allows the electronic designer to easily create and revise electronic circuit designs (digital and/or analog) directly via a very intuitive Macintosh interface. It supports both Simple as well as Complex hierarchies. All of the features that a designer would need, from Rubberbanding, Bussing, Rotation, Auto-Packaging and Multi-page Project Management, to automatic Net List, Parts List (BOM) and SPICE reporting, in a variety of interface formats, are included. Schematics also prepares compatible files for use with other McCAD products such as the PCB-ST layout and auto-routing packages. McCAD SchematicsPlus comes with an extensive 60K+ device library as well as an on-line Library Editor which allows the user to create new parts.

ENVIRONMENTAL

Diversity 1.2

▸ www.apple.com/downloads/macosx/math_science/diversity.html

Diversity is a new tool for entering and inspecting ecological data, and for measuring the diversity of ecological communities. Spreadsheets have long been the standard tool for ecological data entry, but spreadsheets are cumbersome for working with these data. Diversity makes it quick to enter your data and to see the composition of your samples. Standard measures of diversity, including both individual-based and sample-based rarefaction, are made blazingly fast.

AUTOMOTIVE TRADE

PneumaticReserve 0.4

▸ www.apple.com/downloads/macosx/math_science/pneumaticreserve.html

Instrumentation engineers and techs should carefully size reserve bottles used for valve actuators to ensure that these valves will be able to stroke a sufficient number of times without any supply from the air header. Bryce Elliott wrote an excellent article for the January 2009 edition of ISA's InTech magazine. This application utilizes the formulas detailed in the article to calculate the volume required for the reserve bottle.

The Power of Multiple Screens: Optimizing Your Productivity with Smartphone, Laptop, and Tablet Investments

I carry around my BlackBerry and iPad everywhere I go. My laptop goes with me, but not so much. I've also got an iTouch, which I bought when they first came out.

My question is this—most of the time, one or more of my devices is just sitting in its case… or just sitting waiting for a call or a text.

Is there a better way to use my devices? I added up all I'm paying each month and it surprised me how much it is. I'm okay with paying, but I need to feel I'm getting something for all the money I'm ponying up (to use the parlance of Mr. Seymour Burns, of The Simpsons).

So, my question to you is this: How can I use all my devices to improve my performance in my online courses? And do I need to get rid of some of the ones I'm using and use different ones?

I'm ready to optimize!

Sincerely,
Overly Deviced

****

Dear Overly,

I can totally sympathize with you, Overly! I am one of those who has hung on to the old, new, and emerging technologies simultaneously, and I'm here to tell you that I've wasted a lot of money!

A good, solid assessment of your devices, along with a clearly delineated plan of action to achieve your personal, professional, and academic goals is a good way to start. You can start pruning the capacity you have—"culling the herd" to coin a phrase (I'm smiling at my own corniness).

Let's focus on e-learning. That will help us simplify things.

1. **Maximize the number of simultaneous, operational screens. Keep as many up and functional as possible.**

   You'll be amazed at how much it increases your productivity to have two or three devices going at the same time. Make sure they're performing separate functions though. Use one as a dedicated e-text reader, another as your online course access point (log into the learning management system, write your papers, etc), and another as your communication and social networking device (phone/Twitter/text-messaging). You may even have a separate device as a dedicated GPS unit or one for assessments. Separate the functions as much as possible. Granted, you won't be able to separate everything—some things you'll want to integrate.

2. **Use your small screens for multitasking with voice phone/texting.**

   While some people feel quite comfortable reading texts from their iPhones, iTouch, Android, or BlackBerry, there's no doubt that it is a small screen, and you will not be able to see much at once—whether text, graphic, or map.

3. **If you have a tablet, use it as a dedicated reader for your e-text, while you use your laptop for the learning management system and task preparation.**

   Tablets are ideally suited as e-readers because they have scalable/zoomable text. You can zoom in, rotate, and do all kinds of things to enhance your view of the text, image, or map, and it's all with a touch. Other display units (laptops, desktops, etc.) aren't as friendly.

4. **When possible, download to flash drives so you access your**

material from any available computer.

While you'll definitely utilize the cloud for keeping notes, storing items, and accessing materials when you have access to the Internet or a G4 network, it is useful to files on flash drive for when you do not have connectivity.

5. **When you update/upgrade your laptop, invest in high-capacity coprocessors, video cards, and storage.**

This applies to desktop units as well. You'll need at least one computer that has the best you can afford of video processing and storage in order to do the things you'll need to with respect to audio and video editing, etc. Cloud-based computing can be a real coprocessor capacity hog, especially when bandwidth is a bit compromised. The more you can help the situation be having quite a bit of cache space, the better. You'll find this to be the case when you're streaming media as well. One thing to keep in mind is to do as much as you can via a LAN line rather than Wi-Fi—you'll have a more reliable connection, and you won't be as harnessed to the router, etc.

6. **Plan your connectivity.**

Do tasks that require streaming and a lot of bandwidth at a certain time, and don't try to force it when you just don't have the bandwidth or connection speed. There is nothing more frustrating than slow, jerky streaming.

7. **Use one screen to practice active reading; take notes from your e-text, discussion board.**

We've already discussed the importance of separating out your tasks and using your tablet as a dedicated e-textbook reader. However, we haven't yet discussed the importance of active reading. I like to think of active reading as "synthetic reading" which is to say that when you do it, you synthesize your thoughts, ideas, and the main concepts from the reading, and mesh them with the course outcomes and learning objectives.

8. **Practice active information gathering to build your papers and projects in stages.**

While you're working on your courses and activities, you'll find yourself doing quite a bit of research, both on the web and also via your online library or other information repositories. It's a good idea to use multiple screens to maximize your efforts as you build your papers. Put your outline on one computer, and then keep it on the screen so you can refer to it as you do your research. Save your sources in a separate folder which you can place on a flash drive. Also, build an annotated bibliography that contains summaries along with helpful notes (breadcrumb trail) to remind yourself of the intellectual path you blazed as you were working on your project and doing your research.

I hope these suggestions are clear and easy to follow. I think you'll be surprised to see how quickly your productivity ramps up.

As applications expand and information becomes more available, even more tasks will be made easy through multiple screens. The future is now!

Twitter-Enhanced E-Learning

Interaction with your fellow classmates is one of the keys to success in an online course. Using Twitter effectively can take your interaction to the next level very quickly, and you'll gain confidence, avoid frustration, and save time.

How does Twitter fit in with the other ways you interact with your peers and professor? Let's look at the ways you're probably interacting now. Interacting through the discussion board is good, but you have to be logged on to your learning management system in order to do so. There can be a time lag. Sending emails to your classmates can be good, but it often goes to their university account, which they do not check regularly. Sending instant messages or text messages is good, but you have to know their phone numbers or IM addresses, which is not always possible. Further, it can be tedious to build a list for IMs and text messages so that you don't have to send an individual message to each person.

Twitter offers advantages in that you can send messages (tweets) to any number or people in your network at the same time. You can send and receive tweets from your handheld device (cellphone, smartphone, etc.), and you can access archives through your Twitter account online.

Tweet Yourself to an "A"

Develop an outcomes-based game plan to take advantage of real-time information exchange, as well as twitter-accessed information networks. What does an outcomes-based game plan look like? Be sure to keep focused on your overall goal, tweet on topics that pertain to the course. It's easy to get distracted, and, well, a little bit of distraction is fine, since it usually helps you feel a sense of affiliation and being part of the group. However, the majority of tweets need stay on task.

Here are a few examples of good tweets to send and receive:

- Course deadlines
- Insights and guidelines
- Cries for help
- Offers of help
- Links to useful resources
- Links to practice quizzes
- New discoveries, insights (articles you might find, useful websites, research)
- Links to video posts, images (YouTube, Flickr, etc.) relating to the course
- Online research tips
- Links to draft papers for collaborative/peer review

Put Your Plan Into Action: Sign Up for Twitter

Chances are, you already use Twitter (**www.twitter.com**). If you don't, be sure to sign up. You can enable your cellphone/smartphone to receive tweets, or, if you prefer, you can send and receive messages (tweets) from your computer.

You may wish to separate work and play, and to set up a new Twitter account for your academic work. That is often a good idea, because it makes it easier to go back and review the tweets you've sent and received. Plus, you may not want to annoy all your friends with tweets about next week's sociology quiz!

Practice Sending Messages (Tweets)

You can send messages to people who are following you, as well as directly to a specific twitter account. It's good to do both.

To send a message to all your followers, type in a 140 character or less message in the "what's happening" block.

To send a direct message, go to the "Direct Messages" screen by clicking on "direct messages" in the navigation bar in the right-hand column. Then, type a 140-character or less message in the "Send (pulldown menu of your followers) a direct message."

Use Hashtags to Find Tweets on Your Topics of Interest

Hashtags are meta-tags for Twitter. They are useful because you can classify your tweets, and/or find tweets that have been classified in the topics that interest you.

Here is a directory of hashtags: **wthashtag.com/Main_Page**

Final Thoughts

People are finding very innovative ways to use Twitter, not just for social but also for professional networking. It's now time to explore the possibilities in conjunction with academic applications. As you can see, there are a number of ways that you can use Twitter to enhance your interaction with peers, and also to expand your research/resource possibilities.

Useful Reference/Citation Apps
for the iPhone and iPad

I'm really enjoying my new iPad, but I'm lost in all the apps. Are any of the free apps any good? Do I have to pay a lot to have useful apps?

I've already paid for three apps so I can have iWork. I noticed that if I pay for all the different apps that are out there, I'll have spent more on apps than I did on my iPad! What can I do?

App'd Out

****

Dear App'd Out:

You're making a very good point about the hidden and/or creeping costs of iPad/iPhone ownership. It's really easy to get caught up in the quest for the perfect app. Once you've paid for and downloaded one, it seems that you find one that seems to offer even more features—for just a few dollars more!

Here's a way to stop the "cost creep" in its tracks. I'd recommend starting with a few very good, tried-and-true free apps. See how they work for you and then start going to their expanded versions.

I'd like to start with reference/citation apps. They are often the most useful—a failure to cite correctly is one of the quickest ways I can think of to lose points, credit, and even (Heaven forfend!) be accused of a lack of academic integrity. Nightmare (!) So—save yourself a lot of pain and humiliation and download (and use!) citation and reference apps.

Here are my favorites apps for citing references for college papers:

- **My MLA** (iPhone and iPad)

  Based on the *MLA Handbook for Writers of Research Papers* (7th Edition).

- **iSource MLA and iSource APA**

  Creates bibliographical entries (need to purchase a separate app for each style). It allows you to create, save, and even share bibliographical sources. There are definitely a few limitations though. It does not help you with in-text citations, and it does not create full-text bibliographies.

- **EasyBib** (Free)

  Works best with iPhone 4. Scan a book bar code or type in the name of a book. It creates MLA, APA, and Chicago style citations. You can email your citation and/or export them to EasyBib.com's bibliography management service. Can use with iPad and iPhone Touch, but is a bit trickier.

- **iCitation**

  A fairly unique app designed to create MLA-style bibliographies and citations. It works by entering details about the source, and then iCitation will generate a citation for you. Unlike the other citation apps that require you to scan the bar code and then access a database that fills in all the details. In many ways, this tool is a bit more flexible since it helps you with informal sources (interviews, etc.) as well as printed sources.

- **Quick Cite**

  Can snap a picture of a book's barcode and it will send a citation of the book to your email. You can choose the format (APA, MLA, Chicago, IEEE, Harvard, etc.)

- **Sytation Builder**

  This is like other apps in that it uses ISBN numbers and the information affiliated with the ISBN numbers to collect citation information.

Word 2011 for Mac Has A Killer Bug: What Can You Do?

If you have purchased a new Mac and have the new 2011 Microsoft Office suite of programs, you've probably already discovered the bug in MS-Word 2011 for Mac that will cause your brand new Mac to freeze up, requiring you to manually turn off the computer and to reboot.

The problem happens when you start to copy and paste. Somehow, the copying function starts overloading the memory of your computer (I immediately thought of buffer overruns and bad code resulting in endless "do loops") and before you know it, your computer is grinding to a slow crawl and then to a full freeze.

If you go on different discussion boards and help forums, you'll find complaints, but no easy solutions. In fact, there were no solutions presented at all, just outraged users who pointed out that Microsoft and Apple were doing nothing about it, but instead were simply blaming each other's systems for the problem. "The other guy is causing the problem! He should fix it!" is what they are saying.

I'm still searching for a solution for my new MacBook Air's copy of Word 2011 for Mac.

I tried repairing the disk permissions. Here's how you do it:
Go to Applications → Utilities → Disk Utility, select your hard drive and click "Repair Disk Permissions."

I've been afraid to try Word because I don't want to lose the work I'm doing. In the meantime, I'm going to use the following "work-arounds":

1. **Google Docs**
   ▸ www.google.com/docs

   Google Docs has improved a great deal in the last year. It is much more collaboration-friendly, and it plays nicer with Macs. I just opened a few docs I had saved more than a year ago, and they are alive and well. I also started a new one, just for fun. Remember to save often, and when you export, do so as an RTF. That will ensure your paper is compatible with other word processors, even if it does not have all the functionality of bona fide Word products. For example, comments and track changes will not be as easy to work with or save, and you'll need to try a different approach for anything that has graphical input. You might consider saving as a PDF if you do not need to collaborate.

2. **OpenOffice**
   ▸ www.openoffice.org

   OpenOffice is a powerful suite of office-like tools that you can download to your computer (rather than using from the cloud as you would with Google Docs). OpenOffice has spreadsheets and word processing that can integrate, and you can save in Office-compatible formats. I have used OpenOffice and like it, but have to say that downloading it can be rather problematic, and it can be easy to forget to save as an Office-compatible document. Most newer Word and Office versions can open the OpenOffice format, but there are undoubtedly some potential problems and/or glitches.

3. **Bean**
   ▸ www.bean-osx.com/Bean.html

   Bean is a lean, easy-to-use word processing program that has the simplicity of Wordpad, but with more elegance and a bit more flexibility (especially for OSX). If your Mac did not come with Pages, you may wish to download Bean. Bean is not a substitute for Word, and it's not fully compatible. However, it's very quick, lean, and elegant. It doesn't mess up your work with a lot of code and it has an html exporter (which allows you to view the code as you build it in a WYSIWYG environment), so it's potentially nice to use in building webpages and/or embedding/building content in web apps and social networking sites (Facebook, LinkedIn, Wordpress and other blogging programs, etc.).

4. **AbiWord**
   ▸ www.abisource.com

Abiword is a word processing program similar to Microsoft Word. It is not cloud-based, and I have not tried it. It has received good ratings.

5. **LYX**
   ▸ www.lyx.org

Lyx is a robust word processing program that is unique in its support for mathematical formulas.

6. **Lotus Symphony**
   ▸ www-03.ibm.com/software/lotus/symphony/home.nsf/home

Lotus Symphony is a free three-product program that includes word processing, spreadsheets, and presentations. The programs integrate and are effective.

When Mac and Microsoft play nicely together, it's a dream. When it's not, prepare to lose data! Always have a contingency plan, and backup, backup, backup!

Chapter 4

Cultures, Contexts, and Readings

Are People Naturally Bad?
Applying Hobbes to Online Learning

Whether you have a positive idea of human nature or a negative one makes a huge difference in how you respond to other people. In an online course, where you're not going to meet individuals face to face, it's easy to project your ideas and attitudes about people in general. Without the reality check of face-to-face communication, it is easy to assume that your fellow students, your instructor, and others are exactly how you imagined them to be.

One of the beauties of the online environment is its diversity. Imagine a class that is filled with students with differing viewpoints with respect to human nature. They range from those who tend to be suspicious and cynical about people's motives, to those who assume that all people are wise, patient, helpful, and supportive. In most cases, the course content or activities will not put people's values and beliefs into collision. The fact that your fellow students have wide-ranging ideas about the nature of humanity may not come into play.

However, there are cases in which it does matter, and you'll need to keep people's differing viewpoints in mind as you process and respond to their comments in peer reviews, their posts in the discussion board, and their contribution in collaborations. If you're taking an online course that requires you to weigh in on current events, politics, or ethical issues, you'll find such awareness helpful. It is good to know that people interpret events and behaviors differently, depending on their core values and beliefs about human nature.

Some people believe people are inherently good. In Nicomachean Ethics,

Aristotle expressed the notion that the goal of politics and governance was toward the good, and to help satisfy every individual's desire for happiness:

As every knowledge and moral purpose aspires to some good, what is in our view the good at which the political aims, and what is the highest of all practical goods? Most agree in calling it happiness, and conceive that "to live well" or "to do well" is the same thing as "to be happy."

> The function of Man then is an activity of soul in accordance with reason, or not independently of reason.

> —Aristotle, *Nicomachean Ethics*

Renaissance Humanists believed that human beings could be transformed through education. Further, Enlightenment writers such as Rousseau, and others whose ideas shaped the Declaration of Independence, and the documents affiliated with the French Revolution believed that people were good and able to self-regulate. It was not necessary to keep them crushed and cowed by a tyrant king or powerful state.

On the other end of the spectrum is Thomas Hobbes, who held a very negative view of human nature. He, as did Machiavelli, who, a century before, expressed pragmatic (and negative) views of human nature in *The Prince* (1515). Hobbes, like Machiavelli, believed that people are inherently selfish. Hobbes went on to accuse them of being vicious, violent, selfish, and dishonest. For Hobbes (and Machiavelli), it is best to have a strong leader to maintain order and civil discourse. If not, the natural condition of people will be that of perpetual war.

Hobbes wrote *Leviathan*, during the height of the English Civil War. Published in 1651, the text is a classic work of political philosophy. Again, the ideas and attitudes toward men and human nature tend to be fairly negative. After all, it was Hobbes who wrote that the lives of men tend to be "solitary, poor, nasty, brutish and short."

Hobbes also believed that people have a hard time cooperating:

> If any two men desire the same thing, which nevertheless they cannot both enjoy, they become enemies; and in the way to their end, which is principally their own conservation, and sometimes their delectation only, endeavor to destroy, or subdue one another.

To look at things through Hobbes' eyes brings life into focus in a very disconcerting way. It is a view of nature and humanity that is so negative that it's almost hard to comprehend, except in the world of economics and politics. If you accept Hobbes' views, you are likely to feel nervous and threatened by your fellow human being, and may tend to favor a tough, authoritarian leader.

After all, according to Hobbes in *Leviathan*, without a leader, we're in a state of perpetual warfare:

> Hereby it is manifest, that during the time men live without a common power to keep them all in awe, they are in that condition which is called war; and such a war, as is of every man, against every man.

People who have such a negative view of human beings may not appear to be negative. They may seem very otherworldly. After all, such a negative view of humanity and human life may encourage you to focus on the afterlife and to look at the spiritual side of life. Many mystics throughout time had little faith in human beings. Great revivalist movements in which the jeremiad was preached (with the urgent entreaty to repent now because the end is near), or those emphasizing the apocalyptic narrative (some Doomsday cults can be included in this category), were adept at undermining people's faith in each other. They tended to through their lot to a  powerful leader. Sometimes the gamble paid off. Sometimes it did not. Jonestown and Waco come to mind.

How does this apply to online courses?

If your instructor tends to think that the natural state of human beings is competition and ultimately war, then he or she is likely to believe that the correct role is to be the authoritarian leader. Rules are to be obeyed at all costs. People to transgress will be punished. There will be no mercy. Order must be maintained. Punishment will be swift and public. After all, those who break the rules must serve as an example for other.

Thankfully, most online degree programs adhere to a different philosophy of instruction, and focus on maintaining a nurturing, more flexible and encouraging atmosphere.

The one relatively universal exception to this rule is plagiarism. Many instructors are quick to assume that online students copy and paste from the Internet and purchase papers from places such as termpapers.com. Their underlying belief is that students have poor time management skills, procrastinate, hate to write papers, and lack self-confidence.

Such negative views lead to a sense that some instructors are on a plagiarism quest, and are eager to expose and to punish them.

A similar mindset is manifest in the area of assessment and test-taking, which results in an emphasis on making sure that no one cheats or commits academic dishonesty in a test.

So, even thought the dominant attitude in education at this point in time is that human beings are transformable through education, and that learning is one way to make a better person and fulfill one's potential, there are vestiges of a competing view. It can be a bit confusing at times, because an instructor may seem to be easy-going in one area and not in another. Understanding the history of such ideas can be useful.

Here's a final thought, that could be applied to lifelong learning, since it suggests that people are never satisfied, and are happiest when chasing a dream. Framed in the most cynical of manners, it is inspiring nonetheless.

> Felicity of this life consisteth not in the repose of a mind satisfied. For there is no such finis ultimus, utmost aim, nor summum bonum, greatest good, as is spoken of in the books of the old moral philosophers. Nor can a man any more live, whose desires are at an end, than he, who senses and imaginations are at a stand. Felicity is a continual progress of the desire, from one object to another, the attaining of the former, being still but the way to the latter.
>
> —Hobbes, *Leviathan*

After you graduate with your bachelor's degree, it's time to start planning for your master's—after all, you'll be at your happiest when you are pursuing something you desire.

BIBLIOGRAPHY

- Aristotle. (350 BCE). *Nicomachean Ethics*
  - ▸ classics.mit.edu/Aristotle/nicomachaen.html

- Hobbes, T. (1660) *Leviathan*
  - ▸ oregonstate.edu/instruct/phl302/texts/hobbes/leviathan-contents.html

- Macchiavelli, N. (1515) *The Prince*.
  - ▸ www.constitution.org/mac/prince00.htm

Amy Winehouse's Beehive
vs. Marie Antoinette's "Pouf"

Art History and Fashion Design / Business Online

Like much of the world, I was absolutely devastated when I heard that Amy Winehouse had died. I loved her music, especially "Tears Dry On Their Own" from her Back to Black album.

Right now, I'm working in a used (and sometimes vintage) clothing store, and I'm interested in putting together my own retro designs. I'd also like to market them on the web (not just in the store).

What can I do? The city where I live does not have a good fashion design program, and the local college does not offer business courses specific to doing a small business based on creating cool fashion from vintage clothing. What do you recommend?

Sincerely,
Amy-Homage

****

Dear Amy-Homage,

Thank you very much for mentioning Amy Winehouse. I, too, was quite saddened. I loved her songs and her soul stylings.

But, more than anything, I loved her sense of retro style. The 5-inch beehive, the sailor tattoos, the upswept "genie" eyeliner, the "girl group" dresses, the pink ballerina slippers—all were golden to me.

For some reason, people fixate on the beehive and somehow think it emerged in the late '50s and '60s from the ether. On the other side of the coin, some think the style emerged from female members of Pentecostal Christian churches. The women do not cut their hair and consequently they have some serious "big hair."

In reality, there's an antecedent to the beehive: think of Marie Antoinette. Her hair styles—the massive "pouf" creations—were often three feet tall![1]

I think they tended to be a bit foul, though. Contemporary reports mention that elaborate "poufs" often required pomade made of beef tallow or horse fat to keep them in place. The smell of rancid fat tended to attract rodents (and repel humans), so to combat the smell and the rodents, the hairpieces were highly powdered and scented with perfume. Wow! That must have been an amazing spectacle. I just wonder how heavy the creations were!

But anyway, I digress! Let's look at your goals and interests.

I am in total agreement with your business idea! What an exciting idea; create unique new designs from the used and vintage clothing that comes in, and to build a business.

Here are some of the elements I'd recommend in order to maximize your reach:

1. **Take online courses in fashion design, computer graphics, fashion merchandising.**

    You can take these for-credit or not for credit. The Fashion Institute of New York (part of the State University of New York system) has a very highly rated series of courses in design and graphics, as well as an online degree program.

---

[1] en.wikipedia.org/wiki/Pouf

2. **Get involved in virtual worlds and design cool outfits for avatars. I'd recommend Second Life.**

   There are many different fashion worlds, and it's a perfect place to perfect your craft. You can even build outfits and create objects (called "prims") that you can sell for Linden dollars (which convert to real currency).

   - Fashion Institute – College for Fashion Modeling, Design and Arts
     - ▶ pixelook.ning.com/group/fashioninstitutecollegefor fashionmodelingdesignand
   - UK – Couture Island – Main Store –
     Fashion Clothes Skins Boots
     - ▶ world.secondlife.com/place/653fd2ab-bb5a-ea51-96ce-1a5e3364e4eb
   - Fashion Boulevard
     - ▶ secondlife.com/destination/boulevard-fashion

3. **Take courses in small business design and promotion using social networking.**

   Did you happen to hear the A New Dress A Day blog (newdressaday.wordpress.com)? A blogger named Marisa decided to forego traditional shopping and develop a new outfit each day of the year, but to spend no more than $1 for each item (excluding notions, etc. for updating the outfit). She chronicled her progress in her blog. I have to say that many of the outfits were simply good finds at the thrift store. She did not do much beyond putting them on. Other items were shortened, dyed, cut, and shaped using her significant seamstress skills. You could follow the Marisa model but take it even further. Be bold! Create wild fashions based on your thrift store / garage sale finds. If you develop enough buzz, you may be able to develop a nice following and even a retail outlet for your creations.

4. **Take Art History and Fashion History courses online.**
   Many colleges and universities offer online courses, and you can supplement what you're studying by visiting museum sites. In fact, many museum sites offer not-for-credit online courses. Check out the Virtual Shoe Museum (www.virtualshoemuseum .com)—you'll be amazed (and inspired).

Can Your Cellphone Read Your Mind?

If my cellphone could my mind, the first thing it might do would be to sell my thoughts to Amazon. Would it post them on Facebook or on my blog?

I guess we can easily argue that our smartphones already read our minds—at least as our thoughts manifest through actions on the web. Searches, posts on social networks, surfing, registrations, emails, online purchases—we already know that everything is captured and data-mined.

So, we get the "long tail" marketing approach pushed on us: "If you like that, you'll like this!"

Further, when we log into Facebook, Gmail, or Google, we get a customized experience based on our browsing and clicking histories. We get links to locations that we're likely to enjoy, and to follow. Granted, the approach of playing us via our recent searches seems to be a sure bet to get people to click on links.

And we think that we're keeping open and the entire world will flow to us since we're online.

Nothing could be further from the truth.

If anything, our vista is circumscribed by our "click histories" and our search histories. We are consigned to a world of what seems to be narrowing choices (but we're not aware that our perspective has been mapped and controlled).

Our existing interests (along with our prejudices, knowledge, and choices)

are reinforced. Our worldview is made narrower and narrower.

I thought the Internet was supposed to expand our lives.

The bottom line is that in order to keep our worldview open, we need to do searches on random, worldview-expanding topics. Otherwise, all we'll see in our experience is a pathetically self-reinforcing repetition (that we don't even recognize as a repetition or a replication of we already do and/or are).

But, let's say that we manage to introduce randomness into our searches, and we use multiple search engines, and we vary our topics. We may conquer the over-determinacy of the commercial content of the websites we visit.

However, there's another possibility as Web 3.0 times accelerate as they approach us.

Web 3.0 goes beyond the relational databases of Web 2.0 and the social networking and integrated apps (mashups). It proposes to record and store your every move (like the iPhone of today), but with more capabilities. In theory, our devices will record every electronic event around us, including credit card transactions (if we continue to use them, instead of a barcode display from our smartphones.

Good, bad, weird information overload?

The unintended consequences are yet to be explored/unearthed. I personally feel a bit uncomfortable with the idea that a device that I can so easily misplace can be used/abused/hijacked. The possibilities of mischief are almost endless. It's a shame that security always seems to be one step behind the capabilities of the devices.

That said, there is no need to fear the reaper. We're approaching the end of the days, every day. And, at the same time, we witness the birth of the new every day, on a daily basis.

Ethics and the Online Learner

If you're taking online courses that deal with health, business, or the environment, it is very likely that you have had to work with questions of ethics. We live in a world of mixed messages, where everyone loves to judge from afar (or through the Internet), but no one likes to see the ethical quagmire enter into their own backyard. In your courses, the quagmire will enter your life as you're asked to consider ethical dilemmas and either write about them or discuss them with fellow students.

How do you become an ethical person? Can you legislate ethical behavior? If the punishments are severe, will that be enough to keep people behaving ethically?

According to Aristotle, in his classic work, *Nicomachean Ethics*, written in the fourth century B.C. in Greece, it is futile to try to coerce people into high moral, ethical, and virtuous behavior through threat of punishment. Instead, one has to take an approach that relies heavily on teaching and practice.

> Virtue or excellence being twofold, partly intellectual and partly moral, intellectual virtue is both originated and fostered mainly by teaching; it therefore demands experience and time. Moral virtue on the other hand is the outcome of habit.

If you'd like to study ethics, here are 10 online courses to get you started:

» Ethics in Management
» Environmental Issues and Ethics
» Ethics: Health Care and Social Responsibility
» Current Issues in Health Law and Ethics

» Ethics in Criminal Justice
» Organizational Ethics
» Ethics In Education
» Legal & Ethical Issues in School Counseling
» Ethics and Technology in Education
» Bioethics

Thus, Aristotle breaks down ethics or virtue ethics into two parts:

- **Intellectual virtue:** learned through teaching
- **Moral virtue:** learned through doing

So, for Aristotle, the first step involves purposefully teaching people what constitutes ethical behavior and ethical decision-making. The second step is to practice virtue and ethical behavior.

There are numerous approaches used in determining how to conduct oneself in the world, and it is not the purpose of this article to go into all the theories of ethics. Instead, the focus is on Aristotle and the point that he made that one must actively engage in learning and teaching ethics, which must be followed up with practice.

In an online course, the way to approach the problem is to:

Step 1: Identify the ethical dilemma.
Step 2: List the fundamental ethical concerns.
Step 3: List possible ethical approaches.
Step 4: Recommend courses of action.
Step 5: Follow the courses of action; analyze case studies or engage in a field study.

Perhaps one of Aristotle's most enduring contributions to Western thought is the notion of balance. For him, the ideal path of thought and behavior did not lie in exploring extremes (he would leave that to the devotees of pagan cults attached to devotion to Eros and Dionysus, which later emerged as medieval mysticism, courtly love lyrics of the Provencal poets, Romanticism, and more).

For Aristotle, wisdom in governance, economics, behavior, and art (including literature), lay in finding balance—the mid-point, or mean between extremes. Instead, Aristotle focused on finding perfect and harmonious balance and developing a sensibility in the viewer that would appreciate it. His ideas were echoed by the Roman writer Horace, and then revitalized in European NeoClassicism by the French poet Nicolas Boileau and the English Restoration dramatist and poet, John Dryden.

As Aristotle expressed it in *Nicomachean Ethics*:

> Virtue is a state of deliberate moral purpose consisting in a mean that is relative to ourselves; the mean being determined by reason, or as a prudent person would determine it.

• • •

> In regard to feelings of fear and confidence, *courage* is a mean state. On the side of excess, he whose fearlessness is excessive has no name, as often happens, but he whose confidence is excessive is foolhardy, while he whose timidity is excessive and whose confidence is deficient is a coward.

When engaging in an analysis of ethical dilemmas, Aristotle's ideas seem very prudent. While it is very tempting to go into extremes and to take a stand, especially as it relates to sensitive debates on topics such as animal protection, medical experimentation, the treatment of prisoners, it is good to slow the process down. Do not rush to judgment. Listen, and frame your analysis in terms of a map in which you identify positions and place them somewhere in a continuum of possibilities. Then, as you gain a better understanding of all the sides of the issue, start placing each position, stance, or ethical recommendation within the continuum.

While your analysis may not change your ultimate assessment of the ethical situation, you will, at the very least, be more able to describe and discuss the positions along the spectrum. In the end, your papers and projects will be more informed and balanced, and your arguments will be more cogent and reasoned.

BIBLIOGRAPHY

Aristotle. (350 BCE). *Nicomachean Ethics*
▶ classics.mit.edu/Aristotle/nicomachaen.html

Fitness and Cognitive Functions:
Brain-Body Connections in E-Learning

I work full time and am taking online courses. I used to like to go to spin classes at my health club, and I was on a tennis league. I don't have time any more, and I feel tired all the time.

On top of that, I feel mentally very dull, and I'm wondering if I should just give up on school. Maybe I'm too old to learn. Maybe I missed the window of cognitive opportunity when I was younger. I don't know.

All I know is that I felt better when I was active.

Sincerely,
Arggh! from Ardmore

****

Dear Arggh,

We've all heard the old adage, the more energy you expend, the more you'll have. We're also familiar with the idea that you have to exercise your body if you want to exercise your mind.

Now we have even more facts to back up the notion that you really do need to make time for fitness if you want optimal cognitive performance. It's not just about the oxygen going to your brain. Certainly, breathing hard and getting fresh, oxygenated blood to your brain are great. There's a lot more going on, though. Human cognitive function is increased when aerobic activity results in changes in cellular and molecular mechanisms.

- When rats exercise on a running wheel, they experience measurable increases in capillary density in the cerebellum. (Black, Isaacs, Alcantara, and Greenough—1990)
- When old rats run on the wheel, they exhibit higher dopamine receptor density, and also have enhanced cortical high-affinity choline uptake. (Fordyce & Farrar—1991)
- Mice have a higher number of new cells in the hippocampus. (van Praag, Kempermann, & Gage—1999)

One of the most exciting results is that it's not just about kids getting recess while in grade school, although clearly that is important.

We can draw the conclusion that older human brains are like old rat brains. Running on an exercise wheel results in measurable improvements in the brain. If you cringe at the thought of running on a treadmill, think about engaging in an exercise that pushes you, and which you love.

So, Arrgh, here are a few thoughts. Get back on the tennis court. You don't have to get as involved as before—it's not necessary to play matches in a league. However, there's always hitting and running on the court with a friend, and, don't forget the ball machine, and hitting against a wall.

There was something in your letter, Arrgh, that caught my eye. You mentioned wondering if you're too old to learn.

Obviously, no one is "too old" to learn. However, if you don't exercise, you're running the risk of losing mental agility as you age. Here are a few research finding to keep in mind:

- Visuospatial tasks are positively impacted by exercise. The reason for that is because visuospatial processes are more susceptible to aging than verbal skills. (Shay & Roth—1992; Stones & Kosma—1989)
- Improvements in fitness are reflected in enhancements in executive-control processes such as coordination, inhibition, scheduling, planning, and working memory. (Shallice — 1994)
- Executive-control processes and the brain areas that support them are very sensitive to aging. (West—1996)

What is the best way to exercise if you need to optimize the benefits for your cognitive functioning? Colcombe & Kramer (2003) found that the

 greatest benefits were for individuals who exercised from 31 - 45 minutes at a time, who combined strength and cardiovascular training, and who stuck with their training program for six months or longer. Their performance on spatial, cognitive, and executive-control tasks was significantly higher than the control group. In fact, in some cases, it was more than 5 times as high (for women between 66 and 70 years of age).

The bottom line is that you need to make time to exercise, and you need to do it in a way that you enjoy, so that you can put in at least 30 to 45 minutes of cardio and strength training. Make it fun for yourself, and challenge yourself.

You'll benefit right away from fitness. We've talked about how your brain functions will improve, but we have not even touched on the benefits of stress relief and overall well-being. Don't forget you're also providing a great role model to your friends and family.

BIBLIOGRAPHY

Black, J. E., Isaacs, K. R., Anderson, B. J., Alcantara, A. A., and Greenough, W. T. (1990). "Learning causes synaptogenesis, whereas motor activity causes angiogenesis in cerebellar cortex of adult rats." *Proceedings of the National Academy of Sciences*. USA. 87. 5568-5572.

Colcombe, S. and Kramer, A. (2003). "Fitness Effects on the Cognitive Function of Older Adults: A Meta-Analytic Study." *Psychological Science*. (14) 2: 125-130.

Fordyce, D. E. & Farrar, R. P. (1991). "Physical activity effects on hipposampal and parietal cholinergic function and spatial learning in F344 rats." *Behavioral Brain Research*, 43, 115-123.

Shallice, T. (1994). "Multiple levels of control processes." In C. Umilta & M. Moscovitch (Eds), *Attention and performance XC* (pp. 395-420). Cambridge, MA: MIT Press.

Shay, K., & Roth, D. (1992). "Association between aerobic fitness and visuospatial performance in healthy older adults." *Psychology and Aging*, 1, 15-24.

Stones, M., & Kozma, A. (1989). "Age, exercise, and coding performance." *Psychology and Aging*, 4, 190-194.

van Praag, H., Kempermann, G., and Gage, F. H. (1999). "Running increases cell proliferation and neurogenesis in the adult mouse dentate gyrus." *Nature Neuroscience*. 2. 266-270.

Giambattista Vico and the E-Learner

Several classes this semester have required me to read works by Vico. They are from a book called New Science. *Are you familiar with him? Why are so many of my on-line courses asking me to read essays by him?*

Vexed by Vico

****

Dear Vexed,

Because it's in the public domain and is free. Do you ever wonder why almost every anthology has "Young Goodman Brown" and "A Cask of Amontillado"? Their authors died long ago, and no one holds the copyright.

Likewise, Giambattista Vico died long ago. He was a Professor of Rhetoric in Naples, Italy, who died in 1744, just around the time the definitive version of his book, *New Science* was published. Stanford's *Encyclopedia of Philosophy* has an excellent entry for Vico and his work: plato.stanford.edu/entries/vico

Despite the fact Vico died more than 250 years ago, Vico's ideas seem fresher and more relevant than ever. Whenever there are large changes in our world, our societies, the global order, or technology, Vico's ideas about knowledge, history, and meaning-making seem more vital and alive than ever.

Learning Should Be Interdisciplinary

Believes that the best way to know something is to approach it in an interdisciplinary way. To look at things through a single discipline or approach leads to a kind of blindness.

History Is Cyclical

Once you start looking at things in an interdisciplinary way, you can perceive patterns that were never detectible before. Using that approach, Vico proposed that history is cyclical, and that the reason for it was a complex set of causes and contributing factors.

The idea that the unfolding of the history of man takes a certain pattern was nothing new. Ancient Greek and Roman thinkers held that there was once a "golden age" and everything went into decline after that. Jewish and Christian thinkers often looked at history as apocalyptic; which is to say that it was more or less inevitable that man's evil nature would eventually overtake human endeavor, resulting in alienation from all protection, and the ultimate destruction of an essentially thoroughly corrupt universe.

However, Vico believed that the problem with the Ancient Greek and Roman view was that it overlooked specific causes and effects, and so was not very useful for fine-tuned prediction or analysis. For Vico, the key was to look for look for origins, seek causal relationships. Phenomena can be known only through their origins and through causes ("per caussas"), he stated in *New Science*.

For the student of history and humanity, one must build analytical skills and be able to look at the contributing political events, economic pressures, wars, weather, natural disasters, prevailing religious and cultural beliefs, and the structure of society. Only after a careful interdisciplinary analysis can one start to create a complex, yet very useful, model.

But, how does one determine whether or not the theoretical model has any usefulness or credibility? According to Vico, reality and truth should be coherent. They should fit well together. If something does not have a solid base, and can't be supported by multiple viable explanations, then it's probably weak.

Interdisciplinary Analysis Leads to New Knowledge

Vico wrote that when one engages in a complex interdisciplinary analysis, the results are new knowledge. Does the person make the knowledge, or is it a part of the analysis?

For Vico, both are important. It is important for individuals to collaborate and interact with each other and with what has gone on in the past.

How We Make Meaning from Chaos

We set down the rules for making meaning in the areas of philosophy and language.

Philosophy aims at articulating the universal forms of intelligibility common to all experience. How can we tell what is valuable? Vico says it is important to look for the universally true.

Language: a storehouse of customs, a "mental dictionary" used by past, present, and future generations. There are multiple truths embedded in language; cultural, philosophical, existential—we can learn a great deal by reading each other's words very closely.

Vico investigates metaphor and the origins of language. Metaphors have embedded causal chains—once you grasp the connection between the image and the meaning(s), you've embarked on a journey of meaning—what are they to us?

Language articulates the agreed-upon rules of the communication, by which philosophy is made possible. Language, according to Vico, consists of judgment without inner reflection.

For e-learners, the quest for the best way for organizing an overwhelming amount of information is something we can do by creating a mental architecture for it, and developing a strategy for creating categories where we can file away information.

History Holds the Key to Understanding Ourselves and the World

History represents and illustrates the ideal and the eternal. Nations evolve—there is something to be learned in looking at how they approximate the ideal, and how their movements, trajectories are part of the eternal, the timeless, the inescapable

Vico discusses the stages of social, civil, and political order. We can learn from his analysis.

History is inescapable. Language is inescapable. And both are more or less unknowable, or, better said, ineffable and inexpressible.

What does the e-learner do with all this?

Recognize there is power in the individual quest—and also in the collective voice/investigation.

E-learning / mobile learning can tap into two distinct features of human nature: imagination and reflection.

Great Portfolio/Memoir Projects
Using Folktales, Folk Art, Cultural History,
Your Family, Your Life

I'm taking a humanities course and we have to do a portfolio project. We're supposed to explore culture and our own lives. I'm stuck, and I'm not sure what to do.

Sincerely,
Perplexed by the Portfolio

****

Dear Perplexed,

I'm delighted that you're asking this question.

Portfolios are a great way to showcase your research skills as well as your media-generation creativity. You can upload graphics that you've created, and you can share articles and digital objects you've found. On top of that, you're able to combine creative writing, memoirs, and autobiography to create something truly meaningful and unique that helps you understand how your life and times shape who you are today and who you'll be tomorrow.

Please consider focusing your portfolio on folklore and folk art. Why? There's really nothing like folk art or folk tales to provide insight into the beliefs, values, and mores of communities, families, and individuals.

Folklore, combined with folk art and memoirs can provide insight into the socialization process, and how one creates an identity based/formed on shared experiences. Here's a simple series of steps to get started:

1. Recall stories that were told to you as a child and do a bit of research to find the origins, and also similar stories.
2. Conduct online research to find art, crafts, and popular culture items that tie in with your memories of when the stories were told.
3. Detail key historical/cultural events going on at the time.
4. Discuss your family configuration and momentous events going on at the time.
5. Tell your own story about how the convergence of the folktales, the art and crafts around you, and the historical/family context shaped you.

Here are a few good resources for starting your investigation of folk tales and folk art. For information about historical events, check out the U.S. Library of Congress, and also history databases.

*   **American Folklife Center**
    ▶ www.loc.gov/folklife

    Ethnographic Resources related to Folklore, Anthropology, Ethnomusicology, and the Humanities.

*   **Abby Aldrich Rockefeller Folk Art Museum**
    ▶ www.colonialwilliamsburg.com/History/museums/abby_art.cfm

    A resource for bios, essays, and articles on the the people and places of 18th-century Virginia.

*   **Acadian Archives/Archives Acadiennes**
    ▶ www.umfk.maine.edu/archives

    The Acadian Archives documents, preserves, celebrates, and disseminates information about the Upper St. John Valley, a 70-mile stretch of the St. John River running between the U.S. and Canada.

    Archives focuses particular attention on the Acadian & Franco-American history & culture.

*   **The African and Middle Eastern Division (AMED) of the Library of Congress**
    ▶ www.loc.gov/rr/amed

The AMED includes African, Hebraic, and Near East resources, which cover 77 countries and regions from Southern Africa to the Maghreb and from the Middle East to Central Asia.

- **The American Folk Art Museum**
  ▶ www.folkartmuseum.org

  American folk art provides cultural clues into the life, times, and beliefs of communities and individuals in America. The collections cover art, crafts, furniture, and other types of creative expression, often from "outsiders" and other self-taught artists and artisans.

- **American Folk Life Center**
  ▶ www.loc.gov/folklife/archive.html

  The collections of the American Folklife Center online presentations from AFC concerts, lectures, and symposia, photographs, sound recordings,e-books on egg art, memoirs and diaries of veterans,article on Halloween, community roots, and more.

  American memory online collection includes: Buckaroos in Paradise, After the Day of Infamy, California Gold, Life on the Ohio and Erie Canal, Florida Folklife from the WPA Collections, Hispano Music, and more.

  The John and Ruby Lomax 1939 Southern States Recording Trip is a multiformat ethnographic field collection that includes nearly 700 sound recordings, as well as fieldnotes, dust jackets, and other manuscripts documenting a three-month, 6,502-mile trip through the southern United States.

- **World Folklore and Mythological Creatures**

  » **Folklore and Mythology Electronic Texts**
    ▶ www.pitt.edu/~dash/folktexts.html

    Extensive repository of texts from around the world. Many are very humorous.

  » **Storytelling at Ibiblio**
    ▶ www.ibiblio.org

- **For Fun**

  » **Quizlet Flashcards**
    ▸ quizlet.com/1036714/mytholo-
      gical-creatures-65-flash-cards

Mythological Creatures 6.5 – collection of 111 creatures. Unfortunately, they do not have images.

Knowing Your Memory:
A Key Tool to Success in Online Learning

As you work on your courses, you might find it useful to know more about memory, memory functions, and how they can help you in your online courses.

Long-Term Memory

Long-term memories are the events and information that you remember from the past. The past can be the distant past and the recent past. Within the long-term memory, you'll have stronger and weaker memories. Keep in mind that the stronger memories that you have can help you recall weaker memories, which you can access through prompting or reminding.

Long-term memory is always evolving and changing. It is not something that stays static. Instead, it is fluid and dynamic. It is constantly changing, and one set of memories may merge and intermingle with others. As a result, memory is not always completely reliable.

There are several different forms of long-term memory, and all are useful in storing, managing and retrieving information. Long-term memory systems are complex, and they function in different ways. It is useful to realize that there are separate memory systems for different types of information. For example, language is stored in a different part of the memory than life experiences. Procedures and processes are stored in yet another memory system.

Let's take a look at the different long-term memory systems:

- *Explicit Memory*

  Often called "declarative memory," this is a type of long-term memory that requires you to consciously exercise your memory.

Semantic memory is a part of explicit memory which encompasses general knowledge and "textbook learning." It is largely comprised of schema—systems of organizing facts—and they effective in creating classification systems for easy storage and retrieval.

- *Implicit Memory*

    This is an automatic sort of memory which allows you do to things automatically, by rote. Implicit memory is often called "muscle memory" and it involves executing tasks in a certain sequence. Examples include tying a shoe, walking, pitching a baseball, and more. Sometimes, one can lose explicit memory, but can still retain the implicit memories. This can often occur after traumatic brain injury—someone may lose short-term memory and autobiographical memory, but can still drive a car.

    Implicit memory can be reinforced with "priming." Priming occurs through recall of experience or by having heard something recently that triggers memories.

- *Autobiographical Memory*

    This is the memory system used for recalling your life events and experiences. It ties together with episodic memory, visual and semantic memory. Episodic memory helps you remember events that happen to you, and to organize them. It is useful to know that emotionally charged memories are often much more easily remembered than others.

Short-Term Memory

- *Working memory*

    This refers to the brain functions used in managing and manipulating short-term memory. The working memory keeps information in the short-term memory just long enough to use it.

- *Regular Short-term memory*

    This takes place in a rapid space of time. The time that something stays in short-term memory shortens as one ages. The effectiveness of short-term memory can be improved by using different activities that stimulate short-term memory.

Media, Television-Viewing, and Video Games in E-Learning

I know that people have talked about how bad media and video games can be for people who tend to have attention-deficit disorders.

But can video games and media be good for people with attention deficit hyperactivity disorders? It is very confusing to me.

I'm asking not just for my daughter, who has been diagnosed with ADHD, but also for myself. I have struggled with adult ADHD for years. It has blocked me in the past, but now, I am extremely motivated to get my degree.

What do you recommend?

Yours truly,
Mother-Daughter ADHD

****

Dear Mother-Daughter,

Your decision to earn a degree, despite problems in the past due to ADHD, is fantastic. You probably already know this, but for the adult learner with ADHD, e-learning is a great way to go. With online courses, you can avoid many of the distractions that make traditional classrooms so difficult for the learner with ADHD.

I don't know if you remember all the discussions about whether or not television-viewing was bad for school achievement. The argument went something like this: television-viewing is bad because not only does it distract learners, it accustoms them to expect constant stimulation and entertainment. When they have to do something boring—like study for school—they can't. They crave overstimulation.

Some people in the "television-is-bad-for-learning" camp took it even further, and pointed out that television-viewing is passive, and does not encourage interaction. In fact, it may encourage some to retreat to their own private world of fantasy and perfection.

Not surprisingly, we've heard variations of the same arguments when it comes to media, video games, and even serious games and simulations.

Here is what researchers have found, which should give you a great deal of encouragement. Keep in mind that literally thousands of articles have been written, as well as opinion pieces. Very few have conducted the kinds of research needed. The points below are supported by respected research investigations.

1. Television-viewing can be positive when it provides cognitively-enriching experiences, and when the viewers have limited proficiency in English. (Comstock and Paik, 1991)

2. Electronic media can provide effective learning conditions for a wider variety of learning preferences, and can be ideal for auditory learners as well as visual learners. (Kozma, 1991)

3. Video games may improve spatial reasoning skills, particularly when the objects are three-dimensional and are rotated and manipulated. (McClurg and Chaille, 1987)

4. Playing video games can enhance focus, and help improve attention skills, particularly when they have to do with prioritizing and taking note of specific elements. (Green & Bavelier, 2003)

5. Video games may provide the optimal learning conditions with ADHD because they offer immediate feedback and rewards, as well as increasing attention and arousal. Video games are, in this case, even mood enhancing. (Koepp, 1998)

6. Fantasy and imaginary worlds can be motivating when the fantasy can be tied to the content, and the experience stimulates the learner's interest. (Cordova and Lepper, 1996)

7. Games provide motivation for ADHD learners by providing

quickly-achievable goals (Blumberg, 1998).

8. Video games and game-based training can be motivating because the level of challenge can be adjusted to the level of the individual learner. (Schmidt and Vandewater, 2008)

I just read an article that talked about how media, when incorporated in e-learning, actually helps develop and focus attention.

In fact, the study was so positive about how videos, audio, interactive games, and simulations can help people focus, that they were suggesting trying it as a remedy for the problems of learning for kids with attention deficit disorder.

BIBLIOGRAPHY

Blumberg, F. C. (1998). "Developmental Differences at Play: Children's Selective Attention and Performance in Video Games," *Journal of Applied Developmental Psychology*. 19 (1998): 615-24.

Comstock, G. A., and Paik, H. J. (1991). *Television and the American Child*.

Cordova, D. I., and Lepper, M. R. (1996). "Intrinsic Motivation and the Process of Learning: Beneficial Effects of Contextualization, Personalization, and Choice," *Journal of Educational Psychology*. 88 (1996): 715-730.

Green, C. S., and Bavelier, D. (2003). "Playing Video Games Enhances Visual Attention in Children [Abstract]," *Journal of Vision*. 4 (2004): 40A.

Koepp, M. J. (1998). "Evidence for Striatal Dopamine Release during a Video Game," *Nature*. 393 (1998): 266-68.

Kozma, R. B. (1991). "Learning with Media," *Review of Educational Research*. 61 (1991): 179-211.

McClurg, P. A., and Chaille, C. (1987). "Computer Games: Environments for Developing Spatial Cognition," *Journal of Educational Computing Research*. 3 (1987): 95-111.

Schmidt, M. E., and Vandewater, E. (2008). "Media and Attention, Cognition, and School Achievement." *The Future of Children*. 88 (1): 63-85.

Millennials Want Communities:
How Does this Translate to an Online Course?

You've probably read reports about how different generations use the Internet in different ways. Baby Boomers and Gen-Xers tend to use the Internet for direct communication and research. When they take online courses, they often take a very functional approach.

For Millennials, the generation born in the 1980s and after, the Internet is an extension of their own lives and behaviors. They tend to use it to build community, to create a place for themselves within a community.

The Foundation: The Discussion Board

Discussions serve to share impressions and to establish a sense of self. In contrast with other generations, who may use the discussion board to satisfy grade requirements, the millennials take a slightly different approach. They use it as a way to determine the best way to succeed in the course, and they look at it as their first "go-to" place.

They prefer the open forum, and would use it long before they will dig through the FAQ site, or email the instructor.

Learning Communities

Learning communities mean different things to different people. The generational difference between e-learners becomes very clear as people participate in activities that foster the development of learning communities. The activities that foster learning communities range from discussion forums to wikis.

For Boomers, the "learning community" tends to be a group where people have very clearly defined roles. They are most comfortable when hierarchies are clear, and people are treated according to their rank or station. What this means in functional terms is that the students will expect the professor to take a leadership role and to be a repository of knowledge and information. They will expect the professor to not only be a guide, but also a mentor. In addition, students are expected to share information, but they are not accorded any particular authority.

For Gen-Xers, who are naturally skeptical about authority, and who believe it's important for their education to prepare them to be street-smart free-agent entrepreneurs, the discussion board is a place to learn practical, results-focused knowledge. For them, it's the "go-to" place for inside information and tactics—getting more street-smart at every turn.

For Millennials, learning communities are places where students share information, but in a way that accommodates "anytime/anywhere" access. You might think that millennials are freethinkers, but this is not exactly true. The learning community is a place where students learn how to be team players and how to do well in high-stakes standardized tests. Thus, students tend to have a different mindset—they are pragmatic and yet like to feel they are a part of a group. They want to make a personal statement and to express individuality, even as they demonstrate their adherence to the communal ethos.

People learn from each other, and the learning community is an extended socialization process, reminiscent of the scenarios and group learning dynamics described by Vygotsky.

Millennials Will Lose Interest When Communities are Lacking

In every group, there are always self-starters and those who learn best through independent, self-guided study. They are usually the ones who have a very clear outcome in mind, or who are intrinsically motivated due to inherent interests and/or life experiences.

For Millennials, an online course is a place to create a functional community—one that does exactly what they'd like it to do in order to achieve their learning goals, as well as to satisfy needs for affiliation.

Neuroplasticity and the Adult Learner

My mother is 78 years old and wants to achieve her dream of earning her master's degree in Comparative Religion. She's worried that she's too old.

"Saravette, my brain just can't jump through the hoops it used to" is what she tells me quite often.

I've tried to tell her that they're finding that the brain can do all kinds of things. After all, look at stroke victims. They relearn all kinds of things. If our brains can recover from strokes, they can do other things, too, right?

I'm very interested in your views.

Sincerely,
Saravette in Sioux City

****

Dear Saravette,

One of the best things your mom can do for her brain is to embark on an educational journey, particularly one that involves a goal that she is passionate about, and daily engagement with content that interests her on a deep level.

She'll be getting daily brain stimulation, which is part of the process of recovery from stroke. It's also a critical part of keeping the neural pathways working in optimal form. But let's back up a step. What's so wonderful about daily brain stimulation?

One of the most exciting developments in research on the brain is a deep understanding of just how and why the brain exhibits neuroplasticity. Neuroplasticity means that the brain is malleable, adjustable, and "morph"-able—in more ways than we ever imagined. The brain's neuroplasticity is a characteristic related to its overall adaptability. Elements that researchers are now studying relate to how certain proteins and membranes establish networks within neural cells and to regulate neural stem cell survival, self-renewal, and differentiation.

What is neuroplasticity? Here is a more in-depth definition:
▶ www.medterms.com/script/main/art.asp?articlekey=40362

Plasticity Happens Wherever Neuroprocessing Occurs

One of the building blocks of neuroplasticity is an integral membrane protein known as "notch." Notch is extremely important because it signals the brain in ways that influence structural and functional plasticity, including processes involved in learning and memory. (Lathia, Mattson, and Cheng, 2008)

Studies of animal models are giving hope that substances and therapies that influence the function of notch can be effective in several disorders including Alzheimer's.

One of the ways that the brain repairs itself is by creating new pathways. These new pathways can be associated with all parts of the brain, which include cognitive as well as motor skills, language, and regulatory parts of the brain. New pathways are being developed all the time.

Learning changes your brain. Be careful what you learn!
▶ www.sharpbrains.com/blog/2008/02/26/brain-plasticity-how-learning-changes-your-brain/

Dementia slideshow:
▶ www.medicinenet.com/dementia_pictures_slideshow/article.htm

Bipolar slideshow:

▸ www.medicinenet.com/bipolar_disorder_overview_pictures_slideshow/article.htm

The implications make one sit back and think. Yes, we know the brain morphs and changes—but how? One way is through "axonal sprouting," in which undamaged axons grow new nerve endings to reconnect neurons whose links were injured. Does this mean we need to injure ourselves in order to rebuild? In cognitive terms, how do we "injure" old cognitive pathways? One way could be to erase the old pathways. Starve them out. Or, more importantly, replace them with something else.

This is not as outré as it sounds. It's actually scientific support for the familiar "rewriting your scripts" or "rephrasing." It's also scientific support for the efficacy of meditation. Have you been avoiding meditation? No more excuses—just do it! Mindfulness/meditation is worthwhile for the adult learner.[1]

In the meantime, share what you've learned today with your mom. Then, think about your own life and education goals. What can your new knowledge of the brain do for you? With what we're learning every day, truly the only limit to your growth is the limit you place on yourself.

REFERENCES

Lathia, J. D., Mattson, M.P., and Cheng, A. (2008). "Notch: From Neural Development to Neurological Disorders," *Journal of Neurochemistry.* (107): 1471-1481.

---

[1] www.sharpbrains.com/blog/2008/01/29/mindfulness-and-meditation-in-schools-for-stress-and-anxiety-management/

Review of *Drive* (dir. Nicholas Refn, 2011):
OpenPlan Film Criticism
Collaboration Sample/Tool

Co-written with Seth Lynch

• • •

podcast / downloadable mp3:
www.beyondutopia.net/podcasts/drive.mp3

E-Learning Queen is delighted to offer an OpenPlan Film Criticism Collaboration Paper example and template/tool. This OpenPlan offering is designed to help overcome some of the problems that accompany online collaborations. For example, lack of motivation and confusion with course procedures can cause online collaborations to fall flat. However, with wikis and other documents sharing programs (Google Docs, for example), collaborations can be the highlight of an online course.

The key to successful collaborations is having a good instructional strategy that includes a topic that is intrinsically motivating. One of the most engaging collaborations can be to develop movie review teams, and to create reviews. The structure can be very flexible, ranging from a back-and-forth point-counterpoint approach (or a thumbs-up, thumbs-down exchange), to the production of a seamless document that successfully melds together the two voices to create a satisfying, engaging read.

There may be some utility in maintaining a bit of the rawness in the process. In E-Learning Queen's OpenPlan Film Criticism Collaboration Paper in the example below, some of the data is presented at the end as a kind of mini-appendix.

NASH & LYNCH REVIEWS

Drive (dir Nicholas Refn, 2011)
by Susan Smith Nash and Seth Lynch

Drive (dir. Nicholas Winding Refn, 2011) features a gorgeous noir city with sharp-edged skyscrapers and pinpoints of light above the labyrinth of roads that constitute Los Angeles. The opening voiceover refers to the seeming infinity of interweaving streets, the labyrinth of physicality and solitude, which wind and converge. One might think that the taciturn Driver is the hero of the film, but it's much more complicated than that. Like so many self-reflexive films, *Drive* contains interpenetrating references and allusions to elements in the popular consciousness: the first that come to mind are video games (*Grand Theft Auto, Midnight Club*), cartoons (*Speed Racer*), classic car chase sequences (*Bullit, The French Connection*), and the cars themselves—gleaming, fast, classic ('73 Chevy Malibu).

One of the elements of *Drive* is extreme, almost surreal precision. The Driver (or "Kid") meticulously plans his heist getaways. For example, in the opening scene's basketball game getaway has been planned to the second. The film begins with him in a hotel room with the game on the television. After the opening getaway scene, nowhere else in the movie does it show him watching or listening to sports. While in his deliberately anonymous Impala, he simply listens to the game for the timing, knowing the exact moment to lose the cops in the arena's parking lot. He dons a team hat, but he doesn't wear it again. He has no interest in the game other than using it as a getaway. His sole focus and purpose is driving and when Irene asks him what he does for a living, he responds, "Drive." Of course, he follows this by saying he is also mechanic, but only after Irene asks if he drives for the movies.

Precision shows up in other aspects of the film as well: the Driver carefully works on an intake manifold and gangster Bernie Rose (Albert Brooks) slices the veins in the hapless Shannon's arm with surgical finesse so that it bleeds out quickly and "painlessly."

Like the Damascus knives that Bernie Rose collects, precise engineering can either mean the ultimate heist getaway—allowing mere mortals to transcend the limits of our corporeal existence, both in the bodies that bind us, and the laws—or the ultimate meting out of carbon-steel justice. You transgress, you pay.

One might think the gangsters in the film are uniformly clocklike in their precision, as is the Driver. They are not. In fact, the gangsters are refreshing in that they are not filled with hubris and do not have ostentatious lifestyles. Instead, they are fearful and essentially greedy. Their violence is messy but mercifully quick.

The Driver enables gangsters to do what they do, but he is not gangster. Instead, he is a layered, complex, paradoxical presence. The Driver possesses attributes that blur the line between hero and anti-hero. Once he decides to act (violence, expert maneuvers), he doesn't hesitate. He is very controlled under normal circumstances, but has difficulty restraining himself from bashing a mobster's head in with a hammer, and his inner struggle is evident in the fact he is sweating profusely. The audience may notice that the strippers in the dressing room who witness the violence are not shocked, but are still in a kind of frozen tableau that also gives the impression of a scene from a comic book, cartoon, or video game.

The Driver knows he is flawed, and with that self-knowledge, he can detect the flaws of others: when Bernie extends his hand, he is left hanging for a while, then the Driver says his hand is a little dirty. Bernie says his hand is dirty, too. This scene parallels the scene when Bernie reaches out to shake Shannon's hand only to slash the veins in his forearm. Judging character seems to be something one possesses as an instinct. When watching TV, the Driver asks Benicio how he knows a character is a bad guy and Benicio says he just knows.

The overall mise-en-scene reinforces the experience of being the driver and feeling the car, the streets, the omnipresent threats (police, gangsters, and attachment). Panning long shots establish the driver and the viewer in a maze, and prepare one for high speeds and adrenaline, while two-shots where the individuals are on the edges of the frame reinforce the idea that togetherness is something strived for but never quite achieved.

Further, many of the shots are framed within the frame, which gives the sense of looking through a window or from a keyhole. The experience is both distancing and voyeuristic, which adds to the sense that you can never really get to know the Driver, nor can you establish consubstantiality or true resonance. There is a wall that blocks the viewer from projecting too much of one's emotions, except in the sense of alienation and profound existential solitude.

With the modifications made to the cars, and the latex masks and costumes/disguises employed by the stunt driver / getaway driver, identity is problematized. It is always changing, except for the things that do not change—scorpion jacket and a sleek, fast car.

The city itself adds to the notion of problematized identity as drivers make their way in the pristine, dark labyrinth of city streets at night. The implication is that one can ever get free. All roads lead back to an emotional minotaur, or at least to Nino, who will call due your obligations, and will trap you with your own dreams, whether they be of money, freedom, or emotional connection.

The white satin jacket with the embroidered scorpion on the back represents the Driver's life. In the beginning it is clean; likewise, the driver is unencumbered with emotion: he has no real feelings for others. He works for Shannon, but they do not appear to be friends. It is little more than a business relationship, but he is loyal to his boss (he goes after Nino right after he discovers a bled-out Shannon in the garage, though he likely would have gone after him anyway to save Irene and Benicio). In the beginning of the film, when the Driver shows up at Shannon's garage to take out the Impala, he is told about the car (the most common model in California, but with a modified engine), but the Driver does not respond. The Driver only speaks to Shannon twice: he tells him to cut out his joking with Irene, then angrily confronts him after determining how Bernie learned who drove the getaway car in the pawnshop robbery.

The jacket becomes soiled with blood after he assaults Cook in the strip club and later when he viciously kills a hit man in the elevator. The stains on the jacket show parallel a life soiled by the messy relationship he forms with Irene. Though their relationship is mostly pure (while Standard is alive, they do nothing more physical than hold hands), the responsibility he feels for her and Benicio compels him to help to make any sacrifice. The scorpion is emblematic of the driver. He asks Bernie if he's heard the story of the scorpion and the toad, indicating that he is the scorpion and will act accordingly. His fate is to kill those who fail to recognize his true nature. He also knows that Bernie is no different. He instantly sizes him up at the track and does not change his mind. When Bernie offers to meet, the Driver understands what is in store.

They will both act predictably. The Driver knows not to trust what Bernie says to him at the restaurant. When Bernie says he will be let go, only to look over his shoulder for the rest of his life, the Driver simply responds with a smile.

Drive is amazingly intertextual, and the icons in it evoke elements of other films. There are many references / visual allusions, probably too numerous to mention here. However, the Driver's scorpion jacket must be recognized as utterly metonymically intertextual, namely, with another racing film in which the protagonist wears an iconic jacket: *Rebel Without a Cause*.

The Driver wears the mask to conceal his identity while performing stunts. He also takes it from the trailer at the movie set and uses it to stalk and kill Nino. Anonymity provides the driver with a sense of comfort in his violence. He becomes habituated to using it while doing dangerous stunts and it gives him the courage to take out a ruthless gangster. He does not use it as a getaway driver, because these situations call for self-control. He doesn't simply outrun the cops, but skillfully hides from them. In this scene, and in the chase scene following the pawnshop robbery, he uses slick tactics, not aggression, to evade his pursuers.

In a larger sense, masking is the essential mechanism that resonates in an uncertain world, where people can't be trusted, and love is always unattainable, either due to one's own honor codes, or because it's taken away before things can be realized. Masking is the protective carapace that allows one to take action. To be emotive means you're incapable of true action, and, further, you can't be an action hero. To be taciturn and emotionless, means that you are capable of action. You possess the essential attributes of an action hero.

The action hero must live with contradictions and paradoxes. The Driver is at his happiest when he can be himself around Irene, but he has a secret identity as a wheelman. Of course there is another side to him that he tries to hide. He does not tell Irene he about his criminal activity, even when he plans to help Standard pay off his protection debt. He does not want to burden or implicate Irene with any knowledge of the robbery, but wants them to remain pure. Likewise, he does not want to provide them with any knowledge of his violent nature, but when called on to protect them, he will act. He knows he has to kill the hitman in the elevator, yet he understands Irene will be appalled. He kisses her, knowing that what he has to do will change her perception of him. After he stomps in the man's head, he looks at her with a wild sadness as he realizes Irene is too shocked to speak or to stop the elevator door from shutting between them and their relationship closes. The driver knows that whatever happens, he and Irene can never be together. He calls her one last time to conclude things. He tells her that the time he spent with her and her son was the most meaningful experience of his life.

During other times of violence without the mask, it is essential for him to remain in control. After he smashes Cook's hand with a hammer, he has his arm back ready to bash him in the head as he speaks with Nino on the phone. Even after Nino questions the offer to settle things, the Driver does not kill Cook because he hopes the situation can be resolved.

Feelings do not flow freely through a mask, and likewise, the viewer is not likely to see much emotion in the action hero. Blood, however, does flow freely, which allows the catharsis to take place, and the action to have a focus. In *Drive*, as in many other action films, the emotions/blood starts flowing when a loved one is harmed or in danger of being harmed. The anti-hero's flawed nature is what gives him the advantage when dealing with the villains of the film because the anti-hero possesses the same knowledge and perhaps even the same nature. What ultimately saves the anti-hero is the fact that his motives are sacrificial, and that his blood flows almost as freely. The Driver is shot, beaten, and broken—his pain absolves him. It also awakens him, and he feels again. Ultimately, the loved one is spared, and the audience has experienced a vicarious flow as well, either in relating to the sacrifices of the hero, or in a cold recognition that they, too, inhabit a world where the price one pays for being (or seeming) emotionally impervious and distant is a brutal (and often fatal) pain upon awakening.

****

Appendix: Violent scenes

1. Gangster ("Cook") stabbed by Bernie in the eye with a fork and then with a knife in the chest.

2. In Shannon's garage, Bernie slices Shannon's arm and causes him to exsanguinate.

3. In the parking garage, two thugs seek out Standard in order to collect on the "protection" debt that Standard incurred while in prison.

4. In the elevator, the Driver stomps to death a thug sent to kill him.

5. In the parking lot outside pawnshop, there is violence when Standard is shot by someone in the pawn shot (and not someone

in the Chrysler 300 with tinted windows that pulls up as though it's part of a rival gang (startling since you don't see who shoots Standard) expected something to happen because the Chrysler 300 with limo-tinted windows pulled up close to the driver's stolen Mustang and no one got out, but didn't expect shooting to come from the pawnshop; similarity to precision driving because of quick action, must have quick reflexes)

6. In the hotel room (didn't expect Blanche to be killed with a shotgun blast to the head since she was with the mobsters; she called them when the driver leaves the hotel to call Irene).

****

OpenPlan Film Criticism Collaboration Template/Tool

1. List the name of the film, the director, year released, and the key characters and actors.

2. Where and when does the film take place? What is the atmosphere?

3. What is it about this film that makes you care about it? How does it engage you emotionally? Intellectually? What is the primary focus of the plot?

4. What makes this film special? What are the narrative elements that set it apart from others?

5. How do the characters distinguish themselves? How are they special/unique? What do they do or say? (Describe illustrative scenes)

6. What is the dominant camera work? What types of shots characterize this film?

7. What are other films that may resonate with this film? List them, and describe what makes them have something in common with this one.

8. What are some aspects of the film that you're not quite sure how to process, but which linger long after you've seen the film.

9. List a few philosophical/psychological ideas that may relate to the film.

Sports, Physical Therapy, and E-Learning:
The Case of the Tennis E-Portfolio

I'm studying Sports Management, and I love the curriculum. We take a wide range of courses which range from motivation, ethics, physiology, finance, and fund-raising, to the specific sports themselves.

I've been asked to put together an e-portfolio on teaching and learning tennis through e-learning.

Is it even possible? How do I get started?

Sincerely,
Aces in Oceola

****

Dear Aces,

There have always been a lot of books and videos on tennis. It's been customary to tape the big matches and replay them—sometimes for the play, sometimes for the tantrums, sometimes for the fashion.

The question is, are they completely effective for teaching and learning tennis? I think we all know the answer to that: only in a limited way.

Perhaps a better question is, can one really learn tennis, and also learn to teach or coach tennis through an online course? Further, can you put together an e-Portfolio of the elements needed to teach/coach/learn tennis?

Here are elements to include:

1. Historical videos: watching the experts
2. Explanations and discussions: audio files, video
3. Diagnostic videos: posting "live" videos to critique strokes and strategy
4. Field notes and "living journal": notes from the court
5. Discussion board
6. Biofeedback loops and strategy using games, simulations, Wii tennis, etc

   Other fun-to-include elements might be live streaming video that you can archive through Ustream (**www.ustream.tv**), with synchronous chat for analysis and review, after you've archived the transcript.
7. Live streaming video (matches, etc.) for synchronous viewing
8. Discussion to accompany the live streaming video using Twitter, chat, or instant messenger.

As you start to build your e-Portfolio, don't be afraid to start at the beginning. It's okay if you're starting at a low level. More advanced learners can skip through the early units.

Here are a few possible units to include in your e-Portfolio:

Unit 1: Virtual Stroke Clinic

- Video of coaches, tennis pros, and learners: be sure to show at least three or four ways to approach each stroke.
- Text and story: readings and narrative; include audio files.
- Discussion board: discuss questions about grip, strokes, comparative approaches.
- Personal diagnostics: post videos of oneself, encourage peer review/critique.

Unit 2: Building a Serve

- Video of coaches, tennis pros, and learners: be sure to show at least three or four ways to approach a serve.
- Text and story: readings and narrative; include audio files.
- Discussion board: roundtable of experiences (My Serve Story).
- Personal diagnostics: post videos of oneself, encourage peer review/critique.

Unit 3: Match Strategy 101: Singles and Doubles

- Video of coaches, tennis pros, and learners: what they're doing, simple to complex strategies.
- Text and story: readings and narrative; include audio files.
- Discussion board: analyze and discuss videos of matches.
- Personal diagnostics: post videos of oneself, encourage peer review/critique.

Unit 4: Footwork and Drills: Teaching Group Tennis

- Video of drills: group drills, footwork, more. Explain what they accomplish.
- Text and diagrams: readings and narrative; include audio files on different drills and group activities.
- Discussion board: discuss questions about the benefits of certain drills and the potential cons.
- Personal footwork diagnostics: post videos of oneself and invite peers to post critiques.

Finally, Aces, I'd like to commend you on your willingness to be very innovative as you seek ways to teach trainers, coaches, and athletes. It's exciting to see a combination of e-learning and m-learning put to use in a way that helps learners accommodate learning styles.

All too often, we rely on one method of teaching or coaching because it's the way it's always been done, and, because it produces a few star performers, it's assumed that the method works. However, it might not work for everyone. With a variety of learning modes and approaches, there is a much better chance of producing more superstars!

Studying What You Love:
Is It Okay in Today's World?

Is money everything? Should I focus only on how much the jobs might pay when I choose a major?

I know that sounds like a crazy question. After all, guidance counselors always talk about following your dream.

But our world is different. I'm worried that my dream will lead to misery and starvation, not to mention a big student loan bill.

Specifically, I love interior design. I love to think of ways to create interior spaces that evoke specific feelings and moods, and which may even make life a bit more pleasant.

But with all the economic problems the world has today, my interests seem sort of frivolous. At least that's the way they seem to me today. I mean, people are losing their houses, and commercial property is being foreclosed. My friends who were planning to make a lot of money buying old properties, rehabbing and refurbishing them, then "flipping" them are in trouble. My friend Tanda told me she felt like a mouse stuck in a glue trap. The more she tries to move on with her life, the stickier the glue gets that's holding down her feet.

What do you think? Is it okay in today's world and economic climate to study what I love, even if it does not look like it will be a high-paying career?

I don't want to be just another rat in a glue trap.

Sincerely,
Designing Dreamer

****

Dear Designing,

Oh my. Your letter really touched my heart. All I could think of was how sad our world would be if everyone with passion, dreams, imagination, vision, and a creative spark decided that the only way to survive was to extinguish their inner fires and to chase the highest paying job they could possibly find.

How many would get caught up in illicit or unethical activities?

How many would drop out of their degree or certificate program because they just could not face having to push themselves to do something utterly uninteresting to them?

How many people would realize they had set themselves up to fail by playing weaknesses rather than strengths?

I'd like to take a moment to reassure you that your interests and passions are valuable. Granted, it's not always easy to see how to translate them into paying jobs or a career, but I truly believe that with planning, analyzing, and strategic training and education, you'll be able to create a career for yourself that brings you deep abiding joy and satisfaction as well as a solid, fulfilling career.

Let's step back a moment and look at your passion for interior design. It's really fascinating that you're looking at all kinds of interior spaces and thinking about the way people are influenced by their environment. It's very true, and, as you well know, there are numerous studies in architecture, sociology, psychology, and semiotics (the study of signs and symbols) that look specifically at how and why the things that surround us affect our moods and how we assign meaning to the things that happen around us.

It's clear that what you're interested in will always have value in the world. Now, the challenge is to find how to see where your special interests and abilities fit into our unstable and quickly changing world.

Here are a few guiding principles:

- **Identify the big new trends.** How does what you know and what you love fit? Is there a small niche where there is a perfect fit?

- **Build on your strengths.** Don't give up. Be proud of who you are and the talents and gifts that are uniquely yours. See where they match—even if it is a stretch. Do a gap analysis. Where's the gap between what you know and can do, and where you'd like to be? What kind of education and training do you need?

- **Share your passion.** Don't be surprised when others who see your enthusiasm start to follow you and inquire if you're available to do work for them. Let them see your work, and be willing to explain and provide a glimpse into your heart and soul. Put together an e-portfolio and share it online. There are places you can use for your portfolio such as Mahara (**www.mahara.org**), which is open source e-portfolio software. Of course, you can always put something together on Facebook.

- **Find creative ways to volunteer.** One of the best ways to show what you know is to volunteer at an organization that inspires you. Share your gift with the not-for-profit organization that has a cause you identify with. Or, alternatively, offer to do a free internship at a company or organization that matches your interests.

I know it took courage to write your letter and send it in. I'm glad you did—you might be surprised how many people share your worries, and it's good to have a chance to reassure everyone that it's never too late, and there is always time and a way to make your dreams a reality.

The Shish-Kabob Generation:
Skewered by the Recession
and Newly At-Risk Family Members

I thought I was about to enter the Sandwich Generation—taking care of teenagers plus an aging parent. I found out that the Sandwich Generation doesn't exist any more.

In fact, I don't know anyone who is "sandwich" any more.

We are more like shish kabobs: instead of being sandwiched in between two generations, everyone is linked to more family members—a skewer through the heart holding all of us together. I feel like a chunk of bell pepper, in a line with chunks of beef, red onion, chicken, and cherry tomatoes.

Here are the members of my family who live under the same roof:

- *Dad: an aging parent needing long-term health care.*
- *Son: a war veteran deciding not to re-enlist after multiple deployments to combat zones oversea—wants to CLEP out of courses, study using GI Bill.*
- *Husband: just laid off after his company sold his division—he is thinking about a certificate program.*
- *Teenage daughter: working part-time at florist—online AP courses.*
- *Me: studying online—want to get degree in sustainable business; thinking about opening a business having to do with providing services for the elderly who are staying home instead of going to assisted living or nursing homes.*

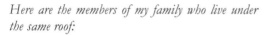

I keep thinking we are the perfect shish kabob. Each piece is different. We don't have much in common. But we are held together by external circumstances. I keep thinking of a sharp, stainless steel skewer that cuts right through the heart of each one of us. We're edgy, sad, "walking wounded."

Sometimes I think that we'd be ideal for a reality tv show—if anyone could deal with the constant ups and downs.

My question is this: Can we transform ourselves so that it is education that holds us together (not just economic and/or physical exigency)?

I'm looking forward to your answer.

Sincerely,
Chunk of Bell Pepper

****

Dear Chunk,

I love your clarity of vision. I think you're seeing family situations as they are now—and you're absolutely right! The so-called "Sandwich Generation" is over. It's too simplistic. What we're looking at now, in our newly complicated and very difficult social and economic landscape is the "Shish-Kabob Generation."

There's are a couple of additional observations that I have that support your thesis that we're living in multigenerational, variably-"abled" households and living situations:

1. It's a multigenerational household, and it mirrors the multigenerational workplace.

2. Education is the best way to unify the vision—start sharing your goals and your success stories/strategies with each other.

3. Identify your strengths. Are some of the strengths typical of specific generations? For example, millennials tend to be comfortable with social networking and communications technology. Can these talents work with the talents of the others in your group?

4. Practice compassion. Stop living with your eyes scrunched shut. Open

your eyes. Recognize the diversity and embrace it. When you see vulnerability, embrace it and accept it.

5. Invest in technology. Then, master it. Share it. The best way for you to bond and survive as a unit is to have the tools that will make you feel confident, strong, and excited—alone and with your group. Feel the joy of discovery. Discuss which items to purchase so that you get the most for your money. For example, talk about getting netbooks. If you do so, buy at least two. That way, you can share your knowledge and build.

6. Reach out to the weakest member of your team. You will soon come to realize that the weak are really the strong. This is a fundamental truth of life and of learning. So, if your aging father seems to be the weakest—at least physically—accept the reality that he's actually the strongest. It's up to you to identify how and where he is the strongest of your home unit, your "shish kabob." ☺

7. Believe in yourself and in your fellow shish-kabob-ers. Be happy that you're being held together by your stainless-steel skewer. If you take out the skewer, will the onions, peppers, chunks of meat, and cherry tomatoes fall apart? Absolutely not! You've skewered yourselves together—by means of a shared vision of the future, a commitment to transformational education, and love.

I'm delighted with your letter, Chunk, and I think your observations are brilliant. You've provided me with fantastic food for thought, and I hope that my response is equally thought-provoking and encouraging.

Viral Ideas, Memes, Egyptian Protests, and Your Online Education

I've been reading about how ideas that go viral can be destructive. How can that be? I've always thought of things that go viral as being just entertaining—like the video of "Spaghetti Cat" whose owner had taught him to feed himself spaghetti with a spoon. (What happened to good old Friskies cat food?)

I'm confused. I'm worried that the information I'm taking as fact could be just a rumor "gone viral."

Could that affect my career planning?

Sincerely,
Cautious in Chicago

****

Dear Cautious,

What a great question! The short answer is "yes," but to really appreciate what is going on, it's worthwhile to go into a few details.

When you say something "goes viral," you're basically talking about a meme, and meme behavior. They spread seemingly instantaneously, and terms like "contagious" and "synchronicity" and "spreading like wildfire" often accompany the phenomenon.

The Internet, blogs, and now social networking are vectors of diffusion. It is amazing to see how rapidly ideas disseminate, and to realize that all information has to be is compelling for it to "go viral." It does not have to be truthful, unbiased, or reliable. It just has to resonate with people and with the particular times and context.

A good example of a meme in action is what happened in North Africa, and the revolts that spread from Tunisia to Egypt. Images, texts, and action combined to create a message that was both extremely contagious in the meme sense, and very hard to keep from following (as in the sense of Albert Bandura's notion of emulatory behavior).

One interesting thing occurred when the meme hit Egypt. Proponents of meme theory have argued that the social networking is absolutely required for the operation of the meme. If you interrupt the dissemination of information via the Internet, the meme stops in its tracks.

In this case, the meme did not stop—if anything it picked up speed and changed its form from a digital manifestation to a physical one. People took to the streets and got their information there. That's when things started to get violent.

One might argue that if the Egyptian government had not shut down electronic forms of communication (Internet, cellphones), then a dialogue could have been established, and individuals could let their voices be heard through civil speech rather than violent physical confrontations.

At any rate, one can see the power of memes to inject a concept or an idea into a group of people, and then to set off a chain of events, some of which are random, and others which are more or less orchestrated by the movement of the meme.

The dream of any mass movement activist, marketing expert, YouTube artist or musician, or Internet entrepreneur is to figure out a way to generate very viral messages that become rapidly-moving memes. They do not want to simply be picked up in blogs or in Facebook posts, but want to provoke individuals to email, text, tweet, and talk about the phenomenon. They want the meme to become personal and for you to consider what you're reading to have a direct impact on you and your life.

    Is Taco Bell "meat" not really meat?
    Will new health care reform include "death panels"?
    Will new jobs emerge in the health industry?

Knowing how to recognize a meme (particularly if it's an urban legend), and how to stop and question the idea that is being promoted is important. Not responding to a provocative meme could save you money, time, and even your life.

Let's consider a meme that's close to home, and the one that inspired you to write me your letter. How valuable is a college education? If you're a recent graduate, will you be able to get a job? Recent reports have tried to paint higher education as fairly useless, and you might as well just forego the student debt and find work without a degree. The bad meme says "stay home."

Don't pay attention to bad memes! In my opinion, there are very dangerous memes and one should stop, research, and reconsider before accepting that idea and acting on the suggestions.

First and foremost are the facts. The unemployment rate in 2009 (published in 2010) for those without a high school diploma was almost 15 percent! However, for individuals with a bachelor's degree, the unemployment rate dropped to 5.2 percent. That is a 10 percent difference, and very important when thinking about investing in your future and in education. Remember, these statistics were collected during the worst part of the recession. A 5.2 unemployment rate is not too bad, everything considered!

Here are the statistics, compiled by the Bureau of Labor Statistics: www.bls.gov/emp/ep_chart_001.htm

The other question is whether it matters where you got your degree. Obviously, your major will affect how many jobs you qualify for, and what the demand is for your skill set. However, that said, you can always customize yourself. Volunteer. Take a second job that relates to your career interests. Write papers and start a blog.

Enhancing your college education with targeted, related experience will make a big difference, and can impress potential employers who will be encouraged to give you a chance.

I hope this is helpful!

Ways of Learning:
What Works for You?

There are many ways of learning, and the more you learn about yourself and the way you learn and relate to others, the more successful you'll be.

LEARNING STYLES AND PREFERENCES:
ARE YOU VISUAL? AUDITORY? KINAESTHETIC?
OR A COMBINATION?

You've probably heard about learning styles and useful it is to understand how it is that you learn and how to adjust your study strategies to maximize learning.

For example, if you're an auditory learner, it's a good idea to discuss the topics with someone and to listen to podcasts, lectures, etc. If you're a kinesthetic learner, you'll benefit from something that allows you to be hands-on—a lab, a video game (serious game), or perhaps a physical activity that incorporates the instructional content.

If you'd like to find out about yourself and your learning styles, here are a few excellent resources:

- Index of Learning Styles Questionnaire: Barbara Soloman and Richard M. Felder
  ▸ www.engr.ncsu.edu/learningstyles/ilsweb.html

- Description of Learning Styles and Strategies: Barbara Soloman and Richard M. Felder
  ▸ www4.ncsu.edu/unity/lockers/users/f/felder/public/ILSdir/styles.htm

- Barsch Inventory
  - ▸ ww2.nscc.edu/gerth_d/AAA0000000/barsch_inventory.htm

The Barsch Inventory is a quick instrument which takes approximately 10-15 minutes to complete. Try to answer the questions by basing your answers on your actual learning preference and not areas which you would like to have as strengths. An explanation and learning tips for each preference is provided in this section.

MULTIPLE INTELLIGENCES

Howard Gardner suggests that each person has a unique set of intelligent attributes and that you can learn best when you understand where your strengths are, and then you find a learning study strategy that plays to your strengths.

Like many theorists, Gardner does not believe in identifying your weaknesses in order to apply some sort of corrective remedy. Instead, he advocates playing to your strengths and developing the maximum amount of flexibility.

Here is a free Multiple Intelligences test (based on Howard Gardner's model)—in MSExcel self-calculating format:
- ▸ www.businessballs.com/freematerialsinexcel/free_multiple_intelligences_test.xls

Intelligence type	Capability and Perception
Linguistic	words and language
Logical-Mathematical	logic and numbers
Musical	music, sound, rhythm
Bodily-Kinesthetic	body movement control
Spatial-Visual	images and space
Interpersonal	other people's feelings
Intrapersonal	self-awareness

LEARNING THROUGH EACH OTHER: TEAM BUILDING FOR ONLINE COLLABORATIONS

Bruce Tuckman developed a widely adopted model of team formation that focuses on the way that team members come together and how they interact. He emphasizes that people learn from each other and that the way people come to exchange knowledge and to develop new actions.

- Forming
- Storming
- Norming
- Performing

How does this apply to collaborative activities in online courses? It is useful to understand the process and the progression.

Smith, M. K. (2005). Bruce W. Tuckman – forming, storming, norming and performing in groups, *the encyclopaedia of informal education*:
▶ www.infed.org/thinkers/tuckman.htm

KOLB LEARNING STYLES: Experiential

Kolb developed a learning theory that holds that there are four distinct learning styles or preferences which flow out of a four-stage learning cycle. Kolb's model is very useful because it gives people a way to understand how people learn through experiencing/involving themselves in a process or learning situation.

For Kolb, there is a progression from the experience itself to reflection and then application. At first, the process may seem to be a bit convoluted, but if one keeps in mind that what Kolb is mapping is a complex interplay of active experience and reflective cognition, and the steps and stages involved in it, it's clearer.

In sum, there are two basic continuums which cover the process from active, hands-on experiencing to abstract reflection.

Concrete Experience (feeling) → Abstract Conceptualization (thinking)
Active Experimentation (doing) → Reflective Observation (watching)

PUTTING YOUR SELF-KNOWLEDGE TO WORK

As you reflect on the ways of learning and working together, think about how you might apply the strategies to your different online courses. If the processes do not seem to work at first, be sure to try a different approach and to be as flexible as possible.

Will the Oil Spill in the Gulf of Mexico
Affect E-Learning?

I recently participated in a think tank / workshop that, among other things, analyzed what might have caused the accident in BP's drilling operations in the Gulf of Mexico. How can we better understand the conditions in the deep subsurface? It might surprise you to know that e-learning is one of the answers.

The blowout and subsequent oil spill in the Gulf of Mexico could affect e-learning in a number of ways, as it points out the need for training, planning, and coordination across different often siloed divisions within organizations. It also points out the need for individuals who have a "big picture" vision of operations and who can make decisions when multiple contractors and outside partners are involved in operations, and when it is necessary to incorporate multiple back-ups and redundancies with respect to health and safety. Further, the accident and the aftermath point out the need for effective communications and public relations in order to give voice to outside stakeholders (including the public at large) and to create effective forums for the exchange of ideas and possible solutions.

The workshop took place in northern California and a group of geologists, engineers, and geophysicists came together in an event organized and sponsored by a not-for-profit global scientific organization. The goal was to advance the science and to apply scientific understanding and new technologies to real-life situations that present themselves in the exploration for and production of oil and gas. In looking at pore pressure and fractures in reservoirs, it became evident that the knowledge would apply to geothermal resources as well.

At the end of three days, the participants of the think tank reached the following conclusions:

1. There is a need for more professionals with a background in earth sciences, both geology and environmental science.

2. There is not enough communication and teamwork between divisions of the company, and across disciplines. Engineers, geologists, geophysicists, geochemists, and environmental geologists need to work together. They also need to plan closely with the accountants and chief financial officers.

3. Companies should hire more graduates from colleges that offer interdisciplinary programs that encourage "big picture" thinking and which provide a combination of theory and practical application.

4. Companies need more tools (technological and analytical) and they need to encourage creativity and extreme "outside the box" thinking.

5. Online degree programs are a "must-have" for individuals in companies who need to continue their education and/or diversify.

6. Online certificate programs can help companies meet short-term competency gaps, particularly when the need is in specialty areas such as green technology, sustainable business, and more.

7. Education should not just be about competency in certain subject matters. It should also be about vision, leadership, and problem solving.

Clearly, there are huge opportunities for e-learners. Online learners can take control of their education and develop a set of skills and abilities. After participating in discussions, I came to realize that the need is more urgent than we may have thought. It is also a widely recognized need. We need new kinds of graduates, and new ways of thinking and communicating. Happily, e-learners are, in the course of their studies and by virtue of the ways they approach learning, fit the profile of the "new view" graduate.

The "new view" graduate is almost always a graduate of an online program and has the following capabilities:

1. An ability to engage in productive dialogues using numerous approaches, which include discussion groups, wikis, social networking, collaborations.

2. Cross-disciplinary education.

3. Mobile learning: familiar and comfortable with obtaining and transmitting information via mobile devices.

4. Philosophy of work that includes life-long education.

5. Outside-the-box networking and sharing, in order to see new ideas grow and flourish.

The oil spill in the Gulf of Mexico is a tragedy of still unknown proportions. Like other tragedies, it can be a catalyzing event and can lead to permanent and positive changes in the way things are done.

World Game-Changers and Your Future:
What TED, Davos, and Others Mean to You

The world is a blur to me these days. I don't know what to study.

How do I know what is relevant and what ideas people are giving credence these days? I know there are some "world game-changers" but I'm not sure where to find out what they're saying, and, further, how it might affect me.

I want to study topics that will put me in the right place at the right time.

Where's the "smart money" going in the world of ideas?

With best regards,
Confused in Kentucky

****

Dear Confused,

There are a few speeches in history that seem to imprint upon us an inescapable destiny. One that comes to mind is President Kennedy's January 18, 1963 speech in which he challenged the American people to envision traveling to the moon, not because it was easy, but because it was hard. While it's true that the speech was heavily freighted with all kinds of Cold War baggage, its core idea—dream the impossible dream and to take technology to extremes—continue to inspire us.

Another notable speech was George W. Bush's "thousand points of light"

speech in which he ushered in idea of a "new world order" and a kind of globalization that has made people feel alternatingly joyous and angry; optimistic and apocalyptic. It's nice to feel connected if there is a tangible benefit. However, if you're connected just to see your jobs and opportunities slipping across the borders, it's frustrating.

Both speeches were eerily prescient, however, and they ushered in at least a full decade informed by the core concepts and ideas contained in the speeches.

They were "zeitgeist" speeches of a sort, and they put their finger on the prevailing moods, tone, and attitudes of the times. They articulated the spirit of the times.

What are today's "zeitgeist speeches"? More importantly, who is making them? Where are they taking place? Do they still predict the prevailing views of the future?

Today is not yesterday.

It's not as easy as it once was to look at the "big" speeches—chances are, you won't get much out of the past half dozen or so State of the Union addresses.

Instead, I suspect you have to go to the conferences where vested interests meet philosophy, where the new moneyed elites meet the old moneyed elites, and they converge in the form of philanthropic initiatives and IPOs.

One place to see new ideas emerge and converge with the old is TED (www.ted.com). There, you'll see Malcolm Gladwell, Brian Greene, Jane Goodall, Al Gore, and any number of people who generate ad promote ideas that result in change—changed ideas or policies. According to TED's website:

> **TED is a small nonprofit devoted to Ideas Worth Spreading. It started out (in 1984) as a conference bringing together people from three worlds: Technology, Entertainment, Design.**

Go to TED and check out the white papers, recordings, and videos. While it might be tempting to focus on the highly-rated ones, the best approach is to listen to as many as you can.

We also see them at the World Economic Forum (www.weforum.org), which took place in 2011 in January at Davos, Switzerland. It is attended by world game-changers, including Bill Gates, Angela Merkel, Queen Rania of Jordan, George Soros, and more.

What are the practical implications for you, your family, and your community?

If you're able to divine the "zeitgeist of the times," you'll be on track to choose the best possible career path, and to identify the industries most likely to experience growth.

You'll also be able to identify the pathways to avoid—what is going obsolete? Which industries will be penalized for unsafe or unhealthy practices? Where are emerging demographics shaping the futures of communities and countries?

For example, for a young person in Japan, which is looking at a population that may soon be predominantly comprised of seniors, it might not be a bad idea to specialize in geriatrics, and also to sensitize oneself to the challenges and realities of eldercare.

For an individual in the U.S., given the strength of the presence of Chinese trade, it might not be a bad idea to learn Mandarin, and to gain a deep understanding of economic relations between the two countries. Further, given the flow of immigrants from Mexico and Central America, if you have interest in Spanish and are entrepreneurial, there are numerous opportunities, particularly as it relates to bridging cultures.

Columbia University economics professor and Nobel Laureate Joseph Stiglitz asserted that the U.S. needs to stimulate investment in research that can provide technological breakthroughs that lead to enhanced efficiencies and new productive capabilities.

Invest in technology. Generate jobs.

Stiglitz says cut back spending on weapons, and increase spending on research and education.

Davos is a gathering of people who can change the direction of history. Granted, there's going to be an element of Machiavellianism, and people will be quick to point to hypocrisy. That said, if the ideas do stick, and more funding goes into research on technology and education, what kind of world can we expect in the near future? Where will the new jobs be?

I'd put my money on innovation. I'd then attach it to the basics—food, energy, health, transportation. Cynics will argue that there will always be a need to anesthetize the masses, so entertainment will be big. I don't see entertainment as toxic. I see it as something we do in order to network in different settings.

We are, after all, social beings.

People need people. We need each other in ways that spill out and cross boundaries. So, that's why I say you must study what makes you passionate.

Don't worry if it doesn't fit today's "hot" topics. If you care about what you do, and you stay current with technology as it applies to your own interests, then you'll be where you need to be, and you'll cross the boundaries and go into the new areas that will give you the satisfaction you seek. You don't need to chase the moving train.

To answer your question succinctly, the "smart" money is going where the new economic narrative is being invented: "Invest in things that will flower and bear fruit; don't invest in turf wars, resource grabs, and killing fields."

Idealistic? Yes, but what else are you to be? Bitter "greed is good" ideas led to boom-bust cycles and collapses. Perhaps it's true that business cycles can't be altogether avoided, but at least you can be on the right side of history, and while you might not ride as high, you won't sink as low as those consigned to chasing the dragon of quick profits, speculation, and other empty pursuits.

Invest in yourself. Affirm your interests. Build your skills.

Above all, believe in yourself. I believe in you!

Chapter 5

C A R E E R S

Construction Career Education Innovations: Smartphone and Tablet-Friendly Instruction Materials

Construction e-learning via smartphones, iPads, tablets? Career colleges and certificate program providers (associations, etc.) are seeking ways to make the learning experience immersive for the student and to harness social-networking power.

They are working with publishers and developers to make sure that the materials that are used move far beyond a textbook or a downloadable series of workbooks. They want to make sure that the media is accessible in a variety of devices, and they'd like to encourage collaborative learning by making it possible to share comments, develop projects together, and to discuss case studies and examples.

Here are just a few examples of the materials that are available now, many of which are free:

Web-Based Math Tutorials— Accessible through Smartphone and Tablets

Construction Management

- Southern Pine Council – PDF download:
  Permanent Wood Foundations Design and Construction Guide
  ‣ newstore.southernpine.com/images/ref400.pdf

- Southern Pine Council – PDF download:

Raised Wood Floors: Case Studies in Progressive Home Construction
- ▶ www.southernpine.com/downloadpdf.asp?filename=RFCaseStudies.pdf

- Raised Floor Basics – 5 videos:
  Note: The small videos are ideal for viewing on smartphone, iTouch, iPad
  - ▶ www.raisedfloorlivingpro.com/video/raisedfloor/
  - ▶ www.raisedfloorlivingpro.com/video/siteprep/
  - ▶ www.raisedfloorlivingpro.com/video/foundationdesign/
  - ▶ www.raisedfloorlivingpro.com/video/crawlspace/
  - ▶ www.raisedfloorlivingpro.com/video/framingoptions/
  - ▶ www.raisedfloorlivingpro.com/video/porchesdecks/

- Board Foot Calculator
  - ▶ www.woodbin.com/calcs/tabulator.htm

- Board Foot Calculator
  - ▶ extension.missouri.edu/scripts/explore/G05506.asp

- Calculating Loads on Headers and Beams
  - ▶ bct.eco.umass.edu/publications/by-title/calculating-loads-on-headers-and-beams/

- The Math Carpenters Use
  - ▶ www.xpmath.com/careers/jobsresult.php?groupID=7&jobID=3

- Maintenance, Construction, Remodel Converters and Calculators
  - ▶ www.csgnetwork.com/constructionconverters.html

Carpenters

- Maintenance, Construction, Remodel Converters and Calculators
  - ▶ www.csgnetwork.com/constructionconverters.html

- Designing Stairs and Laying Out Stair Stringers
  - ▶ www.hammerzone.com/archives/framecarp/technique/stairs/outdoor.htm

Construction / Carpentry Layout and Design Shareware

EZ-Pix (www.xequte.com/megaview) is a fast, highly functional shareware image viewer and editor with support for all common image formats, including JPEG, GIF, BMP, TIFF and PNG. It has a streamlined interface, and can be used to retrieve images from scanners and digital cameras.

All Trades

GIMP (www.gimp.org) is an acronym for GNU Image Manipulation Program. It is a freely distributed program for such tasks as photo retouching, image composition and image authoring. It has many capabilities. It can be used as a simple paint program, an expert quality photo retouching program, an online batch processing system, a mass production image renderer, an image format converter, etc. GIMP is expandable and extensible. It is designed to be augmented with plug-ins and extensions to do just about anything. The advanced scripting interface allows everything from the simplest task to the most complex image manipulation procedures to be easily scripted.

Electronic Health Records and the Boom in Medical Records Careers

Tailor-Made for Working Moms and Online Students

Related Degrees:

- Associate's Degree in Medical Billing and Coding
- Certificates in Medical Billing and Coding
- Degrees in Medical Informatics

The individuals in this article are based on real-life e-learners who participated in interviews, but names and details have been changed.

Marina sat in the pediatrician's waiting room as her nine-month-old daughter, Peleixa, fussed and fidgeted. Marina sighed. Another ear infection? She hoped not.

As she went back to the examination room, she was surprised to see that the rooms that had formerly held files were completely empty, except for a few workstations and what appeared to be rack of servers.

"What happened to all the files?" she asked the assistant who took her to the examination room.

"We're required to be 100% paper-free. All medical records are digital. It took a long time to scan all of the files, and we're still not finished. We have to go back and scan all the old files we have in our storage area now," said the assistant. Her voice sounded exhausted.

"Is it a part of the new electronic health record program?" asked Marina. "I heard about it."

"Yes, there's a new law that requires that there are electronic health records, which will be very helpful once the new health care programs are in place," said the assistant.

After they chatted a bit, Marina found that the new requirements were fairly stringent, and it had resulted in a boom for those who could provide the service.

There were very particular requirements for various sub-groups. For example, there were special requirements for health records for pediatrics.[1]

"You seem very interested in the subject," said the assistant. "We are looking for people who can help us scan the records and build a database."

The assistant's comments inspired Marina to look into online courses and programs. She found that she could get a certificate in medical records and coding within 8 months, and an associate's degree within 18 months.

New doors would be opened, and ones with a true future. After all, once everything was encoded, there were databases to be maintained, and installation, maintenance, and new use issues to be addressed. Change management with electronic health records would become increasingly important. [2]

Once the databases were created, there would be a need to update the records quickly and easily. In fact, every day, new electronic devices that could synch with the database and the records would allow quick uploading. They could avoid delays in that way. [3]

---

[1] www.ncbi.nlm.nih.gov/pubmed/17332220

[2] www.ncbi.nlm.nih.gov/pubmed/19911542?itool=EntrezSystem2.PEntrez.Pubmed.Pubmed_ResultsPanel.Pubmed_RVDocSum&ordinalpos=4

[3] www.ncbi.nlm.nih.gov/pubmed/19911534?itool=EntrezSystem2.PEntrez.Pubmed.Pubmed_ResultsPanel.Pubmed_RVDocSum&ordinalpos=5

The medical records and health information technicians job outlook was outstanding. According to the Department of Labor, the growth of jobs between 2006 and 2016 was estimated at 18 percent.[1]

Many jobs could be flexible, with some work from a home office, which made both studying for the degree and working ideal for a mom with a small child at home.

As Marina stood in line at the pharmacy to fill the prescription for Peleixa, she felt calm, even though her little daughter was fussier than ever. Things might be a bit edgy and nerve-wracking right now, but she could see a future for herself that truly felt satisfying.

---

[1] www.bls.gov/oco/ocoS103.htm

Empty-Nest Moms
and Urgent Care Administration

The individuals in this article are based on real e-learners who participated in interviews, but names and details have been changed.

When Soffia's youngest daughter graduated from high school and left home for college, a new chapter opened. Soffia, who had been a stay-at-home mom and volunteer for the "Kats for Kids" pet therapy program at the local hospital, decided to get a job at the hospital. Her dream was to be in health care administration, but her general associate's degree in business administration was something she earned 20 years ago, and it did not specifically deal with health care administration. So, she looked for something that built on her volunteer work, and which might put her in a position to learn how and where to get the education she would need to achieve her goal.

Soffia was lucky. She found part-time work with the public relations office of the hospital, where she was surprised to learn that the recession, coupled with health care reform, was likely to change the medical employment in a profound way.

Soffia learned about the changes on the horizon as she spoke with Maridor, the manager of the emergency room.

"Once everyone has some sort of insurance, we're going to see emergency rooms slow down," she said. "We won't get the asthma attacks, small accidents, and stomachaches. They will go to urgent care centers," Maridor explained.

Administrators at large hospitals and highly-specialized practices worried that health care reform could cause them to have to slash staff and cut services. At the same time, urgent care entrepreneurs wondered how they would expand quickly enough to meet the anticipated burst of demand.[1]

"Aren't doctors the ones in charge?" asked Soffia. She contemplated the doctors she saw making rounds at the hospital. It was rather unlikely that they would have the time or the temperament to spend a lot of time with the complex paperwork, compliance issues, and insurance filings. For one thing, they would not have time.

"Most doctors don't have time," said Maridor. "And, frankly, they don't have the background."

Maridor went on to point out that the best urgent care administrators were ones with business administration skills, as well as specialized knowledge of how the health profession works, both in large hospitals and in small urgent care clinics.

New jobs would be created in booming new care areas: general practitioner-led urgent care facilities, nurse-headed clinics in pharmacies of national drug stores, providers of secure storage for medical records. There would also be jobs in home health care and eldercare.

Rural health care would be an area of opportunity as well. Rural communities have difficulty attracting qualified registered nurses, and there is a need for health care professionals of all types. For moms in rural areas, distance education is definitely the way to go.[2]

Encouraged, Soffia signed up for an online bachelor's degree program in business, with an emphasis on health care administration. She was glad to find she could take her courses online, and also that she could use her job in the required internship. It was a path that was perfect with her interests and good organizational skills. In addition, she was able to find partial financial aid, which was a huge help.

---

[1] www.immediatecarebusiness.com/articles/0791practice.html

[2] www.ers.usda.gov/amberwaves/may07specialissue/features/policy.htm

Extreme Longevity
and the Workplace of the Future

I've been reading that our world is going to change in really dramatic ways due to extreme longevity. While part of me feels really skeptical about our health care system in ten years, and I do not really think the trend of longevity will continue, who am I to disagree with the studies?

And, well, that said, what does extreme longevity portend for the future workplace? Where will the new jobs be?

Sincerely,
Long in the Tooth in 2040

****

Dear Long in the Tooth,

Love your name. The concept of "long in the tooth" always makes me smile—I get the visual image of a large, wily lioness whose teeth get sharper with age.

That said, I want to compliment you on your question. It's something we should all be paying attention to because there are very real opportunities for those who recognize the trends and prepare themselves with education, training, and visionary skill-building.

According to many studies, increased longevity of our population, combined with diminishing benefits/pensions means that people will be working long past the traditional age of retirement, age 65.

Here are a few things to keep in mind:

- Older workers will work alongside younger workers in digital teams. You may or may not know the ages of anyone in your team.
- Assistive technologies will be standard in most computing systems/software/websites.
- Knowledge transfer will privilege the problem-solving skills, integrative thinking and convergence of technologies. Experienced and older workers who can help build new bridges/approaches by reconfiguring perception/thinking/paradigms will be in high demand.
- Knowledge architectures will change rapidly. Older workers who think of ways to make the new approaches accessible and practical will prevail.

What are the careers that will be in demand given a long-lived population?

- Home health care providers
- Assistive technologies
- Team-building / Team training
- Integrated technology design
- Entrepreneurship
  (assembling teams of technical specialists to achieve certain goals)
- Convergence cultures

The practical skills you'll need will include the following:

- Communications (written, which also includes social networking—however it evolves in the future)
- Math
- Humanities (creative problem-solving, new configurations of thinking)
- Science (especially chemistry, physics, biology, and environmental-earth)
- Social Sciences

- Systems thinking (Project management)
- Business (International/inter-related economics)
- Specialty skills (healthcare/computers/legal/trades)

You might think that what I'm talking about sounds quite vague and/or general. It does, but what I'm trying to get across is the fact that in ten years, we'll be in a completely different set of conventions, codes, and labels.

The fact that people will be living longer will just accelerate the process, since it means that competition for scarce resources will intensify, and as new networks (family, affiliation, etc.) start to gain power and traction.

I hope this is helpful!

Geographical Information Systems: Expanding Uses, Growing Jobs

What do you think about careers that use geographical information systems (GIS)? While I was first alarmed by the fact that geographical tracking devices are everywhere, I've now embraced it, and am intrigued by the way that geographical information systems can help improve efficiency, coordination, and communication, as well as keeping you from getting hopelessly lost in a new town.

I love the fact that geographical information systems are at the backbone of automated operations, too.

Are there jobs that allow me to immerse myself in geographical information systems? Where would I get the training? Can I do it online?

Sincerely,
Getting started with GIS

****

Dear Getting Started,

It is very exciting that you're interested in equipping yourself for a career that incorporates the use of geographical information systems.

As you have already noted, knowledge of GIS is useful across many disciplines and fields. You may not want to be a GIS specialist, but knowledge of GIS will enhance your career opportunities immensely.

When GIS was in its nascent phase, you'd generally find the programs in the geography departments of universities. That made sense because it tied into things like the early stages of remote sensing (satellite mapping), and other kinds of maps that were generated by information gained by means other than physically traveling to the locations and measuring them.

If you're interested in developing maps and looking at land usage, geography departments are still a great way to go. You can earn a bachelor's degree or a master's, and you'll be prepared to go to a number of jobs in industry and the government:

- government agencies (water, land, soil, public transportation. urban planning, geological resources, weather)
- security agencies (governmental and private)
- private map companies (marketing/demographics/highways, etc.)

With the advent of robust geographical information systems, along with programs that help you bring together different types of information, GIS is basically everywhere. Here are just a few broad areas where your knowledge of GIS is at the center of operations:

- Law Enforcement and Criminal Justice
- Marketing
- Engineering and Surveying
- Transportation
- Mobile Workforce and Asset Management
- Site Selection and Real Estate
- Emergency Preparedness and Management
- Demographics
- Health and Human Services
- Environmental
- Agriculture

Currently, to get started in GIS, you may choose among options:

- Certificate in GIS
- Associates in Applied Science in GIS
- Bachelor's in GIS
- Master's degree in GIS

Alternatively, you can take courses through one of the main providers of

GIS software, Esri. Esri's software includes a number of programs that allow you to integrate and manipulate GIS information along with cultural and other data:

- ArcInfo
- ArcView
- ArcEditor
- ArcGIS Server
- ArcIMS
- ArcPad

By the sound of your letter, you've already become familiar with the basics of GIS and what a career would entail. As you know, you'd need a good background in computer graphics, computer applications, along with math (primarily statistics). It would also be very important for you to take geography courses, and also to understand the way that you use multiple streams of information. For that reason, data management and workflow development are absolutely vital.

Salaries tend to be all over the map, but as a beginning GIS specialist working with a company that needs the expertise you have with an Associates in Applied Science, you can expect to make between $40,000 and $55,000 per year after you have some experience. With experience, and a bachelor's or master's degree, you can earn more. The ranges are quite broad, however, and start at around $45,000 and go all the way to $105,000. I found these numbers at the Bureau of Labor Statistics, so they're fairly solid.

If you're not a huge math whiz, don't worry about it too much. What you really need to do in GIS careers is to problem-solve and to think spatially. This means that you need to be able to think of how things relate to each other over time, and how the variables you're concerned with (trucks, criminals, clouds, etc.) move, make patterns, and trigger cause-and-effect relationships.

It's great that you're checking out degree programs. In the meantime, you may wish to play around with some free downloads:

DIVA-GIS

▶ www.diva-gis.org

PC only – Free GIS application specializing in analyzing species distribution and climate data; includes tools for modeling distributions (Bioclim, Domain) and evaluating models.

LandSerf

▸ www.soi.city.ac.uk/~jwo/landserf

Unix, Linux, PC & MAC – A Java-based program so runs in any environment that supports Java (e.g. Linux, Unix, too). Fully functional GIS application with a new version coming soon that will allow macro programming and map algebra.

GRASS GIS

▸ grass.fbk.eu

Unix, PC & MAC – Stands for Geographic Resources Analysis Support System, an open-source application that is constantly being improved (since 1982). They even have a Wikipedia entry. Natively Unix, so PC users must first install Unix compatibility software (easy); next version is supposed to work directly in Win (easier)! Powerful.

Google Earth

▸ earth.google.com

Linux, PC & MAC – What it lacks in spatial analysis chops, it makes up for great visualization tools and easy to use format.

Green Jobs in More Places Than You Might Expect

If you read the news and all the stories of alternative energy, you may start to think that to be a part of the "green economy," you have to be able to climb a 150-foot wind turbine, brave high winds and inclement weather, to install parts in under the nacelle (the streamlined enclosure that covers the engine and gears in the wind turbine).

What you might not realize that, thanks to the nationwide smart grid system, tax incentives, new environmental regulations, and cost savings associated with energy efficiency, green is almost everywhere. Chances are, you can pursue the career of your dreams and still be green. And, by being green, your job has a good chance of being in a sustainable industry that will thrive in the new business environment.

Let's take a look at a few major "green" industries, and then list the green jobs and careers that are primarily concerned with energy, environment, and waste reduction. Next, we'll list the ones that are green-focused jobs. The "green focus" jobs are ones that are flexible and require an understanding of core green concepts, but are broader in responsibility and scope than the specialized green jobs.

Alternative Energy / Renewables

Specialized Green Jobs:

- Solar Energy Engineers and Technicians
- Biomass Engineers and Technicians

- Geothermal Engineers and Technicians
- Wind Energy Engineers and Technicians

Green Focus Jobs:

- Marketing
- Business planning
- Support staff (sales/administrative)
- Transportation

Green Buildings

Specialized Green Jobs:

- Green architects/design
- Green plumbing
- Green electricity systems
- Green HVAC / indoor climate control
- Green construction
- Green Construction management

Green Focus Jobs:

- Marketing
- Business planning
- Support staff (sales/administrative)
- Rental/maintenance

Electric Power/Utilities

Specialized Green Jobs:

- Smart Grid computer programming/design
- Smart Grid electrician
- Smart Grid systems and support

Green Focus Jobs:

- Monitoring/statistics

- Auditing/trouble-shooting
- Business planning
- Public relations
- Billing / support / administrative support

So, as you can see, green jobs are often a matter of degree (not just the kind you earn in college!) If you are in a specialized green job, you may be 100% "green"—which is to say that your job is specifically about sustainable business, energy, waste management, environmental conservation, etc.

However, more likely than not, your job will require between 15 and 30% "green" knowledge and skills. What is important to keep in mind is that by taking a pro-active approach and getting "green" training and certification, you'll have a competitive advantage. Plus, you may be able to have a job in what you love, while simultaneously being in synch with new trends, new jobs, and new opportunities.

Green Technology Training:
Jobs Created Outnumber Graduates

Related Online Degrees:

- Master of Business Administration – Environmental and Social Sustainability
- Bachelor of Science in Business / Green and Sustainable Enterprise Management

When Marilisa realized she needed to go back to school, she was worried. She could not afford to fail. So, should she take a low-risk course that would yield a quick degree, or should she pursue a technical degree that would take longer and where she had a higher risk of failing?

Marilisa decided to go the low-risk route, but immediately regretted it. Her degree in General Studies would not open the doors she wanted to open.

So, the first step was to decide what she really wanted to do with a degree, and which industries she wanted to enter.

After careful consideration, she decided that being able to work with renewable energy was where she wanted to be. She lived in a part of the country that was experiencing a boom in wind farm construction.

"Should I be a wind turbine technician?" Marilisa asked her parents. They were not encouraging.

"It's just a fad," said her mom. "Where will you work once they've finished building all the wind farms?"

Marilisa probed the issue. She quickly found that incentives to construct wind energy facilities are in place for years, and that growth is expected well past 2015, both in Europe as well as North America. Job growth would continue for a long time. In fact, worker shortages were continued to continue because of two reasons: 1) an insufficient number of training programs; 2) hesitation on the part of students who were afraid of failing an expensive and time-consuming course of study, and who opted to go for "easy" degrees that did not involve subject matters such as math where students convince themselves they have a phobia.

"I thought you were afraid of heights," said her dad.

Marilisa paused for a moment. "True enough. I do not want to go up on a tower. But I can work on designing the facility and also in the integration into the electricity power grid, or in the integration of renewable and non-renewable energy."

Her parents were convinced. Plus, they had read articles in their local newspaper that detailed how employers in the "green tech" industry could not find qualified workers.

So, Marilisa made an appointment with an academic counselor. What her counselor told her gave her pause yet again.

"I had no idea I had to take so many math and engineering technology courses," said Marilisa. Her counselor could hear the hesitation in her voice. "I have never been good at math. In fact, I think I have a math phobia," Marilisa continued.

The counselor was not surprised to hear this. It was her experience that the majority of non-traditional students she worked with were convinced that they could not succeed at math.

"We understand," said the counselor. "We have designed a series of Math Success courses for people who may need to have a refresher because they've been away from school for years, or who decided at an early age that they did not like math. We tell our students that it is never too late to develop a love for math."

With that, Marilisa embarked on a program to help her become a renewable energy specialist. In order to succeed and to expedite her progress, she followed a clear set of steps:

- Start with Certificate Courses
- Credit by exam for general education courses where appropriate
- Credit through ACE-approved training courses
- Supplemental "Math Success" courses
- Virtual tutor for tricky courses
- Support network of "study buddies"
- Practice assessments
- Networking to meet potential employers

Marilisa enrolled and found that it was true that green jobs were growing at a phenomenal rate. In fact, even traditional jobs were starting to require individuals to have some abilities to incorporate sustainable technologies (equipment and materials to maximize energy efficiency, and also new software that simultaneously gathers information and monitors remote sites).

Health Care Reform: New Jobs, New Training

I've been hearing a lot about health care reform, and I'm confused. On the one hand, it seems that it will mean a lot of new jobs and opportunities. On the other hand, people are saying it might mean fewer jobs because there will be fewer services and health care providers will start shutting down.

What should I believe?

Thank you for your time,
Confused in Connecticut

****

Dear Confused:

The need for lower cost and more efficient health care is already leading to big shifts in the health care landscape. Big, inefficient operations will be streamlined. Waste of all kinds will be reduced. An emphasis on green technologies will continue to change the way we look at operations.

So, where will the job loss occur? Where will the jobs be?

For everyone who's involved in a nursing program, especially one that leads to an RN, there's no need to panic. The Department of Labor projects that there will continue to be significant growth—from 2.5 million to 3.0 million from 2006 to 2016—an increase of almost 24 percent.

However, everyone will need training. They will need to know the new approaches to medicine, there could be problems. You'll need to show you've had training in new legislation and in energy-efficient, environmentally friendly processes and procedures in order to keep your license. Those who do not get the training run the risk of having limited employment options.

What are the new trends?

The key to new, efficient health care is to bring it to the people. That means having smaller clusters of primary care facilities, where, instead of doctors and expensive equipment and labs, there are nurse practitioners and very basic diagnostic equipment and lab facilities.

Nurse Practitioner-Level Primary Care / First Responder: They will be at the first level of contact. The result will be a large demand, especially in areas that have been underserved in the past. If you're working on becoming an RN, it is worthwhile to take the next step and become a nurse practitioner.

Home Health Care: As the population ages, and technology assists health care providers and allows them to remotely monitor conditions and also to be able to pay productive visits, there will be more of a shift to home health care. Nurses, home health care aides, physical therapists, and massage therapists will all benefit from these trends.

Green Health Care: Environmentally-friendly health care practices are very important, along with energy efficiency. Green health care practices will require facilities management, waste practices audits and more. There will be a number of jobs available for individuals who can work with renewable energy for health care facilities, and who can install and maintain equipment that will fit in the "smart grid." Green health care also concerns itself with controlling emissions and avoiding harmful chemicals that could harm people and the environment.

Change is occurring quickly. You're right, Concerned, to be nervous.

Don't worry, though. There are ways to stay on top of the changes and to succeed. The key is to continue to take courses and to be willing to branch out. For example, you may not feel interested at first in green building standards, but once you start seeing how it fits into your future and your life, chances are, you'll appreciate having the knowledge.

High-Pay and High Prestige vs. Extinction:
What Happens If You've Chosen a Career
Slated to be Replaced by Computers?

I am studying to get a degree in radiology. I like the idea of being in a health-related field, and the subject is interesting to me.

Imagine my dismay when I heard a computer scientist describe how many of today's jobs will be fully automated—basically run by computers.

Radiology was one of them. There were a number of science professions among them as well.

Do you have a good feel for what will happen in the future?

I may need to change my major!

Sincerely,
Fearful in Fentonville

****

Dear Fearful,

You're right. Most of our careers and career paths will be affected by technology. Will they go obsolete? The specifics might (think of horses and buggies, rather than the general concept of transportation).

Before I address your core question of the career of radiology and the impact of technological innovation, I'd like to respond to your expression of fear and uncertainty. You letter makes me step back and think a moment. It is amazing how many people who write me and express a feeling of fear.

Fear is a natural feeling, and it can protect us from dangerous, life-threatening situations.

Fear is natural in a world like ours, where we've been in and out of economic catastrophe since 2008.

But, is fear such a good thing? Fear can paralyze, and it can lead to a mindset that seeks the negatives instead of the positives. Sometimes the best way to overcome fear is to look at the situation and to turn it inside out.

Let's look at your desire to become a radiologist and the fact that many of the tasks that are now performed by a human being will be automated. Does this mean that your chosen profession is disappearing? It might. But, more likely, it means that you'll need to focus on the underlying reason you're drawn to the profession and to identify the new technologies that will be a part of it.

Then, ask yourself if you're willing and able to pursue competency in the new technologies. If so, you're in good shape.

- State your long-term objectives.
- Look at them closely.
- Find a logical path to your overarching objective—identify the new technologies you'll need to have.
- Set intermediary goals—acquire the skills you've identified, put them into practice.

Radiology is just one of many professions that will be affected by changing technologies. I would like to list a few other professions that will be similarly transformed. As I make the list, I'd like you to keep in mind that the new technologies are doors that are opening wide—even as old ways of doing things are doors slamming shut.

Here are a few careers that are being affected by new technologies to the point that the old career classifications may be completely defunct within 10 years.

Here are a few professions that will eventually be more or less automated, and conducted by computers.

However, human beings will need to priorities projects, do the "selling" to partners, develop business strategies, and bring together the worlds of finance, science, engineering, and project management.

- Petroleum Geologist will become an Integrated Petroleum Geosciences (geology / geophysics / computing / statistics and probability).
- Petroleum Engineer will become Integrated Subsurface Earth Engineer (combine science, mechanical / electrical / earth systems engineering).
- Geophysicist will become Integrated Earth Modeling (combine applied math, physical properties, earth sciences, computer modeling).

Now, to return to the "fear factor," I would say it is perfectly legitimate to feel fear if you cling to the old paradigm and you refuse to evolve.

Make fear your friend, which is to say get to know it so well you're ultimately bored by it (!)

I hope this has been helpful! Let me know how you're doing and how you've planned out your own live and approach.

Innovative Uses of Educational Technology in Quickly Changing Medical Professions

I work in the billing office of a hospital, and I'm concerned about the changes that are occurring in the medical profession.

I love my job. How can I keep up? Are colleges and universities doing anything to offer courses to help me maintain certification?

I don't need continuing education, per se. I need something more in-depth, which helps me reinvent myself as it becomes necessary. What do you suggest?

Sincerely,
Contented Coder

****

Dear Contented:

Your question is an excellent one, and the timing is excellent.

If you're certified to do medical coding for insurance and reporting, you are already aware that the 30-year-old standard, the International Classification of Diseases, version 9 (ICD-9), is going away. It has been outgrown, thanks to innovations in technology and in procedures. It's also been found to be too vague and too general for the needs of statisticians, health care demographers, and, perhaps most tellingly, health management organizations, government reimbursement policies and insurance companies.

The changeover is required by law, and will take effect in 2013. To help individuals update their certification, to provide training those who would like to enter the field, and to provide guidance for organizations that need to change their policies and procedures, many colleges and certification providers are incorporating videos, interactive quizzes, animations, guided presentations, and synchronous/asynchronous webinars and help.

To get the word out, colleges are using social networking tools, primarily Twitter, Facebook, LinkedIn, and YouTube. They are also using other networking tools where readers can review and comment on the effectiveness of various manuals and printed resources, such as Goodreads.com.

Texts, Videos and Archived Presentations

Textbook publishers are developing online resources that will accompany their textbooks. As you sign up for the course, be sure to review all the materials in your ebook, which will include texts, charts, videos, interactive charts, guided presentations, and review quizzes.

Not For Profits and Government Information Sources

- Noblis
  - ▶ www.noblis.org
  - ▶ www.noblis.org/MissionAreas/HI/Solutions/Pages/ICD-10Videos.aspx

- Center for Medicare and Medicaid Services
  - ▶ www.cms.gov/ContractorLearningResources/Downloads/ICD-10_Overview_Presentation.pdf

iOS Apps: Comparisons and Information Repositories

A number of iOS apps are being developed to help with the ICD diagnosis and procedures coding. It is important to keep in mind that college for-credit and certificate courses can provide the framework for the appropriate use of the apps and tools that are being developed. My impression is that if you use an app without having training, it's about like driving your car blindfolded. Take a course!

Some of the existing ICD-9 codes can be compared with new ICD-10 codes.

Here is one app provided by AAPC (**www.aapg.org**). While it is not a conversion (and not a crosswalk or a General Equivalency Map (GEM)), it is helpful in the learning process.

▸ www.aapc.com/ICD-10/codes/index.aspx?gclid=CMvSOK6gsakCFYRa7Ao dvVyqMg

Another app provided by the AAPC (free to members), is a implementation tracker / benchmarking tool which helps organizations plan their conversion and implementation.

▸ www.aapc.com/memberarea/ICD10/intro.aspx

ICD-10 Lite

Description from the publisher: The 2011 ICD10-CM diagnosis codes are instantly searchable and also browsable by their traditional categories. Search by code or diagnosis, through the whole ICD10-CM or through just a category or selected nonspecific code. Images within the list indicate whether a code is specific or nonspecific. Tap to view the diagnosis and the full text of its standard ICD-10 long description and to add it to your Favorites list for immediate access later. The same features are available for the ICD10-PCS procedure codes, too, used primarily for facility billing: search, browse, view long descriptions, and add to your Favorites list.

▸ iphone-apps-search.com/iphone_ipad_apps/344568/ICD+10+Lite+2011/

Here's an app that sounds quite helpful:

ICD 10 AM Lite

This app definitely needs to be reviewed by a medical coding professional to find out how effective and accurate the app is. The price is definitely right, but free could be costly if the information is incorrect.

▸ itunes.apple.com/us/app/icd-10-am-lite/id434073649?mt=8

ICD10 Codes for iPad

This iPad application provides a handy reference to all ICD10 Codes, along with detail notes on their usage. Black Knight Labs.

▸ itunes.apple.com/us/app/icd-10-codes-for-ipad/id418486253?mt=8

ICD10 Codes

This iPhone/iPod application provides a handy reference to all ICD10 Codes. Black Knight Labs.

▶ itunes.apple.com/us/app/icd10-codes/id413924956?mt=8

In conclusion, Contented, I hope that I've provided some good information that help guide you on your path. Good luck, and keep me posted on your progress! You're in a great field!

Learning a Skill via the Internet:
Practice Is Key

I'm a big believer in The Food Network. I've streamed every episode of every cooking show and I feel very confident that I can perform as well or better than the chefs.

So, now I have two questions.

One: Is there any way to fast-track a degree from a culinary institute? I'd like to test out using CLEP exams if I can.

Two: What's the best way to launch my own web-based food show?

After immersion in cooking shows, I fully understand the theory of food preparation, presentation, menu selection, and marketing. I know I may sound a bit overconfident, perhaps even delusional, but I truly believe in the efficacy of multimedia in imparting skills and abilities.

Sincerely,
Foodie in Philly

****

Dear Foodie,

I love your enthusiasm, but I'm a bit worried.

When you watched the cooking demonstrations, were you in your kitchen and did you follow along? Practice is really vital in developing the ability to perform, regardless of if you're talking about sports or taking an exam for a math class.

Practice involves two phases:

1. Mental rehearsal and conceptualization, which requires you to develop a mental model of how/what you're going to do.

2. Physical practice, which involves performing the activities in as close to the real-life circumstances as possible.

Practice is the repetition of demonstrating the retrieval of long-term knowledge of principles and techniques. Effective practice exercises in e-learning shows ways to select, integrate and apply new knowledge.

Exercises are a way to interact with a learning environment and are found in a variety of formats; for example, multiple choice or drag-and-drop questions to answer or more elaborate games. The variety and the complexity of interactions in applied practice examples show a higher order of processing knowledge.

Instead of simply regurgitating information acquired by rote memorization, applying acquired information in an assortment of practical applications leads to a greater probability of retaining knowledge. The latter method of demonstrating learned techniques requires more thought.

So, how does practice in an e-learning environment apply to becoming an expert in something?

One becomes an expert in a chosen profession not simply by learning theory, but by the application of concepts. Imagine yourself as someone who learns to be a chef by watching episodes on the Food Network, but has never actually cooked. Would you trust that yourself to prepare a complex recipe?

Clearly, it is important to apply your knowledge and in a focused, outcome-centered activity. Outcomes are important because without them it is hard to evaluate your performance, and to make corrections when they're needed.

Some research supports the conclusion that the amount of time invested in practice makes a profound difference in the application of learned techniques (Sloboda, et al., 1996, 287-309). Conversely, other research shows practice is important to a point, but has a negligible impact, if at all, thereafter (Plant, et al., 2005, 96-116).

You're very motivated to obtain a degree or certificate in culinary arts. I get the sense that you feel that certain activities that are required by traditional programs could be a waste of time. These are interesting questions. At what point does practice become a waste of time and effort? Further, what types of practice is conducive to enhanced performance?

Deliberate practice (as defined by Ericcson) is not the "mindless repetition" of applied knowledge, but requires concentration on instruction relating to gaps in knowledge and leads to expertise.

Notice, you're bringing together cognition (reflective/reflectionable knowledge). Practice in demonstrating knowledge not already mastered is most likely learned in environments absent from distraction. Practice should be in the form of realistic situations where knowledge is to be applied. Educational activities should be as close to possible as real-life instances and should be presented in such a context. In such a manner, a narrative is helpful to set up a context for the student to imagine a vocational environment and the requisite demonstration of capabilities.

Explanatory feedback shows learners corrective actions in areas where they need to improve. It does not simply involve telling a student if an answer is incorrect, but why it is so. This method inevitably requires more work on the part of the instructor, but is essential to stimulate the desire to learn and in the application of knowledge. In addition, explanatory feedback works best while progressing from basic to more complex situations.

Practice is useful up to a point, but then provides diminishing returns. This axiom is what is known as the power law of practice. Why is this principle important in the learning environment? In the e-learning environment especially, time and resources are expensive. It is simply a measure of maximizing cost efficiency. Practice is important, but it is up to the trained educator to decide how critical an exercise is in relation to job performance. Some vocations require an automatic demonstration of knowledge, while others permit a worker time to reflect while thinking-through what is required of them. The latter instance requires more development in underlying concepts of knowledge and is obtaining more so by the quality of education, than by the amount of repetition of a particular skill.

Spacing out practice sessions during segmented learning has an advantage over practicing larger amounts of course material. Long-term retention of knowledge is far greater (Bahrick, 1987, 344-349).

Education is constrained by schedule, so finding the right amount of spacing between practices is key. It is essential, however, to incorporate practices throughout lessons rather than placing it all at the end of a course of study. What's more, varied multimedia approaches to practice reinforce retention of information.

As you view the food network shows, it would not be a bad idea to change modalities. Read a recipe. Listen to audio while you look at diagrams. Switching the emphasis to audio, graphics, text, and video engages different types of learners and, for the individual learner, supports and enhances cognition.

It is important for various approaches not to be redundant, but complimentary to each other. It is equally significant to remove extraneous information or sensory input to reduce the learner's cognitive burden. Once again, a tranquil learning environment is crucial.

So, the bottom line is that I think that you can definitely successfully learn from multimedia presentations. But, you'll need to apply the knowledge and practice in a way that is meaningful and result-driven.

REFERENCES

Bahrick, H.P. (1987). "Retention of Spanish vocabulary over eight years." *Journal of Experimental Psychology: Learning, Memory, and Cognition*, 13, 344-349

Plant, E.A., Ericsson, K.A., Hill, L., & Asberg, K. (2005) "Why study time does not predict grade point average across college students: Implications of deliberate practice for academic performance." *Contemporary Educational Psychology*, 30, 96-116

Sloboda, J.A., Davidson, J.W., Howe, M.J.A., & Moore, D.G. (1996), "The role of practice in the development of performing musicians." *British Journal of Psychology*. 87, 287-309

Looking for an Income Boost?
Try a Certificate Program

A good certificate program led to an immediate $15,000 per year boost in income. That is what more than one person has found out after returning to school to obtain a certificate on top of their associate's degree.

After Marriya graduated with her associate's degree in general studies, she was able to get a job at a document processing center where her job was to scan checks, receipts, deposit slips, and other items from a local credit union. It was not a bad job, but there was not much opportunity for advancement. Someone mentioned to her that a good way to get a boost in her career and find a job with a future was to finish a certificate program.

After looking at several different certificate programs, Marriya decided on a certificate in sustainable business. It seemed a bit vague at first, but after Marriya looked more closely, she began to realize what a positive program it really was.

"It's great, Mom," she remarked as she and her mother were drinking coffee at a local bookstore and perusing a stack of books in the section entitled "Careers for the Future."

"What I like about the certificate program is that it covers so many areas. Sustainability has to do with new regulations, new technologies, and 'green' planning—across the board. For example, the place where I do scanning also has a copying and printing business. They need people who know the laws governing environmental issues and also they need to find ways to conserve energy and reduce costs," said Marriya.

"What did your certificate program require you to do?" asked her mom.

"I took all five courses online. At the end, I had to do a project as well as a brief internship. It was rigorous, but I was able to finish it in one semester," Marriya told her mom.

What Marriya found at her workplace was that her employer had an opening for someone with the kind of credentials that Marriya now had. While Marriya was considering applying for that position, she found another company that managed hotels. They needed a person to help them develop sustainability plans for the hotels they were updating and refurbishing. They loved Marriya's educational background in sustainable business practices and were willing to give her a $5,000 signing bonus, which essentially paid for Maria's certificate program. After deliberating, Marriya accepted the job. She now had a job with potential as well as immediate benefits. Her new salary was $15,000 higher than before.

Marriya was delighted. She was not alone, however. Two separate studies that tracked the earnings of individuals after college found that for a quick boost to earnings, the best and quickest approach was to obtain a certificate in a program that is in demand.

According to one report, *Changing the fortunes of America's workforce: A human-capital challenge*, certificate programs are key elements in helping workers make the transition from a manufacturing-based to a service-based economy (McKinsey & Company, 2009).

Another study, *Pathways to Boosting the Earnings of Low-Income Students by Increasing Their Educational Attainment*, found the biggest gains in social mobility were found in individuals from at-risk backgrounds who obtained funding to go to a career college and completed a certificate program centered on a specific job category (The Hudson Institute, 2009).

Marriya sat quietly as her mother leaned forward. She could tell her mother was very moved.

"Marriya, I am so proud of you. You have had a tough time, with the kinds of lives we've had. But you're fearless and persistent. You are a true leader."

REFERENCES

Jacobson, L. and Mokher, C. (2009). *Pathways to Boosting the Earnings of Low-Income Students by Increasing their Educational Attainment.* The Hudson Institute and CNA.
▸ www.hudson.org

McKinsey & Company. (2009) *Changing the Fortunes of America's Workforce: A Human Capital Challenge.* McKinsey Global Institute.
▸ www.mckinsey.com/Insights/MGI/Research/Labor_Markets/Changing_the_fortunes_of_US_workforce

Math and Science:
High-Paying Careers of the Future

It may not be self-evident that majoring in math or science for your undergraduate degree would lead to a high-paying job. After all, who hires zoology majors? However, if you scratch the surface, you'll find that many high-growth careers consist of "applied" science or math. This ranges from nursing to engineering and computing.

In many ways, it's better to have a degree that is a general, foundational science or math, and is not a trendy application. If you have the core courses, you can always specialize or customize your education later, either with a certificate program, or by getting involved in an internship program or specialized electives that give you hands-on experience.

What are some of the core science and math clusters, and where might you be able to develop a career? Let's take a look.

Earth Sciences

Studying geology or geophysics may not be your first choice. However, if you're interested in climate change or theories of global warming, and how communities need to adjust their carbon footprint and the patterns of using renewable and non-renewable energy, you may wish to focus on the following areas:

- Climate change
- Environment
- Energy
- Earthquakes and Volcanoes

Biological Sciences

- Allied Health (Nursing, Physician Assistant, etc.)
- Plant Science (Genetic engineering for agriculture, etc.)
- Pharmacy
- Genetic engineering for humans and animals

Chemistry

- Industrial hydrocarbons (plastics, etc.)
- Geochemistry (unconventional hydrocarbon resources such as shale gas, shale oil, etc.)

Math

- Statistics & modeling
- Imaging (GIS, geophysics, etc.)
- Computer Forensics
- Computer programming
- Mapping/Imaging (GIS)
- Foundation/Math

What's the best approach? Take courses in science and math, build a foundation. Why do it now? You may find it's very hard to go back and fill in the gaps if you avoid math and science.

It is very useful to have the core courses for maximum flexibility.

Avoid the easy General Education type of degree if you're just starting out. Why? You won't be taking enough math and science.

However, if you're in the military and you can receive credit for your courses and experience, it might be worthwhile to obtain a degree so you have a degree. However, you can build on that—perhaps have a double-major or a second degree.

If cost is an issue, consider self-study and CLEP tests for some of the coursework.

Oil Industry Careers

Since the Gulf of Mexico Spill (Macondo) and the controversy surrounding massive hydraulic fractures used to help produce gas and oil from shale plays such as the Marcellus in Pennsylvania and New York, I've become very aware that there are a number of job opportunities in the oil industry.

My question is this: Are most of them related to environmental cleanup? That's the impression I get when I watch the news.

I'm a very fervent believer in the environment. I also realize we need clean fuel for our future. What do you recommend?

Sincerely,
Energy Career Seeker

****

Dear Energy:

You make a good point about the public perception of oil and gas. It's really hard to find an industry that has been the target of more negativity—despite the fact that we use and need oil and gas-derived energy every day, even if we aren't driving our cars. Natural gas is used to generate electricity, which you're using right now, whether you're plugged in with your laptop, or are working off the battery in your phone or tablet.

If you're interested in being involved in environmental regulatory compliance issues, the following careers could be for you:

- **Environmental Quality Technologist:** You can put your general biology or earth science degree to good use in this career, especially if you combine it with courses in law and political science (focus on regulatory agencies).

- **Geographical Information Specialist:** If you get a degree or certification in geographical information technology, you'll be able to use data to monitor the environmental quality of offshore and onshore operations. You can also monitor water quality for surface impoundments, and track air pollutants, and the way that drilling and production locations are impacting the landscape.

If you're interested in exploring for oil and gas, and you'd like a job that is potentially higher paying (but, could be volatile, thanks to the cyclical nature of the oil industry), the following careers could be of interest:

- **Geotechnician:** This position usually requires a four-year geology degree, and a number of additional courses in geographical information systems and petroleum geology. Your job is to monitor operations and create maps.

- **Petroleum Engineer:** Engineers can focus on upstream operations (drilling and reservoir calculations), as well as more downstream (production, enhanced oil recovery). Some engineers focus on well log interpretation and petrophysics.

- **Geophysicist:** If you're a geophysicist, you've had a lot of math as well as some computer science courses. You'll be doing a lot of work with computer programs designed to process seismic information and to gain an idea of what the structure looks like in the subsurface. The information is used to select drilling locations and to determine where to steer the well while drilling horizontally.

- **Geochemist:** Geochemists often look at the impact of drilling fluids on the formations and the try to help avoid problems during drilling and production. The also evaluate the composition of different formations to determine whether or not they're prospective for petroleum production.

- **Geologist:** To be hired as a petroleum geologist, you'll need a master's degree in geology, and your thesis will need to have dealt with a petroleum-related problem. Your job will be fairly interesting as you evaluate locations for drilling and you use an array of information determine the likelihood of good oil and gas production. It's a fairly technical position, and you'll be using a number of computer programs to develop workflows from which you'll build maps and models, and will evaluate well logs and other information.

If you prefer a more physical job which puts you in the field, you may wish to look at certain technical positions:

- **Welding and construction (rigging up / transportation):** You'll need to get training in construction sciences as well as welding from a career college.

- **Oil Field Chemical Transportation:** You'll be trained to handle chemicals, as well as in the operation of vehicles, and methods of transfer.

- **Pipeline Specialist:** You'll be in charge of monitoring pipelines, which includes flow, transportation, and corrosion.

- **Drilling Operations (driller, tool pusher (supervisor)):** This is a rather specialized position which requires quite a bit of training on the different operations on the drilling rig floor, as well as the rigging up and breaking down phases.

- **Oil Field Safety:** This is a very critical position, which encompasses all aspects of operations.

- **Production (pumper):** Although this position is often referred to as simply the "pumper," the job is really all about being a production supervisor. You're in charge of monitoring producing wells and determining the amount of production, troubleshooting if there are problems, making suggestions, and overseeing repairs.

- **Lease Records Specialist (Landman):** You'll be in charge of managing leases and lease records, along with other legal documents (division orders, etc). During the leasing stage, you may get involved in developing mineral take-offs, preparing leases/drafts, and negotiating terms with mineral owners.

If you have any questions about these careers, please contact me and I'll give you more details. It might be nice to follow up with a list of programs and colleges, with links.

Renewable Energy Careers

One of the most exciting areas for new jobs is in the energy sector, specifically in renewable energy. However, what are the jobs and where can one obtain training? Renewable energy sector jobs include design, engineering, installation, auditing, and programming for green power, which includes solar, wind, biomass (cellulosic ethanol), hydropower, and geothermal energy.

Where are the jobs?

- **Energy auditing:** For the smart grid to really work, it's necessary to identify the true patterns of energy consumption, and to be able to make recommendations for more energy efficient substitutes. This involves learning how to audit to determine costs, ways to increase efficiency, and to test new design.

- **Solar design:** Graduates should demonstrate an understanding of photovoltaic principles, the current manufacturing facilities, and the places where photovoltaic energy can be implemented.

- **Energy modeling:** Being able to model energy from different sources enables the individual to be able to work on hybrid solutions—the energy "farm"—that may have three or four sources of energy on a single expanse of land. Education in this area allows one to integrate geothermal, wind, solar, biomass, and fossil fuels.

- **Wind farm design and operation:** Wind farms can be small or large, and they can be locations that range from remote rural to win farms on the edge of a town, where the wind turbines are owned by the local municipality.

- **Wind turbine installations—residential, small farm-light commercial, large commercial:** The jobs are literally all over the globe, and they range from massive wind turbine installations to small windmills used for residential or light industrial purposes (taking the load off diesel generators, for example).

- **Photovoltaic manufacturing:** Technology is advancing rapidly in the area of the manufacture of photovoltaic cells used in solar panels.

Colleges and Universities offering Renewable Energy Programs

- **Crowder College – Neosho, Missouri**
  ▸ www.crowder.edu/MARET
  Missouri Alternative and Renewable Energy Technology (MARET) (associates degrees in solar, wind, geothermal, and biomass technologies)

- **Lane Community College - Eugene, Oregon**
  ▸ www.lanecc.edu
  Lane has three two-year degree programs with a sustainability focus:
  - » Energy Management
  - » Renewable Energy Technology
  - » Water Conservation

- **San Juan College, Farmington, New Mexico**
  Renewable Energy Program
  ▸ www.sanjuancollege.edu/documents/MathSci/RENG/content/REeFly ergfxlres.pdf

- **Bronx Community College, Bronx, New York**
  The Center for Sustainable Energy
  ▸ www.bcc.cuny.edu
  ▸ www.csebcc.org

- **Humboldt State University, Arcata, California**
  B.S. and M.S. programs in Environmental Resources Engineering
  ▸ www.humboldt.edu

- **Appalachian State University, Boone, North Carolina**
  Undergraduate Program in Appropriate Technology
  ▸ www.tec.appstate.edu

- **Illinois State University, Department of Technology**
  Renewable Energy Program
  ▸ www.tec.ilstu.edu/renewable_energy

- **Arizona State University, School of Sustainability**
  ▸ schoolofsustainability.asu.edu

- **Slippery Rock University, Pennsylvania**
  M.S. degree in Sustainable Systems
  ▸ www.sru.edu/pages/6781.asp

- **University of Wisconsin – Madison**
  Solar Energy Laboratory (SEL)
  ▸ sel.me.wisc.edu

- **Oregon Institute of Technology**
  Renewable Energy Center
  ▸ www.oit.edu

- **Washington State University**
  Renewable Energy Program
  ▸ www.energy.wsu.edu/projects/renewables/bioenergy.cfm

- **Farmingdale College, Farmingdale, NY**
  Solar Energy Center
  ▸ www.farmingdale.edu

- **State University of New York-Canton**
  4-year degree program in alternative and renewable energy
  ▸ www.canton.edu/csoet/alt_energy

Software Architect:
In the Future, Every Organization
Will Need One

I recently read that one of the hottest new careers is in software architecture.

It's projected to grow, even as work for regular computer programmers, web developers, network support, and other computer-related positions are projected to maintain merely modest growth.

What is software architecture? What does a software architect do?

Yours,
Software Skyscrapers

****

Dear Software,

Do you ever wonder how companies keep all the databases and online services/products straight? How do they keep from having the entire enterprise become an inefficient mess, with overlaps, obsolescences, and redundancies?

Part of the answer is the "architect" of the organization. In some organizations, it's the "enterprise architect" and in others, it's the "software architect." In any case, it's the "big picture" person who helps mesh things together in a way that builds a strong organization that does not collapse beneath its own weight, or have people lost for years in its dark, digital labyrinths.

The software architect is a very important person in an organization—especially one that relies on digital products and digital systems as its core business. This could apply to many enterprises, especially if they have multiple locations and many users—external and internal—who need to access systems. Companies that deal in the knowledge industry and those which provide services are clear beneficiaries from the systems architecture approach.

Enterprise and software architects are not architects in the literal sense. They don't have to take CAD and be licensed in order to design buildings. They do, however, understand the structures of organizations, and they look at both the design of workflows and the overall organizational mission. They also take stock of the resources of the company—human, financial, physical—and they seek to maximize efficiency and return on investment.

Instead, they have to do with system design and engineering, and in that way, they help companies bring together the knowledge functions. Software architecture contributes to competitive advantage in two primary ways:

- The software architecture provides the technology platform that supports the product characteristics and development processes which differentiate a business from its competitor
- Having a "map" of the software architecture helps address system complexity.

What are the key characteristics of a systems, enterprise, or software architect?

- Interdisciplinary
- Analytical
- Big picture thinkers
- Creative/innovative systems thinkers
- Good leadership skills

What kind of education do you need?

There are numerous ways to approach the same goal, but some of the majors you can explore would include:

- Software engineering
- Industrial engineering
- Business management (emphasis on systems)
- Information systems management

What kind of courses should you take?

- Business management
- Software families / systems overviews
- Information systems management (with case studies)
- Technology Leadership

Some of the jobs available today for software architects include those companies that develop applications used in cloud computing:

- **Developing new commercial software solutions in cloud environment.** The goal is to provide software engineers with the tools and infrastructure to untangle the web, using the structure of the web to develop application interfaces.
- **Make existing software work in cloud computing architect.** For example, the architect could figure out a way to support QuickBooks' millions of online customers during all times, including peak loads.
- **Complex business solutions / customer relation management.** Finding a way to analyze valuable data collected from millions of small businesses and use that data to develop new business lines that help the small business customers grow, speeding up our nation's economic recovery. The new product could something like "GoGrow" and could help clients set up, develop, and expand their presence on the web. The architect would work with designers to create innovative tools that make setting up a business online and growing your customer base simple, elegant, and collaborative.
- **Functional regulation software.** Used in "green" purposes.
- **Remote/Mobile Meet Land-based Systems.**
- **Smartgrid.**
- **Security and Computer Systems Designs.**

I hope this overview had helped you, Software. Please do investigate further and as you do so, think of your own skills and interests. Be sure to blend/meld them as you can to see the emerging opportunities and times.

Stay at Home Military Moms
and Online Degrees in Green Jobs

The individuals in this article are based on people who participated in interviews, but names and details have been changed.

Talibria had been a stay-at-home mom for the entire duration of her husband's military career. There had been times when she wanted to find a job near base, especially when they were stationed in locations where there was a significant population center and, hence, lots of jobs nearby.

Now that her husband had retired from the military, she wanted to find a good job with career potential, but she was not sure where to turn.

Talibria and her husband had decided that it was better for her to stay at home with their four children and to provide a stable base as they relocated to new duty stations every two or three years. At one point, she tried college, but with her husband's deployments and her children's needs, it was not viable.

With her husband in retirement, she found herself at a crossroads. When she took courses before, she had been interested in early childhood education. However, raising four children had pretty much cured her of that dream, and so now she was more interested in green living, renewable energy, and sustainable business practices.

As she looked up possible degree programs, she found a number of programs in sustainable business. So, she decided to start with a certificate in sustainable business.

Then, she took an internship at a supermarket chain that was in the midst of updating its processes in order to be more environmentally friendly, as well as to move from non-renewable to renewable energy. In addition, she would learn about how they were focusing on water conservation services.

After she looked at the skill sets and the education she would need, Talibria decided to go to a career college and to obtain certificates that included understanding the basics about green plumbing and power.

At the same time, she focused on an associate's degree that would open the doors to a career with employers who needed someone who could help them turn their businesses around, and to become green, sustainable, and future-focused. She would also look for scholarships for older women. A good link, "Grants for Older Women Returning to College" may be found on eHow.com.
▸ www.ehow.com/facts_5202746_grants-older-women-returning-college.html

Talibria's husband and four kids were excited. Markus, her youngest, was still in junior high school, and he was very proud of having a mom who was interested in the things he was studying in school. Dray, her husband, was excited, too. He was looking at post-military careers, and he thought it might not be a bad idea to see how Talibria's experience went.

As she communicated in the college's discussion board for prospective students, she found there were a number of women who had been laid off from jobs at large companies.

Many of the women were planning to try to go into nursing, but there were a few interested in green technologies. Talibria decided that scaling wind turbine to work on the nacelle was not quite for her—but understanding the basics of wind, solar, geothermal, and biomass energy sources would help her.

Talibria did her homework. She knew that going back to college would involve challenges. However, she was ready to tackle them, especially with the support of the group of returning to school moms who regularly posted on the discussion board.

Talibria knew it would be a great experience.

The Globally Connected Workplace in 2035

I've been reading discussions of what the workplace will look like in 2020 and which degrees I should get.

Frankly, I don't want to go down a path that will only buy me 9 years of usefulness. Isn't there anything we can do to prepare ourselves for 24 or 25 years from now?

In 2035, I'll be 45, and my mom, who used to work in the auto industry will be 66, and, as she says, probably just hitting her stride, with no intentions of retiring. We're both studying to be in the health industry. I'm studying to be a nurse. My mom is getting training in medical coding and billing. What do you recommend?

Yours truly,
Future Fitness

****

Dear Future,

I think you're smart to look ahead to 2035. We know that technology is changing so quickly that some things we take for granted will be long gone.

For example, data storage and the way we use computers will be different. The way we read and preserve information will change, and our ways of traveling, communicating, and interacting with each other with technology will not be the same.

What will stay the same is the fact that basic fundamental facts will stay the same:

- Human populations will have needs (food and water, transportation, shelter, clothing, communications, work).
- Plants and animals will have special needs (either in the wild or in human-organized structures).
- Cities will continue to grow, resulting in mega-cities so large we might as well call them giga-cities.
- Governmental structures and ways of governing will change.
- Security will have a different meaning.
- Privacy/identity/freedom will be augmented in ways we may not expect.

What are the skills you'll need?

I'd say that instead of trying to predict just which careers will be flourishing, it is better to focus on the fundamental skills and abilities that you'll need. You'll need good communications skills, with a foundation of computing, business, math, science, humanities, and social sciences.

When it comes to specifics, I'd recommend finding what you love and then dedicate yourself to it. Let yourself put as much energy as you can in doing what you love.

Then, flow and adapt with the times—keep up to date with what you like to do.

So, for example, if you're studying to become a nurse, stay up to date in new developments in pharmaceuticals, infomatics, data storage and tracking, public health, web/mobile-assisted training (including simulations, games, and virtual worlds).

Invest in yourself. When an aspect of your career comes up that you like, go ahead and sign up for training and continuing education.

Be as inter- and multi-disciplinary as possible.

Through it all, stay active and eat a healthy diet, get exercise, and plenty of sleep. Let me know your thoughts.

The Paralegal Profession:
Better than Ever, with More Specialization

Since going to work for a technology company, I've been really interested in patents and how patents work. I would love to work with engineers and inventors who have new processes and products and help them protect their intellectual property.

I'm also intrigued by the market for patents and want to know how to purchase a patent or two, and perhaps even fight the patent trolls.

I do not want to become a full-fledged attorney at this point. I want to jump right in with both feet and try out these ideas within a year. Is it possible? What can I do?

Sincerely,
Patently Insane About Patents

****

Dear Patently,

I think your goals are very admirable, and there are people who really need the skills you'd like to develop.

You asked what career you're describing—I'd say you're right on track to enjoy the career of Paralegal (legal assistant). With the training you'll receive, you'll be qualified to conduct legal research, prepare and file legal documents, and do many of the tasks that an attorney does. You will not be able to practice law, but you can put your knowledge to use in many ways. Not only can you work in a place where you're directly involved in the law and legal processes, you can also work in businesses that need the abilities of a paralegal.

Your best bet is to specialize, which is precisely what you're doing as it relates to intellectual property.

People often ask me if it's a good idea to go to law school, and my answer that it's always a good idea to expand your knowledge and skills in areas where you have a passion.

At the same time, you may wish to do other things besides the law. For example, your interests seem to be in the area of technology / new technologies. In this case, you're in great shape with paralegal training.

You're in a great career path. You can find paralegals in many organizations. Of course, the obvious fit is with law firms and legal departments, but you might be surprised how many other places they can be found. Paralegals are essential in places that are involved in litigation, personal injury, criminal law, human resources, intellectual property (patents!), bankruptcy, divorce, immigration, real estate, and not-for-profit associations.

With a background as a paralegal, you can assist attorneys as they prepare contracts, agreements, benefit plans, and corporate incentive packages. You can also help develop and maintain records for corporations and not-for-profit associations.

The Bureau of Labor Statistics (www.bls.gov/oco/ocos114.htm#outlook) reports a great outlook for paralegal, with a 28 percent group from 2008 to 2018, and salaries that range from a low of $36,000 to a high of around $75,000 per year. The median tends to be around $55,000 per year.

So, Patently, you're in a perfect spot. Talk to your company and see if they could use your help. In the meantime, check out the online programs. There are a number of one-year certificate programs as well as two-year degree programs.

Good luck to you—but please use your knowledge for the good and not the bad! Continue your desire to fight the patent trolls (rather than becoming one of them!)

About the Author

Susan Smith Nash has had a passion for e-learning since the mid-1990s, when she started developing companion websites for her face-to-face literature and humanities courses. Since that time, she has been involved in all phases of e-learning course and program development for Open-Courseware, professional development, career training, and degree and certificate programs. Delivery methods include both 100% distance and hybrid programs for delivery with e-learning/m-learning across an array of devices and technologies.

A believer in diversification, Susan has taken a multi-disciplinary approach to life, bringing together environmental, energy, and geological sciences and technologies with economics, literature, film, and the humanities.

Susan's publications include peer-reviewed articles and chapters on aspects of e-learning, as well as literature, humanities, film studies, and petroleum technologies. She has written short stories and novels, and her poems have been collected in several volumes. Her hobbies include cartooning, tennis, and admiring D.I.Y.